A NEW MATRIX FOR MODERNISM

MAJOR LITERARY AUTHORS
VOLUME 18

STUDIES IN
MAJOR LITERARY AUTHORS
OUTSTANDING DISSERTATIONS

edited by
William E. Cain
Wellesley College

Routledge
Taylor & Francis Group
New York   London

A New Matrix for Modernism

Modernism

A Study of the Lives and Poetry of Charlotte Mew and Anna Wickham

Nelljean McConeghey Rice

Routledge
Taylor & Francis Group
New York   London

This edition published 2011 by Routledge:

Routledge
Taylor & Francis Group
711 Third Avenue
New York, NY 10017

Routledge
Taylor & Francis Group
2 Park Square, Milton Park
Abingdon, Oxon OX14 4RN

Published in 2003 by
Routledge
29 West 35th Street
New York, NY 10001
www.routledge-ny.com

Published in Great Britain by
Routledge
11 New Fetter Lane
London EC4P 4EE
www.routledge.co.uk

10 9 8 7 6 5 4 3 2 1

Library of Congress Cataloging-in-Publication Data

Rice, Nelljean McConeghey, 1947–
   A new matrix for modernism : a study of the lives and poetry of
Charlotte Mew and Anna Wickham / by Nelljean McConeghey Rice.
      p. cm. — (Studies in major literary authors ; v. 18)
Includes bibliographical references (p.) and index.
   ISBN 0-415-94140-7 (hardback)
   1. Mew, Charlotte Mary, 1869-1928. 2. Feminism and literature—Great
Britain—History—20th century. 3. Women and literature—Great
Britain—History—20th century. 4. English poetry—Women
authors—History and criticism. 5. English poetry—20th
century—History and criticism. 6. Poets, English—20th
century—Biography. 7. Feminist poetry—History and criticism. 8.
Modernism (Literature)—Great Britain. 9. Women poets,
English—Biography. 10. Wickham, Anna, 1884-1947. 11. Feminism in
literature. I. Title. II. Series.
   PR6025.E8 Z87 2002
   821'.912099287—dc21
                                                  2002009236

First issued in paperback 2013
ISBN13: 978-0-415-94140-2 (hbk)
ISBN13: 978-0-415-86706-1 (pbk)

Contents

Preface

Much of the feminist writing of the last several decades in both the U.S. and England has been determined by the critic's desire to reconfigure the modernist movement. This book is my contribution to the project. While most of the writers on gendered modernism have begun with a thesis and then set out to prove it, I began with two poets, Charlotte Mew (1869–1928) and Anna Wickham (1883–1947), whose work I have admired ever since I found their poems many years ago in Louis Untermeyer's anthologies. These women pair eclectic poetic styles with feminist content. Yet as I pursued my interests in literature and poetry, it was easy to forget about them because they didn't feature in any university courses, they were no longer being anthologized, and I learned to apply a formalist, male-modernist poetic aesthetic which revised my initial opinion of their poems.

During the early years of the feminist reclamation project, by chance I bought Louise Bernikow's *The World Split Open: Four Centuries of Women Poets in England and America, 1552–1950* (1974). Here, Charlotte Mew and Anna Wickham are represented by five poems each. Re-reading poems such as "Fame" and "Rooms" by Mew and "Nervous Prostration" by Wickham reminded me of what I had been missing. As much as I admired the technical skill and vision in poems by T. S. Eliot, Ezra Pound, and W. H. Auden, and the women modernists such as H.D. and Marianne Moore, the poems by Mew and Wickham affect me more profoundly, and intimately. The lack of interest in their work mystified me. Why were they not routinely presented as important modern poets in scholarly writing about modernism?

A New Matrix for Modernism is my answer to that simple question. Since I begin with the poets themselves, I have to consider their lives and times as the context for the poems. My critical and theoretical approach is best described as cultural biography. Literary history, feminist theory, other contemporary trends in literary criticism, and cultural studies help me to frame my answer. Drawing on feminist, gender, new historicist, and post-colonial theories, the introduction discusses the concept of a gendered modernism, tracing the styles and writers that influenced its development. Following a matrilineal line from Charlotte Brontë through Alice Meynell and May Sinclair, the book explains the emergence of a distinctive women's voice in the Victorian era, and locates its presence through the Edwardian, Georgian, and modern eras. There has been some discussion about whether Charlotte Mew should be classed as a Victorian or modern poet, and whether both Mew and Wickham should be considered Georgian, even though neither appeared in Edward Marsh's anthologies that promoted the Georgian poets. I classify both Mew and Wickham as coeval modern poets, because, despite the fourteen-year difference in their ages, they were both writing and publishing poetry at the same time and with the same group—Harold Monro's Poetry Bookshop. Wickham's first book of poems, *The Contemplative Quarry* (1915) and Mew's *The Farmer's Bride* (1916) situate their production at the same time as Pound's *Lustra* (1916) and Eliot's *Prufrock and Other Observations* (1917).

In my quest to establish a permanent place for Mew and Wickham's genius, I treat as meaningful whatever information I find. Tangents abound because I cannot separate the personal from the poetic. Claude Lévi-Strauss's definition and treatment of the term *bricolage* in *The Savage Mind* (1962) and *Totemism* (1962) enables me to search through all the bits and pieces left over from previous renderings of the era, or even to rehabilitate ideas or concepts dismissed as irrelevant by some critics. His understanding of the mytho-poetic nature of *bricolage,* and the excitement inherent in a total re-working of the relationship between the real and the imaginary, has been a key factor in my understanding of the conjunctions between these two women and their culture. I have tried to interrogate all the elements of their lives and work that I could, to discover what each of the elements might possibly signify. I use this debris to craft a new matrix for modernism, sometimes deliberately destabilizing the term in the process. I think this is the only possible way to approach Mew and Wickham's contributions to their era because it is exactly what they themselves were accomplishing with their writing. While both theoretical and poetic paradigms can narrowly focus the critical eye, they also can limit the reader's view of the broader *milieu,* which initially engenders the need to write the poem. A narrow focus slights the life of the poem, as it tends to ignore the importance of readers, who are, after all, what keeps the poem alive. In this book, the poems, which reached and touched some important twentieth century writers, always come first, but they are presented as parts of the historical-biographical-cultural conjunctions (in other words, the matrix) from which Charlotte Mew and Anna Wickham emerge.

The late nineteen-nineties and early part of the twenty-first century have seen a resurgence of interest in the lives and events of the previous *fin de siècle* and the early years of the twentieth century. Especially among feminists, historical reflection often concludes that "the more things change, the more they stay the same." In the world of poetry, women poets are still not as widely anthologized as their male counterparts, nor are their poems discussed with the same critical complexity because the task of developing a tradition of an un-gendered or feminine poetic aesthetic has not been accomplished. Women poets, Mew and Wickham included, have always fashioned masking strategies to negotiate the language, critical paradigms, and reception practices of the male literary establishment.

Therefore it is instructive to revisit the first wave feminist project of recovery, late-Victorian and Edwardian culture and their influences on the modernist movement, and both the fiction and poetry of the era to discuss, once again, the critical and aesthetic formulations that have separated the poetess from the poet. *A New Matrix for Modernism* began as a larger project, which included fiction writers Dorothy Richardson and Mary Webb. In the course of discovering a body of feminist analysis focused around Richardson's "feminine sentence," I realized that my proposed study was too large for one book, and, since I initially trained in poetry and poetic theory, I decided to concentrate on the poets.

My primary question has always been: "Why have these excellent poets been forgotten by all but a few?" To address the inherent complexities of this pursuit, I have had to examine not only Mew and Wickham's *milieu*, but also the strategies of rereading and subsequent ranking that have been feminist projects for the past thirty to forty years. The resistant readings accorded many women poets by male readers have been adopted by some feminist literary critics. Even in the process of recovery, there can be an unconscious acceptance of male-modernist hermeneutics. Virginia Woolf, one of the few women writers of the time who was also respected as a critic, germinated a viable means of evaluating women's fiction, but her critical apparatus was never really applied to her poetry-writing contemporaries. May Sinclair also focused her analytical acumen on prose rather than poetry. Lacking a critical framework fashioned by a woman contemporary of both Mew and Wickham, I craft an etiology out of disparate and, perhaps, unusual sources. For this reason, cultural considerations sometimes have been more important to my thesis than have poetics.

After brief contemporary review notices of their books, there is no word about either Mew or Wickham, except for Untermeyer's continuing to include them in his anthologies and *Lives of the Poets*. They are mentioned in sections on women poets in several other overview compilations of nineteenth or twentieth century poetry. The lone scholarly exception must be mentioned here. All searchers after the enigma that is Charlotte Mew start with Mary C. Davidow's 1960 Brown University PhD dissertation, *Charlotte Mew: Biography and Criticism*. It is a measure of the lack of interest in Mew that this excellent work was never published. Penelope

Fitzgerald's lively and engaging biography, *Charlotte Mew and Her Friends* (Addison 1988) draws on and expands Davidow's work. Another dissertation, Jennifer Vaughan Jones's *The Poetry and Place of Anna Wickham: 1910–1930* (1994) from the University of Wisconsin is a thorough discussion of Wickham's poetic place, which benefits from Jones's friendship with George and Louise Hepburn and Margaret Hepburn, Anna Wickham's surviving son and daughters-in-law. This work awaits a publisher. Before Jones' work, the only full-length treatment of Wickham's poetry was R.D. Smith's *The Writings of Anna Wickham: Free Woman and Poet* (1984).

There were waves of interest in their work in the seventies and eighties, which I detail in the introduction of the book. Most recently, Elaine Showalter's *Daughters of Decadence* (1993) analyzes Charlotte Mew's short story, "A White Night," describing it as a feminist counterpart to Conrad's *Heart of Darkness*. Kathleen Bell's essay, "Charlotte Mew, T.S. Eliot and Modernism" in *Kicking Daffodils: Twentieth-Century Women Poets* (1997), edited by Vicki Bertram, makes a strong case that there is much work to be done exploring the conjunctions between Mew and Eliot, an idea that was first broached by John Newton in a *TLS* Commentary in April, 1995. Newton himself contributes an important essay, "Charlotte Mew's Place in the Future of English Poetry" in the *New England Review* (1997). He makes a persuasive argument that Mew be considered a major figure in early twentieth-century English poetry. However, Newton's most important contribution to a Mew revival is his edition of *Charlotte Mew: Complete Poems* (2000), but this invaluable collection with preface, and textual notes, is already out of print. Val Warner, the initial instigator of renewed interest in Mew's poetry and prose pieces, whose *Collected Poems and Prose of Charlotte Mew* (1981) is also out of print, has contributed solid scholarship on Mew both in her introduction to the above and in "New Light on Charlotte Mew" *PN Review* (1997). Warner's introduction and notes on the text for *Charlotte Mew: Collected Poems and Selected Prose* (1997) continue to refine our understanding of the enigmatic poet. My work would not have been possible without the contributions of Davidow, Newton and Warner on Mew, and Smith and Jones on Wickham. A long overdue scholarly interest in Mew's unusual prosodic techniques begins with Jeredith Merrin's "The Ballad of Charlotte Mew" in *Modern Philology* (1997). Dennis Denisoff discusses Mew's contribution to the genre of graveyard poetry in "Grave Passions: Enclosure and Exposure in Charlotte Mew's Graveyard Poetry" *Victorian Poetry* (2000). James Persoon's *Modern British Poetry: 1900–1930* (1999), a work in the Twayne Critical History of Poetry Studies series, has much of interest to say about both Mew and Wickham.

Aside from Jennifer Jones's work on Anna Wickham, little recent scholarly work has been written about her. Because Wickham grew up in Australia, there has always been an interest in her work and her place in modern letters among Australian feminist scholars. Ann Vickery's chapter "Between a Modernist Passport and House Arrest: Anna Wickham and the Question of Cultural Identity" appears in *Soundings: Poetry and Poetics* edited by Lynn Jacobs and Jeri Kroll (1998). Vickery's impulse is to examine the cultural parameters that Wickham felt forced to negotiate. The latest collection of her works remains Smith's *The Writings of Anna Wickham: Free Woman and Poet.* Another collection, preferably with textual notes, is long overdue.

A New Matrix for Modernism sets out to show where Charlotte Mew and Anna Wickham originate in terms of their poetics as well as their persons. I use the simplest framework, the chronology of Mew and Wickham's births and deaths and the conjunctions of their personal and publishing histories, to order my chapters in the body of the book. To tie the two together I found Coventry Patmore's "angel in the house" metaphor to be instructive when it can be seen for what it is, rather than what most feminists, following Virginia Woolf's lead, interpret it to be. Using this dominant Victorian metaphor for women as female children allows me to join Mew and Wickham's work, relating their literary production to family politics. Chapters two through four discuss Charlotte Mew's life and work, following her personal and aesthetic development. I place her in a cultural context that explains her importance in an alternative, gendered modernism. These chapters detail Mew's personal, sexual, cultural, and poetic exiles. Beginning her publishing career as one of the New Women who contributed to *The Yellow Book,* she was referred to as the greatest living *poetess* (my italics) by both Virginia Woolf and Thomas Hardy. Chapters five through seven detail Anna Wickham's life and poetry. Considered by Harold Monro, D. H. Lawrence, Amy Lowell, Natalie Barney, Louis Untemeyer, and others to be one of the most innovative and interesting poets of her time, Wickham wrote her life in verses scribbled on pub coasters and kitchen walls, grocery lists and domestic inventories. Like Mew, Wickham suffered a variety of exiles that kept her writing from receiving the prominence it deserves. Although both Mew and Wickham were published in many of the important little magazines of the era, most twentieth-century literary historians have slighted their contributions to the modernist movement and their affinities with their male contemporaries.

Late in the writing process, I discovered Gaston Bachelard's provocative phenomenological inquiries, *The Poetics of Space* (1964) and *The Poetics of Reverie* (1969). These texts encouraged my belief that I not only have workable metaphors, the matrix and the child in the house, but also ones which reveal the heart of any poet's creation of images. Bachelard uses the terms *topophilia* and *topo-analysis* to explain eulogized space in terms of both body and house, and body *as* house. His descriptions of the germ of the essential in our habitations, his chapters, "Miniature," from *Poetics of Space,* and "Reveries toward Childhood" in *The Poetics of Reverie,* link his philosophy to Lévi-Strauss's work in the "Science of the Concrete" chapter in *The Savage Mind,* thereby informing my readings of both Mew and Wickham's poems. Most important, a close reading of the Bachelard texts provides a philosophical underpinning for my contention that Mew and Wickham's poetry must be read through the habitats of these two poets.

As with many such projects, this book started its life as a doctoral dissertation; however, the ideas were born even earlier, in my first doctoral course, "Family Fictions," taught by Judith Giblin James at the University of South Carolina. Her insightful understanding of feminist, literary and cultural politics set me on my path. To navigate, one needs a map; Patricia Gilmartin, professor of Geography and Women's Studies at the University of South Carolina, helped to provide that metaphorical map. Near the end of the dissertation writing, my passion, for Charlotte Mew especially, was refueled by Ed Madden's gracious agreement to serve on my committee. His knowledge of poetics and his personal response to Mew's work boosted my morale at a time when I needed it. I owe my largest debt of gratitude to Thomas J. Rice, my dissertation director, who let me plunder his library, and his brain, for years without complaint and with a calm certainty that this was a workable approach to an important issue.

At Coastal Carolina University my dear friend, Margaret Fain, reference librarian par excellence, has provided whatever I have needed. In this, Peggy Bates, Jeri Traw, and Alison Faix in reference and Sharon Tully in the inter-library loan department have aided her. I would also like to thank the librarians, especially Wayne Furman, Office of Special Collections, at the Berg Collection of English and American Literature, the New York Public Library, Astor, Lenox and Tilden Foundations for their help and permission to quote from a letter from Siegfried Sassoon to Edith Sitwell housed in the collection. Dr. Richard Price of the Modern British collection of the British Library and Joyce Nield and Pam Heaton of Carcanet Press were a great help with copyrights and permissions. Permission to quote from Val Warner's *Charlotte Mew: Collected Poems and Prose* has been granted by Carcanet Press Limited.

Many thanks to the Hepburn family and John Newton whose kind replies to my queries have yielded much valuable direction in putting together the final draft of this book. All the Anna Wickham material is printed by permission of George Hepburn and Margaret Hepburn. Damian Treffs of Routledge Press answered all of my questions promptly and cheerfully. I thank both Mr. Treffs and Professor William Cain, general editor of the series, for their help.

Finally, I would like to thank my husband S. Paul Rice and our children, Jesse and Emily. Our ongoing project of making a family and a home has provided me with the best "poetics of space" in which to work.

A New Matrix for Modernism

CHAPTER ONE

The Bohemian and the Dandy
"The *permanent child* alone can return the fabulous world to us." [1]

The cultural biographer faces a daunting task. Every aspect of society must be considered for its significance in a complete rendering of the social, cultural, and literary nexus that explains the authors or works in question. What the scholar as *bricoleur* searches for in the welter of historical, anthropological, sociological, psychological, and political details are the several conjunctions between these factors and the personal. The trajectory of an individual artist's career, and that artist's place in the literary history of an era, cannot be explained without a careful sifting of the details of the times. The cultural biographer's hope is that attention to the details of elements related to each other through their congruity will reveal aspects of importance that critics or biographers with fixed agendas could not. Literary theory that focuses narrowly on the work itself does not interrogate all the elements that comprise the making of that work. Instead, it should be used to explain the implications revealed by a close attention to cultural and biographical detail. None of the means of exploration and revelation is an end in itself. Their conjunction is necessary for a more complete understanding of the era under discussion. The critic and scholar must become a *bricoleur* who delights in finding useful scraps and discards, which then can be fashioned into something new. The combination of all these factors forms a cultural *poesis*, reconstituting the subject through discursive practice, a careful examination of the conventions of the disciplines, and the exclusions they foster. In the case of this study, that era is modernism, and the poets are Charlotte Mew (1869–1928) and Anna Wickham (1883–1947). A crucial metaphor of Victorian sensibility must be examined before a detailed explanation of how the cultures of Victorian, Edwardian, and modern England, and more specifically, the culture of the city of London shaped the writing of these two women can be formulated.

That metaphor is exploited thoroughly in Coventry Patmore's famous poem, *The Angel in the House*. The ostensible subject of the poem is

Patmore's wife; however, the poem is dedicated to his daughter, Emily Honoria. His wife Emily died in 1862 of tuberculosis and so "Patmore's favorite daughter stood in for her mother as a very present and intimate angel" as John Maynard remarks (152). Maynard postulates that she became Patmore's muse and audience as well as a little mother to her siblings. She was a figure representing (at least in Patmore's mind) man's potential for redirecting physical passion toward a religious ecstasy. In Emily Honoria's mind, her father stood as the patriarchal God of the Old Testament. This symbiotic relationship is the true basis for one of the dominant metaphors used to explain Victorian domestic and sexual mores. However, most critics search no further than the broad implications of the poem.

They follow the lead of Virginia Woolf, whose excoriation of the trope has led them into a clichéd attitude toward a complicated emotional and social construct. First presented as a speech before the London/National Society for Women's Service, January 21, 1931, Woolf's comments on the angel in the house state that she was "a dream, a phantom" that needed to be killed if a woman was to succeed as a writer, because a writer's province and the angel's is the same—the house and all matters of crucial importance to its functioning (*The Pargiters xxvii–xxxiii*). There is no doubt that the latter half of this statement is true, but the first half sets up a false dichotomy between the angel in the house and the woman writer. Woolf does not suppose that the angel is the female child who can grow up to be a writer, just as she herself did. Her manipulation of the metaphor creates an opposition where none need exist. If a woman chooses to write like a man, then, perhaps, the angel needs to be killed. But there are other ways to deal with this specter. Woolf analyzes the bind that the metaphor places on women; however, her words intensify a scrutiny of the general male/female relationship instead of focusing it on the relationship between a man and his child. Perhaps this angle of contemplation was too close to reality for her. She felt that her sister Stella had been sacrificed upon the altar of the metaphor. But again, the Woolf family dynamics is an example of the woman *child* being the angel in the house, substituting for the dead mother. Woolf's problematic relationship with Leslie Stephen, her father, may have colored her reading of *The Angel in the House*.

Charlotte Mew and Anna Wickham were more modern than Woolf in the sense that they, differing from Emily Honoria and Virginia Stephen, who were perhaps stifled by their fathers' successes, were able to reject the influence of their fathers. Mew and Wickham's fathers were social, emotional, and business failures. Rejecting the father enabled them to have a flexible relationship with God. At times rejecting, at times accepting, neither worried too much about His *word*. Instead, they attacked it with their own renderings of the *materna lingua*, the language of the angel in the house, creating a matrix for modernism.

Alice Meynell, whose relationship to Patmore has been documented in many sources, explains Patmore's angel in a way that exposes another, perhaps more applicable meaning. From 1891 to the end of his life in 1896, Meynell became the center of Patmore's life. She was a literary daughter to him, replacing Emily Honoria, who had entered a convent, and then broken with her father when she neared her early death. Maynard proposes that the rupture was caused by the same doubts that Jane Eyre has about Rochester. That any merely mortal man could stand between a woman and her intimate relationship with God put her immortal soul in peril. Patmore's final words to Meynell were, "'Our meeting again in Heaven depends upon your fidelity to the highest things you have known'" (153–59). Although critics have speculated wildly about the nature of the Patmore-Meynell relationship, it is best not to forget or disdain the words of the participants themselves. About *The Angel in the House* Meynell contends:

> It is possible that this early poem is contemned because the reader takes the 'Angel' to be the woman, and an angel obviously feminine is a kind of sentimentality. But I prefer to take the 'Angel' to be Love. [. . .] Together with Love, Patmore's subject was the Child in the House, before ever Pater had so varied Patmore's title. Together with the revelation of youthful love he has coupled all the sweet revelations made to a child:
>
>> This and the child's unheeded Dream
>>
>> Was all the light of all his day. (*Prose and Poetry* 134)

Love and the child's unheeded dream, which is dreamed in the house of its parents, are themes that resonate particularly for Mew and Wickham as women modernists. These ideas take the critic backward to eventually go forward. A *bricoleur* must be retrospective, remembering that the predetermined features of any particular cultural artifact will always limit the possibilities. Again, the perception of Alice Meynell is pivotal. It takes the seeker to the Brontë sisters, whose use of the language of feminine perception helped to define literary Romanticism. In "The Brontës," Meynell characterizes Charlotte as one who knew well the experience of dreams, and as one whose "noblest passages are her own speech or the speech of one like herself acting the central part in the dreams and dramas of emotion that she had kept from her girlhood." And of Emily she remarks "her great words sound at times in paltry mouths" (*Prose and Poetry* 106). Emily is the mistress of disguises; she is one who does the emotions in different voices. Charlotte, in her position as oldest living daughter, functioned as the angel in Haworth parsonage.

The Brontës' literary style stands as a talisman for several generations of women writers. Although Alison Light is writing about the Brontës' influence on Daphne du Maurier when she says, "We might look to the Brontës too for the fascination with the margins of polite society [. . .] and for the familiar themes of bourgeois transgression," and for "the idea of a tumultuous inner life and [. . .] a language of a developing selfhood," her statement holds true for both Charlotte Mew and Anna Wickham (165). They come to the Brontës seeking literary models. In the work of Charlotte and Emily Brontë, women writers read sentence patterns and poetic rhythms that authentically represent the linguistic flow of women's intellectual and emotional concerns. The Brontës were exemplars for the leading late Victorian women writers Mrs. Humphrey Ward, Alice Meynell, and Mrs. Gaskell, and Mary Robinson, who wrote a biography of Emily Brontë for W.H. Allen's *Eminent Women Series* in 1883.

The Victorian Aesthetic Movement, Theosophy, Positivism, and what Warren Smith calls the London heretics also affected the literary development of Mew and Wickham. Mew learned to love the Brontës at the Gower Street School under the influence of its headmistress, Miss Lucy Harrison. Mew's association with *The Yellow Book*, through which she was able to socialize with writers Henry James and Arthur Symons, and the New Women of Grant Allen's *Keynotes* series, influenced her early fiction pieces. The short stories are Mew's first experiments with a variety of styles and voices. While her stories are interesting as forerunners of her poems, they are viewed by several critics as pieces "in the style of" Henry James, Thomas Hardy, popular novelist Rhoda Broughton, and as Penelope Fitzgerald, Mew's biographer, attests, her "overwrought narrator has something about her of Lucy Snow in *Villette*" (60). It is not until one reads them as written in the language of a developing female selfhood that one is able to understand their modernity. *The Yellow Book* authors also showed Mew the pleasures of both literary and literal disguise. For the rest of her life, she made a political, sexual, and literary statement by talking like and dressing as the dandy. This pose functions as a totem of sorts for Mew; in its social, psychological, and ritual elements, she can fashion a mask distinct from her family's class. In dress, actions, and most especially in her writing, the dandy Mew has *killed* the angel in the house.

Wickham, on the other hand, through her parents' interests and connections, lived on the outer circles of the Fabians, the Positivists, and the Theosophists. Her poetry is an intriguing blend of the tone and style of early nineteenth-century wits and the ideas of "Bohemian feminist" Olive Schreiner. While Harry Blamires characterizes Charlotte Mew as "one of those rare minor poets precluded from greatness only by quantity," he castigates Wickham as a versifier of "heartfelt feminine belligerence" with the personality of an "early beatnik" (61–64). Wickham, like Mew, felt compelled to present an image. She became the bohemian, the gypsy, and an earth-mother type whose layered garments fluttered as she walked Hampstead Heath in the company of D.H. Lawrence. Both her look and her work proclaim her essential stance as "Free woman and Poet." Again, as with Mew, the label has totemic significance. The Celtic word for the people of Bohemia is *Boii*—fighter. Wickham spent her life fighting for causes and people, and her right to write.

Philosophically, the two poets share mentors. However, they responded differently to the ideas espoused. The key figure here is the philosopher T.H. Green. With Walter Pater, Algernon Swinburne, John Symonds, and others, T.H. Green was a member of the Old Mortality Society at Oxford (1856–66). A radical literary group, they were "dedicated to social amelioration, liberty of thought, and the ultimate validity of human reason in matters secular and sacred" (Monsman 26). Mew encountered Green's philosophy through her friendship with the novelist May Sinclair. She (and Wickham) almost certainly would have read the bestseller, *Robert Elsmere*, by Mrs. Humphrey Ward, which is dedicated to Green. The novel is about a minister racked by religious doubts who, on the advice of a philosopher (a thinly disguised portrait of Green himself), gives up the ministry to work among the London poor, founding The New Brotherhood of Christ. Warren Smith claims this group is modeled on the actual Fellowship of the New Life which drew many future Fabians to its early meetings, and which, by 1891, had acquired the group-living facility that they named "Fellowship House" at 29 Doughty Street. That was just three years after the Mew family moved from 30 Doughty Street to Bloomsbury (131–39, Fitzgerald 41). Green's philosophical idealism colors all of Sinclair's novels, as it perhaps also influenced the work of H.G. Wells, Dorothy Richardson, E.M. Forster, and Henry James (Zegger 20–21). From Sinclair, then, and perhaps from *Robert Elsmere*, Mew gets several of her central poetic themes, including the "image of a purely human Christ" and the idea that renunciation and sublimation elevate human life (Zegger 354). Anna Wickham absorbed Green's philosophy through her mother's association with several major spiritualist movements and through her own friendship with T.E. Hulme, who was Green's student. The differences between pupil and teacher occur as Hulme pulls away from his mentor's romantic idealism and positivism toward a more classic pessimism, which is the aspect of his philosophy most interesting to T. S. Eliot.

Because neither woman had the systematic education available to an upper-middle class British man, any connection with the dominant ideas of the times is poetic, rather than academic. Gaston Bachelard, in *The Poetics of Reverie,* states that this is the ideal mode for the true poet. He says "[p]eople are so well educated nowadays that they have to be 'taught' their memories—stuffed with sociability and objectivity in able to enter the zone of family, social, and psychological conflict" (107). *Au courant* ideas and images that struck Mew and Wickham personally, they used. The inner psychology of the poetic moment and the idea of poetry as images, and analogies, are points Hulme stresses which resonate with them (Coffman 52–53). Bachelard continues and expands on these ideas in both *The*

Poetics of Space and *The Poetics of Reverie*, phenomenological inquiries into the origins and nature of poetry. His exploration of *topos* as the key to the imagination leads the reader to an understanding of the importance of the house and the room in the house. The intimacy of writing (and reading) a room joins writer and reader in an intuition of the world's space where we can share "the thread of our history as told by others" (*Space xxxi–ii, Reverie* 99). Virginia Woolf claimed that a woman could not write without a room of one's own. Also important to an understanding of how the house trope functions for Mew and Wickham is Shelly Skinner's suggestion that lesbian writers like Radclyffe Hall transform the idea of keeping a house in order by disordering the metaphor to erect a new order that creates a space for the lesbian voice. The writer's voice becomes the house of the soul, and for many women writers this is the only inviolate, intimate space.

Although neither writer articulated her desire to do so, both wrote for the disenfranchised. In their efforts they followed a pattern begun by the Romantics and carried on throughout the nineteenth century. However, their feminist emphasis and frank discussion of female sexuality is modern. Stylistically they practice an intriguing blend of ballad stanza, nonce forms, free verse, and anything that seemed to work. Perhaps what stands out the most about their styles is the ease with which each poet varies her style to fit a particular theme or tone. That they are not limited by anyone's notion of correct prosody or subject matter makes them interesting, rather than "lumbering, halting, and prosaic in texture" as John Gould Fletcher characterized Wickham's work in a contemporary review (165). As much as further study needs to be done on their ties to the great ideas of the times, another study on their innovative use of prosodic devices would reveal their place in the progression of modern prosody.

However, in this study, their function as daughters, as the metaphorical angels in the house, trying to keep faith with outmoded obligations but also attuned to a modern vision of women's place in the twentieth century, is the focus through which their lives and works will be examined. In significant ways during their adulthood, both women still functioned as children in the house. For the person stuck in a real or metaphorical house, the house has to be the site of aesthetic development. Walter Pater's essay "The Child in the House" delineates the child's discovery of its powers so that "the early habitation thus gradually becomes a sort of material shrine or sanctuary of sentiment; a system of visible symbolism interweaves itself through all our thoughts and passions" (152). Bachelard agrees that the house is the key to intimate secrets of the child, and, most importantly in terms of Mew and Wickham's poetry, he confirms that houses and their rooms are the poetic tropes of primary significance (*Space xxxii, 38*). Both Charlotte Mew and Anna Wickham desired the passionate presence of physical love in the house; this work is the story of their search through many rooms.

Like Pater they wished for the inward and the outward to be "woven through and through each other into one inextricable texture" (148); as artists, it is their hope that their words can do the weaving. This kind of weaving is what Margot Norris calls "an unmasterable play of styles" which disrupts the presence and unity of the subject (10). The sites of secret joys and sorrows, these domestic rooms are the supposed provenance of the nineteenth-century woman poet whose capacity for pain provides her inspiration (Walker 89).

Yet in the twentieth century, the modern individual is assumed to be "an autonomous male free of familial and communal ties," and modernity is often read as an Oedipal revolt against the tyranny of Victorian authority (Felski 2–3). Many feminist critics have pointed out that this reading of modernism leaves out the historical significance of the Suffragist movement, to name just one aspect of the contemporary culture, and limits our understanding of an era to the ways it was defined by the work of a small group of men and women who were the intellectual and stylistic avant-garde. Instead, there need to be more studies that discuss the relationships among a variety of factors affecting gender and poetic production at a given historical moment. More balance between the approaches of close reading and historical scholarship is needed to de-homogenize previous analyses of the time period. Rather than approaching the era as existing in defiance of and outside of its own culture, literary historians need to examine its matrix, the surrounding substance from which it originates.

One issue that Norris highlights is the necessity for understanding the modern artist's dilemma. Art that reproduces political ideology and social relations must disavow this fact about itself so that it will not be accused of fostering them. Therefore, the seemingly radical and avant-garde writers who deny any social agenda for their art actually are lying, because this essentialist aesthetic reinforces the status quo (118). Anti-sentimentality is a stylistic position that up to this point has been used to distinguish the modern writer from others. When writers such as Mew and Wickham are accused of being sentimental, they are relegated to the modernist margins because the sentimental, identified with mass culture, was the avant-garde's enemy. The intelligentsia disparaged the semi-educated, making *suburban-ite* a dirty word.

The suburb, on the margins, represented the unknowable, and "the antagonisms, divisions, and sense of irrecoverable loss [the expansion of suburbia] generated, were major shaping factors in twentieth-century literature" (Carey 50). This attitude associates topography with intelligence, or a lack thereof, relating human worth to habitat. A home-style colonialism, which fueled the artistic exodus to the continent, this trend denies its origins and its family. Abandoning the sentimental as weak, or even worse, aesthetically obscene, means moving out of the house and forgetting from where one has come. Conversely, the suburb also stood as a site for daring

new ideas like women's rights. As Carey affirms, the suburb was the loca-
tion of a poetic voice that "avoids and undercuts the kinds of dignity and
authority that males have appropriated." These poems are not pretentious;
they achieve cultural significance because they are not interested in achiev-
ing it. Their tone wavers between a joke and a cry of pain (69). A confla-
tion of women and mass culture captures the ideological bind modern
writers place on themselves. As Suzanne Clark, who believes that mod-
ernist critics used sentimentality to demonize mass culture as a feminized
enemy, writes:

> In order to avoid admitting the rhetorical situation of literature, which
> engages it inevitably in culture, history, and desire [. . .] modernist literary
> criticism endorsed a formalism which avoided ideology by calling women
> ideological, and rejected their sensible attachments to the everyday. [. . .]
> Modernism transferred the lover's discourse from the interior of persons
> to the interior of a text. (6–7)

In doing so, the modernist writer (mistaken as he already was about the
meaning of the angel in the house) began to sentimentalize the angel in the
text just as he said the Victorians had done to woman as angel in the house.
If modernism is defined as an Oedipal struggle, then it has to disregard the
pre-Oedipal narcissism and melancholy, the tones of the sentimental, where
subject and author have not yet delineated the difference between self and
(m)other.

But what of the women poets from the modernist time period who did
not discard the sentimental? They chose to remain in the house. For too
long they have been considered old-fashioned and therefore bad writers.
Because they chose to remain in the womb/room in the suburb, the breed-
ing-ground of the sentimental, their literary production was suspect. If they
took as subject the tensions of their position in this site, in their undifferen-
tiated state, in other words, in their childishness, metaphorically rendered as
angel in the house, then the truths that they told about this condition were
viewed as lies by modernist critics who were busy perpetuating a contrast-
ing myth or lie. Their reputations could not recover. Yet, as Bachelard
reminds his readers: "With poetry, the imagination takes its place on the
margin, exactly where the function of unreality comes to charm or dis-
turb—always to awaken—the sleeping being lost in its automatisms"
(*Space* xxxi). And again, "The *permanent child* alone can return the fabu-
lous world to us" (*Reverie* 118).

When we ponder the fall into obscurity that the standing of some writ-
ers takes, we have to consider many factors. In the late nineteenth and early
twentieth centuries, a nexus of occurrences that sometimes had little to do
with the actual writing produced created literary status in England. The
discarded writers from various periods deserve a closer reevaluation, if for
no other reason than the fact that their lives and works fill out a picture of
certain literary movements or impulses that have been too narrowly

defined. Neglected writers, such as the World War I poet Ivor Gurney, have re-emerged as worthy subjects for literary scholars. Others, such as Walter de la Mare, are now being examined for their influence on their fellow writers, and for stylistic innovations which were ignored or dismissed by several groups bent on highlighting their own poetic agendas at the expense of the broad spectrum of British poetry and its loyal readers. As Robert H. Ross remarks, "For a few years, amid shouts and jeers, behind dust and tumult, the postwar coteries succeeded in obscuring the voice of English poetry, but they could not choke it into silence" (200).

The task set before a woman writer who wished for her work to be considered seriously by other writers, publishers and reviewers, was formidable. In order for historians of modernism to begin to tell a more inclusive truth about its contours, both Charlotte Mew and Anna Wickham must be returned from exile; contemporary critics must reevaluate their contribution to one of the most influential and exciting periods of poetry. This period has often been defined as a male revolt against the authority figures of the Victorian era. It is now time, Felski urges, to construct a counter-myth of emblematic *ostranenie* (de-familiarization), which disrupts the previous automatic reading (23). *Ostranenie* is best accomplished in a site that is itself disruptive. For many women poets that site is the suburb. The suburb has been dismissed as an artistic no-man's-land full of philistines, but it is just this dismissal by widely acknowledged and accepted writers that makes it such an attractive site for the woman writer. The border between places is always an area of tension, yet the high modernist dismissal of the importance of the suburb negated this concept. The emotional and physical center of the suburb is the single-family home.

As Victor Turner explains it, the boundary is a liminal site where the state of the subject is ambiguous. This realm has few or none of the characteristics of either the past or the coming state (5). Suburbs are neither country nor city but are in the stage of becoming something different from both while retaining some of the characteristics of each. To express this idea in a way that conforms to Turner's paradigm, the suburb is an adolescent. The *personae* in this stage are invisible, complex, bizarre, and thought of as at once both living and dead, wandering in a realm of pure possibility. "Their condition is one of ambiguity and paradox, a confusion of all the customary categories," and they are symbolically either sexless or bisexual, or assigned characteristics of both sexes so that they are often regarded as human *prima materia* (Turner 7–8). Turner's discussion of the liminal state maps the emotional location of Mew and Wickham's product and theoretical stance. Although the suburb is not a force in every one of their poems, it is featured in several of their most powerful statements. Mew's "In Nunhead Cemetery" is set in the SE 15 section of London, and Wickham's "Nervous Prostration" begins "I married a man of the Croydon class" referring to the southeastern suburbs surrounding the Crystal Palace

site. Using Turner's paradigm to describe both an actual place and an intel-
lectual or emotional response to a location allows the critic to conceptual-
ize a space and a shape that explain these women's artistic movements
more completely and accurately than do previous literary groupings.

The case of Charlotte Mew, who was considered at her death to be the
greatest living poetess by both Thomas Hardy and Virginia Woolf, shows
what can happen to a writer's life work when that writer refuses to play the
game of cliques, or jump to one side over the city versus country divide. She
also refused to do the job of self-aggrandizing so necessary for one's liter-
ary reputation. At the height of the poetry public's interest in her work, for
several understandable reasons, Mew retreated into a deliberately created
enigmatic public persona which put others off, and isolated her from the
necessary social situations that could have cemented the contacts she need-
ed to foster a wider interest in her poetry. She did this, for the most part,
because of the straitened economic circumstances of her family, which did
not allow her to reciprocate any entertainments. Also, she was most clear-
eyed about the issue of being taken-up by poetasters. As she says in
"Fame":

> Sometimes in the over-heated house, but not for long,
>
> Smirking and speaking rather loud,
>
> I see myself among the crowd,
>
> Where no one fits the singer to his song,
>
> Or sifts the unpainted from the painted faces
>
> Of the people who are always on my stair [. . .]
>
> (*Collected Poems and Prose* 2)

Although both Mew and Wickham have been identified with the
Georgian poets because of their association with Harold Monro, in fact,
neither was ever published in Edward Marsh's Georgian anthologies. Still,
this casual association has served to prevent close study of their books. If
Mew were to be categorized as a *type*, then perhaps she must be called
either a New Woman or a *Yellow Book* aesthete; yet neither of these des-
ignations fully explains either her poetic subject matter, or her style. Critics
such as Angela Leighton and Celeste M. Schenck differ on their placement
of Mew into a tradition. Whereas Leighton classifies Mew as the last
Victorian, Schenck views her as one of the founders of a female modernism.
Leighton's discussion of Mew's style is thorough, but I believe that it
strengthens the case for Mew's modernism, rather than her Victorianism.
Mew's career as a poet came after she had already garnered a following as
a short story writer.

At the turn of the century, she was one of the cadre of writers who pub-
lished in *The Yellow Book*. As such, she fraternized at editor Henry
Harland's Saturday evenings with Henry James, Arthur Symons, Max

Beerbohm, and George Moore, among others. Through her association with Mrs. Dawson Scott, founder of International PEN, and the novelist May Sinclair, Mew was introduced to a circle of poets and writers which included Evelyn Underhill, the religious mystical poet; Elisaveta Allen, the publisher Grant Allen's ex-wife; Edward Garnett; Austin Harrison of the *English Review*; and Ezra Pound who was at the height of his influence on literary England (Warner "Introduction" *Collected Poems and Prose x*). Her poetry was published in *The Egoist* and *The Nation*, and earlier, between 1899 and 1905, the magazine *Temple Bar* published many of her prose pieces.

As well, her work had come to the attention of Harold Monro of the Poetry Bookshop through the auspices of Alida Klemantaski (later to become Mrs. Monro), who had been so deeply affected by Mew's poem "The Farmer's Bride" when she read it in *The Nation* in 1912 that, as she notes in "Charlotte Mew-A Memoir," she had memorized it (*vii*). It would seem that Charlotte Mew's place in the history of early twentieth-century English letters was assured. Yet after the Poetry Bookshop publication of *The Farmer's Bride* in 1916, its reissue in 1921 with eleven new poems, and its publication in the United States as *Saturday Market* by Macmillan in 1921, Mew's only other book of poetry, *The Rambling Sailor*, was published posthumously by the Poetry Bookshop in 1929. In 1953 Duckworth published *The Collected Poems of Charlotte Mew*, which included the memoir by Alida Monro, but this reissue did not generate a corresponding critical reevaluation of her place in English modernism. Her short stories were not collected until 1981 when Virago, in association with Carcanet Press, issued *Charlotte Mew: Collected Poems and Prose* (hereafter noted as *CPP*), introduced and edited by Val Warner. In 1984, as part of the Radcliffe Biography Series, Penelope Fitzgerald published *Charlotte Mew and Her Friends*. A thorough, but somewhat idiosyncratic view of Mew's life and work, which includes a selection of fifteen of Mew's poems, it is characterized by Brad Leithauser in his foreword as lucid and respectfully restrained (3). Such an approach is helpful for the generalist interested in Mew's life, but it does not address the problem of Mew's neglect by a generation of literary critics. Neither does Warner's introduction to the collected work; however, Warner's most recent essay, "New Light on Charlotte Mew" and her introduction to *Charlotte Mew: Collected Poems and Selected Prose* (1997) correct Fitzgerald's inaccuracies. Most importantly, Warner's efforts have kept Mew's work in print and Warner's approach to Mew's life and work always foregrounds poetry over politics. *Charlotte Mew: Complete Poems* (2000), edited and with a preface and notes by John Newton, is indispensable for any Mew scholar. While both Newton and Warner believe that Mew deserves to be acknowledged as one of England's foremost poets, Ian Hamilton, in his introduction to *Charlotte*

Mew: Selected Poems (1999) is primarily pejorative; yet his overall assessment is that she is a poet of lasting value (10–16).

As Celeste M. Schenck notes in her introduction to Mew's work, which appears in Bonnie Kime Scott's *The Gender of Modernism: A Critical Anthology* (1990), "critics have only begun to reevaluate the corpus so admired by Mew's contemporaries" (316). In this short introduction and in "Exiled by Genre: Modernism, Canonicity, and the Politics of Exclusion" in *Women's Writing in Exile* (1989), Schenck makes the point that there are varieties of modernism that must be analyzed in order to dismantle the monolithic movement of "white, male, international Modernism" ("Mew" 320 n.1). She notes that both Charlotte Mew and Anna Wickham have been neglected by students of modern poetry because, like other female modernists, they have been both exiled "from and to poetic form," both condemned for their poetic gentility and for their feminist and/or sexual radicalism ("Exiled" 231, 235). Women modernists have a kind of cultural self-consciousness that causes them to use varied *personae*, and varied forms to place their themes in front of a public, which might not have been ready for either the ideas or the style in which they are presented. Schenck also points out that while the radical poetics of male modernists sometimes masks conservative politics, so do the conservative, even genteel, poetics of some women modernists mask a radical sexual politics ("Exiled" 231). It is now time to peel away the careful stylistic layering of poets like Mew and Wickham to reveal just what they have contributed to the shifting dimensions of modernism.

Some of the factors mentioned above, which, while contributing directly to the power of Charlotte Mew's poetry, had on the surface little to do with it. Yet the juggernaut of white, male, international modernism caused Mew's powerful effect on her contemporaries to dissipate after her suicide in 1928. When Thomas Hardy died shortly before Mew herself, Mew lost her most influential mentor. At home, her position as the angel in the house of her family, and the family's secret shame that her only living brother and one sister were schizophrenics confined to institutions, caused the mysteriousness of her personality that was much remarked upon by all who met her. Her rigid demarcations between public and private life left her at death with few intimates. Alida Monro, Florence Hardy, and Sydney Cockerell were the only literary people who communicated with her in the weeks before her death.

The other mystery, the puzzle of Mew's sexual orientation, also plays its part in Mew's social and artistic isolation. It is my contention that Mew's family life and her sexual orientation caused a withdrawal of interest in her poetry in the early days of the cult of personality which has stipulated that the character of a writer must be on display so that the work can be marketed in terms of a personal interest as well as a more detached professional interest in the quality of the product. This focus on personality applied especially to women writers. As well, Mew was a writer for *The Yellow Book* when the scandal over Oscar Wilde broke. Even though the publication had nothing to do with Wilde himself, because of Aubrey Beardsley's illustrations it became associated in the public's mind with Wilde's homosexuality. Therefore, Charlotte Mew could not allow herself to have anything further to do with it. Because of these constraints, Mew never felt safe displaying her true self, and, after several painful rebuffs, she gradually withdrew from all activities that brought her to the attention of her peers.

In spite of receiving a Civil List pension of seventy-five pounds per annum, recommended by John Masefield, Walter de la Mare, and Thomas Hardy in 1923, Mew wrote very little after 1916 (Alida Monro *xx*). Still, her influence on her fellow poets was an important aspect of modernism. Although several writers have acknowledged her debt to Hardy, only Robert Gittings in *Thomas Hardy's Later Years* acknowledges that Hardy might have caught an echo of Mew in his poem "Nobody Comes" (203). As well, there are definite correspondences between her poems and T.S. Eliot's. These are outlined briefly in "Another Handful of Dust" by John Newton in TLS, April 28, 1995, and by Gary Day and Gina Wisker in "Recuperating and Revaluing: Edith Sitwell and Charlotte Mew" (1995). Kathleen Bell's essay, "Charlotte Mew, T.S. Eliot and Modernism" continues to find parallels between Eliot and Mew's work. Bell focuses on Mew's "The Quiet House," comparing it to "The Love Song of J. Alfred Prufrock." Bell believes that Mew's modernism is more clear than Eliot's because it carries the logic of the modernist agenda to its end: to self-destruction. Mew's gaps and fragments and the underlying intense, but suppressed emotion of a range of alienated, marginal *personae* make her a plausible (though unacknowledged) model for Eliot's work (13–24). John Newton's "Charlotte Mew's Place in the Future of English Poetry" reads Mew beside her mentor, Thomas Hardy, and her contemporary, T.S. Eliot. Newton makes his case that Mew's "bald and stark directness in tragic representation" and her absolute authority and timelessness mark her as one of England's greatest modernists. He believes that the direction of English poetry would have been better served by the Mew model which would help to teach poets how " to be powerfully direct, passionate, and charged in the simplest and purest English language [. . .]"(32–46). With champions like Newton, Mew is assured of her rightful place in the re-visioning of modernism. The American poet, Richard Howard, declares, "[s]he had found a way of making a poem, big long poems, important statements, not at all wispy or minor" (*n. pag.*) and wonders in an interview why she was not one of the poets introduced to him when he was a student at Columbia University.

The restrictions that obligations to her family placed on Charlotte Mew link her to Anna Wickham. Both writers spliced writing into their family life, and both suffered in reputation because of their conflicting desires to be the mainstays of their family and to have the freedom of a poet's empty hours. Mew and Wickham were hampered from their childhood by the burden placed on them by their families. They, like Patmore's daughter Emily, served as mother, daughter, and most importantly as moral touchstone for Victorian families fissured by death and the misunderstandings between husband and wife.

With the poet Anna Wickham, four mysteries about her mother's paternity, Wickham's birth, her husband's death, and her own death must be explored. She had great natural talent as a singer and versifier, but her career as an artist ended long before her suicide in 1947. A brief resurgence of interest in her work and life occurred in the late 1970s with the publication of Margaret Newlin's essay, "Anna Wickham: 'The Sexless part which is my mind'" in *The Southern Poetry Review* (1978), and "Feminist Themes in Anna Wickham's *The Contemplative Quarry and The Man with a Hammer*" by Myra Stark in volume two of *Four Decades of Poetry* (1978). Most recently, Ann Vickery's "Between a Modernist Passport and House Arrest: Anna Wickham and the Question of Cultural Identity" appeared in *Soundings: Poetry and Poetics* (1998).

In 1984, R.D. Smith's *The Writings of Anna Wickham: Free Woman and Poet* (hereafter noted as *WAW*) appeared. Admirable as an introduction to the poet, and the most wide-ranging compilation of her writing to date, this work does not delve into the factors that determine the complete contemporary lack of interest in her writing, even from feminist critics who have decried the dearth of information about early twentieth-century models. However, it does include "Fragment of an Autobiography: Prelude to a Spring Clean" begun by Wickham on March 4, 1935 (hereafter noted as "Fragment"). I have employed this long prose piece as a key to the mysteries of Wickham's situation as both woman and poet. By examining the verbal clues that Wickham drops, I have been able to form a picture of Wickham, which opens further possibilities for scholarship. Smith's editing of Wickham's work includes changing the titles to some of her poems and correcting "evident nonsenses" in her punctuation, which Smith characterizes as "impatient and erratic" (Editor's note *xxv*). From the viewpoint of scholars, even more damaging to a full understanding of this poet is Smith's heavy editing of the first two chapters of "Fragment," which contain "long-winded historical speculation" (Editor's note *xxvi*). I submit that it is just this kind of historical speculation that drives one of Wickham's greatest impulses, namely her sense of feminist and class outrage. Any contemporary critic approaching Wickham's work from a post-colonial, new historical, or feminist critical standpoint would need just the information that R.D. Smith rejected. In 1986 *The Women's Review* published two important pieces of Wickham material. Volume five contains "I & My Genius," another autobiographical fragment, in which Wickham details her incarceration in an asylum precipitated by her husband's objections to the publication of her poetry. James Hepburn, Anna Wickham's oldest son, contributes "Anna Wickham," an account of Wickham's final poem and suicide to volume seven.

Celeste Schenck has contributed important work on Wickham. Schenck's contributions are critical to reviving an interest in the work of Wickham and her contemporary, Charlotte Mew. Yet Schenck's focus is on the "politics of canonicity and even [. . .] inadvertent feminist adherence to a politically suspect hierarchy of genre," not on the poetic contributions of the writers themselves ("Exiled" 231). In 1994, Jennifer Jones's dissertation, *The Poetry and Place of Anna Wickham: 1910–1930* appeared. This thorough discussion of Wickham benefits from Jones's friendship and correspondence with George Hepburn, Anna Wickham's only surviving son, and Margaret Hepburn, James Hepburn's widow. Jones's stellar scholarship provides the groundwork for any future discussion of Wickham and her writing. I hope to build on Jones's scholarship, and on Schenck's hypothesis, expanding and strengthening her points about both Charlotte Mew and Anna Wickham. The most important points that Schenck makes about Wickham's poetry are her urging that the poems "should not merely be read as unsophisticated concessions to the popular conventions of the day" and that we acknowledge our collusion as feminist critics in the exiling of writers like Wickham whose poems do not easily fit into the prescribed poetic dicta of Ezra Pound or T.S. Eliot, or even of H.D., Virginia Woolf, or the Sitwells ("Exiled" 239–42). The point Schenck does not make is that Wickham's feminism, as well as her poetry, might be too divergent from the prescribed feminist dicta. Jones notes that critics almost always mimic each other in categorizing Anna Wickham and her work (11). In this sense, Mew is an easier study because feminist critics can focus on her cross-dressing and lesbianism as indicators of her modernism; however, Mew's poetry remains problematic for the feminist modernist critic more at ease with the spare austerity of an H.D. or the detached and whimsical irony of a Marianne Moore. Illuminating the web of relationships among women modernists is a process in which critics sometimes still have fallen into a politics of exclusion based on poetic style. In the rush to establish a feminist body of work, we also need to be aware of our tendencies to exclude or include writers based on their lifestyles.

I will delineate Anna Wickham's career, and the demise of interest in it, paying special attention to publishing decisions, poetic fashion, socio-cultural considerations, Wickham's family history, and her life as a daughter, wife, mother, and poet. Looking into the several mysteries that surround her personal, poetic, and publishing history, I hope to be able to answer why Anna Wickham is not still hailed as the "free woman and poet" that she fashions herself. Because Anna Wickham does not fit neatly into a particular category, she and her writing have been given cursory attention by the many feminist scholars whose work on other forgotten writers of the period has been exemplary. Even in recent feminist studies of the era, Wickham has been relegated to the margins, or only given a cursory nod, because no one has found a school or a political/feminist niche in which to place her. I submit that a study of Wickham's life and work would tell us much about her own and other lost voices of the time because she is more representative than hasty examinations of her career reveal. Often, both Wickham and Mew are included in anthologies or critical discussions about the gender of modernism merely to make the point that women who did not follow all the stylistic innovations of the modernist males, or followed them sporadically, or erratically, or who used them to delineate a feminist political agenda, were not the ones that male literary arbiters, such as Ezra Pound and T.S. Eliot, chose to help with their careers.

The women poets whose careers were helped, especially poets like H.D. and Marianne Moore, have, until recently, been seen as writers who toed the imagist and formalist lines. This happened because their other work, which did not conform to the precepts of their mentors (for example, H.D.'s "Notes on Thought and Vision," or Moore's "Marriage"), was seen to have subject matter "[t]oo close for comfort" as Marilyn L. Brownstein says (330). Therefore these works were ignored in the discussions about their style. Much of the poetry written by women of the early modernist era was about subjects too close for comfort for their fellow writers; and these fellows ignored it, disparaged it, or argued *ad feminam*.

R.D. Smith recounts Harold Acton's reaction to Anna Wickham's charisma, which he found not *comme il faut*, and, although he does not say who it is, Smith describes an American "culture-snob" who characterized Wickham as a "'burly lady fortified in advance with garlic and wine'"(2). Often, Anna Wickham's person blocked readers' reception of her poetic *personae*. The reaction to Charlotte Mew's look, and by extension, her work, focuses on her size two hand-made boots, her velvet-collared Chesterfield coat, and the pork-pie hat that she wore rammed straight down on her brow (Alida Monro *viii*). Most firsthand accounts of Mew describe her as a woodland sprite or elf dressed as an Edwardian dandy. The fact that both Mew and Wickham often favored a male-voiced persona over a female or androgynous one has never been thoroughly discussed, although it is one of the reasons that their work is hard to classify. They "do" "in different voices" just as Eliot did, but unfortunately, or perhaps fortunately, Ezra Pound did not take up their cause with as much enthusiasm as he championed Eliot's.

Perhaps one day Anna Wickham's over one thousand unpublished poems will be published, or at least edited into a more comprehensive collection than David Garnett's *Selected Poems by Anna Wickham* (1971), R.D. Smith's *The Writings of Anna Wickham*, or Jane Dowson's collection of twelve poems in her *Women's Poetry of the 1930's: A Critical Anthology* (1996). T. I. Fytton Armstrong, using the pseudonym John Gawsworth, edited the final compilation of her poems while Wickham was alive. It appeared in 1936 as *Anna Wickham: Richard's Shilling Selections*. Of these thirty-six poems, thirty were new (Dowson 165–66). More close scholarly attention, along the lines of Jones's investigations, needs to be paid to this treasure-trove of material.

That there would be considerable interest now in a more complex presentation of both Mew's and Wickham's work is evidenced by their inclusion in the New York Public Library's popular exhibit, "The Hand of the Poet: Part One: John Donne to T.S. Eliot" (November 3, 1995 to July 31, 1996). This exhibit included a holograph signed manuscript of Mew's "Love Love Today," a letter to Mew from Florence Hardy, and a letter lamenting Mew's death from Siegfried Sassoon to Edith Sitwell, as well as several photographs of Mew and two editions of *The Farmer's Bride*. Five poems of Wickham's appeared, copied out by D.H. Lawrence, along with a photograph and a copy of *The Contemplative Quarry* (*The Hand of the Poet* exhibit catalogue 8–9). Reviewing the exhibit, Amy Gameran states, "For me, the great discovery is a poet named Anna Wickham." She praises Wickham's poem "Bridegroom," which appears "neatly copied out by Wickham's good friend, D.H. Lawrence," calling it "a mysterious poem with the simple language and rhythms of a hymn" (A13).

Serious study of the lives and works of Charlotte Mew and Anna Wickham is long overdue. Their connections to prominent modern writers, and their heterodox poetry need to be explored to reveal a further facet of the ongoing expansion of our understanding of the modernist enterprise. We should allow them, as Wickham says, to "reveal our common mystery"; to reveal "more I's than yet were in one human"; to "give you *woman*" (R.D. Smith 1). The cultural-biographical approach, combining information from a wide variety of disciplines, can be the means for understanding these angels in the house in the most comprehensive way; since it combines whatever aspects of the late nineteenth and early twentieth century that are necessary for our appreciation of these women's work, it does not leave out details which do not fit a predetermined critical stance. Rather, it focuses on answering why and how Mew and Wickham were forgotten.

Anna Wickham herself acknowledges the impact her life has on her work, so she violates the formalist dictum that art stands separate from life and that the life of the poet is not important in evaluating the work. My discussion of Wickham's style and themes will show how she wrote for her life, scorning the mask. As she states in the lines used to preface all her work, "Here is no sacrificial I," and as she says in "Self Analysis," "The tumult of my fretted mind/ Gives me expression of a kind;/ [. . .] My work has the incompetence of pain" (*WAW* 192).[2] Using several key poems as examples, I shall show that she must be given a place in the revised, more inclusive history of modernist poetry.

Anna Wickham stands beside Charlotte Mew, and Mina Loy, H.D., Marianne Moore, Amy Lowell, Laura (Riding) Jackson, Edith Sitwell, Nancy Cunard, and others whose work has been neglected in the accounts of a masculine-centered modernism which focuses on the poetry and prose of Ezra Pound, William Butler Yeats, T. S. Eliot, D.H. Lawrence, and James Joyce, and their male followers. In Mew and Wickham's cases especially, an evaluation of the work must begin with their lives, or as much of them as they choose to reveal. Because their poems can be read as cultural representations of the experience and perception of marginalized segments of early twentieth-century British society, the matrices of their poems must be explored. To refute, in some cases, and to strengthen, in others, the evaluations of their work by their contemporaries, serious consideration must be given to the poems and prose of Mew and Wickham, not only reading them as cultural representations, but, most importantly, to continue reading them as writings which have the power to delight and move their readers throughout the years.

Charlotte Mary Mew 1869–1894
"The moon's dropped child"[1]

Like Thomas Hardy, her favorite fellow poet, Charlotte Mew's father was an architect. When she was born in 1869 Fred Mew had become the junior partner in the firm of Henry Edward Kendall, Junior. The Kendall firm, under the direction of the first H.E. Kendall, was responsible for building or remodeling the houses of the Earls of Bristol, Egremont, and Hardwicke, as well as many churches, prisons, workhouses and castles in the Gothic manner ("Henry Edward Kendall, Architect" 33). Unlike Hardy, both Kendalls were considered gentlemen, so when Fred Mew, the son of an Isle of Wight innkeeper, married the daughter of Kendall junior, Anna Maria Marden Kendall, in 1863, he was expected to transform himself into a gentleman for the sake of his wife's expectations. The young Mews took a good address at No. 30 Doughty Street, W.C.1, which overlooked Mecklenburgh Square, to be close to Anna Maria's parents, who resided in the much more superior Brunswick Square. Like Hardy, Fred Mew was a good jobbing architect. His father-in-law, a busy, successful builder and designer of private homes, Ecclesiastical and Board Schools, and County Lunatic Asylums for Essex, Sussex, and Dorset, and the district surveyor of Hampstead, needed a confidant and helpmate. Both Kendall's own son, Edward Herne, and a nephew had been articled but never finished their training and never practiced ("The Late Mr. Henry Edward Kendall, Architect" 883–84, Fitzgerald 13–14). Kendall's sister had married Lewis Cubitt, a pupil of her father's and one of three brothers who all became notable Victorian builders. Lewis Cubitt designed King's Cross Station, which, when it was completed in the mid-1850s, was the last station complex designed entirely by one man (Metcalfe 70). However, the firm of William and Lewis Cubitt still was not as successful as the royally sanctioned architectural firm of the third brother, Thomas Cubitt. The Cubitt connection conferred status on the Kendalls and the Mews. So, as was the case in many *petite bourgeoisie* Victorian homes, the women harbored great expectations of the country-bred in-comer, Fred Mew. He was to rise and prosper. But Fred Mew stubbornly refused to do so. Perhaps, like Hardy's, his heart was not in designing and building. The evidence is clear.

When Kendall junior died in 1885, Mew was only able to keep the firm going under reduced circumstances. In fact, the only jobs he finished after Kendall's death were two, both of which had been commissioned before Kendall died. Why this was so illustrates much about the Victorian temper concerning reputation and social class. The family's personal tragedy must have also contributed to the destruction of Fred Mew's desire for success, but a public scandal was the ostensible cause of Mew's dive into obscurity. In 1876 Kendall and Mew won the competition for the building of the new Hampstead Vestry Hall. However, a losing competitor wrote to the local newspaper, the *Hampstead & Highgate Express*, about a vestryman who had been touting the merits of a design that he had seen previous to the competition. The loser asserted that said design did not really meet the requirements of the project. Shortly thereafter, it was rumored that Henry Kendall, who had been Hampstead's district surveyor since 1844, had an unfair advantage in the contest. By the time the building was completed in November, 1878, Hampstead residents had complained in their newspaper about the bright red brick façade that made them dizzy, about the vestry having to crouch in the half-finished hallways, and that the date carved over the entrance, 1877, was foolishly optimistic for a design whose motto was *cavendo tutus* (caution means safety). The cloud of suspicion and innuendo that grew over the building of the Hampstead Vestry Hall damaged the reputation of Kendall and Mew. By 1878 Fred Mew was forced to borrow a hundred pounds to keep the business going (Fitzgerald 39–41). For another seven years the firm manages, somehow, to survive.

At the time of his death on June 9, 1885, Henry Kendall, who had recently moved his family from the elegant Brunswick Square to the much reduced circumstances of Burlington Road, Westbourne Park, near Paddington Station, left an estate valued at a mere six hundred pounds ("The Late" 883–84, Fitzgerald 41).

How the Cubitts must have gossiped about the man. He had worked on many illustrious projects, including ones for Lord Lytton; the Earl of Kilmore; at Farnborough, the residence of the Empress Eugenie; and at Pope's villa at Twickenham. How could his fortunes have fallen so low? The winner of Royal Academy medals, a founder of the Royal Institute of British Architects, the noted author of *Modern Architecture* (1846) and *Designs for Schools and School Houses* (1847) advocating the Gothic style, Henry Kendall had to suffer the ignominy of having his last work summed up in his obituary as "the erection of the new vestry-hall at Hampstead, &c" ("The Late" 883). However, the business burden of the disgrace would have fallen squarely on Fred Mew's shoulders because Kendall had withdrawn from the firm, in all but name, by the early 1880s.

Fred Mew was a convenient scapegoat for a number of reasons. His tradesman attitudes and country ways could be blamed for the lack of new commissions, because someone of the stature of Lord Lytton would prefer to deal with a gentleman, even if that gentleman were in a profession that had its *in trade* side. Further, even though Kendall had made Mew the executor of his will, not the beneficiary, the Kendall women felt somehow that Fred was after the money. Fitzgerald mentions that Mrs. Kendall's will, made in 1883, gives one-third of her Cobham family money to Anna Maria "'for her sole use and benefit separate and apart from and exclusive of her said husband Frederick Mew, and that she may hold and enjoy and dispose of such share in the same manner as if she were unmarried'" (41). The Kendall women blamed Fred Mew because he was not a gentleman, much as Anna Wickham's grandmother and aunts would sneer at her father, Geoffrey Harper, for the same reason. Alida Monro reinforces this view (and where else would she have gotten the idea if not from Charlotte) saying Fred "seems to have been a man who took his responsibilities very lightly [. . .] leaving nothing, having spent all his available capital on living" (*ix*). When Fred Mew died in 1898, his architectural accomplishments were so little remembered that *The Builder* did not even print a memorial; although Penelope Fitzgerald mistakenly says they did print one a year later, I have found no record of it.

Lest too much blame for the failing family fortunes be placed unfairly on the shoulders of Fred Mew, several other factors about the Kendall and Mew family dynamics must be taken into account. The senior Henry Edward Kendall lived almost one hundred years, dying on January 4th, 1875. His obituary in *The Builder* terms him the "Nestor of architects," mentioning that his father was a banker from York and that Kendall had been a pupil of both Thomas Leverton and "the celebrated Mr. Nash."[2] Kendall senior built the London house of Thomas Kemp, the developer of Kemp Town in Brighton, and he built churches in Ramsgate; Trent, Middlesex; and Bantry, Ireland. For fifty years he was the surveyor of St-Martin's-in-the-Fields and St. Anne, Soho, as well as being (with his son, whose idea it was) one of the founders of the Royal Institute of British Architects ("Henry Edward Kendall, Architect" 33).

There is in Kendall senior's obituary the faint hint that he was a *bon vivant*, if not a full-fledged Regency rake. The adjectives "tall," "handsome," "noble," "generous," "refined," and "winning" are all used to describe him. It also mentions that he was an avid shooter who lost his left thumb when his gun burst, but that this did not deter him from his sport. Perhaps his autumn shooting trips took place at the country homes of his relative by marriage, Thomas Cubitt (1788–1855) whose building business was so successful that at his death he left over one million pounds (Dixon 57). However close the Kendalls and Cubitts might have been, the Kendall men did not mirror the Cubitt business acumen. Old Kendall had left very little beyond the Brighton property because he had entertained lavishly all his life. Or perhaps he left the bulk of his estate to his second wife rather than to "the fruit of his first marriage" as the obituary so poetically calls them. One last anecdote from his obituary serves to paint the Kendall attitude. Although Kendall senior's designs won both the first and second prizes in the contest for a Gothic chapel for Kensal-Green cemetery, the design of Sir John D. Paul, chairman of the company that owned the cemetery, was chosen for execution. *The Builder* applauds Kendall senior for refusing to undertake the commission. It is more likely that the Kendall men, instead of the maligned Fred Mew, are the ones who spent all their available capital on living and keeping up their wives' responsibilities as the women of "one of the first families" of Brighton, which they became because of their Cubitt connections.

In a small way, the Kendalls were part of an important English architectural moment—the Gothic Revival.[3] Kendall senior was a friend of Augustus Charles Pugin, a French nobleman who fled the revolution. The architect, John Nash, used Pugin's decorative, detailed drawings and probably Kendall and Pugin met in Nash's offices. Both Pugin and the Kendalls exhibited at the Royal Academy and Pugin wrote many books on European Gothic and picturesque architecture (Dixon 184). One of the Kendalls' cherished pictures was Pugin's line drawing of Kendall senior's design for the Sessions House at Sleaford ("Henry Edward Kendall, Architect" 33). His son, Augustus Welby Northmore Pugin, was one of the leading thinkers, writers and designers of the Neo-Gothic architectural movement. He believed that the devotion of the architect to his work must be the same devotion as a religious feels toward the order. He also declared that all Classical architecture was false, pagan, and Utilitarian, championing the Picturesque and Gothic as more functional and practical for a variety of activities such as those that occur in churches and schools.

Welby Pugin was extremely scornful and sarcastic about those contemporaries who pursued architecture as a business (Dixon 22, 184–5). The Kendalls, who contributed articles to *The Ecclesiologist*, a publication begun in 1841, shared Pugin's attitude. This journal grew out of the Cambridge Movement, which focused on church building and the reformation of liturgy while the Oxford Movement stood for doctrinal reform (Dixon 194). An amateurish, enthusiastic, gentlemanly approach to their profession set the Kendalls apart from their relatives the Cubitts, who were some of the most successful speculative builders in Victorian England, completing projects in Belgravia; Banbury Estate, North London; and Kemp Town, Brighton, in the Classical style (Dixon 59).

Although Charlotte Mew was only six when her great-grandfather died, she and her sister Anne, rather than the oldest Mew son, inherited the obligation to Kendall standards for keeping up appearances and genteel behavior at all costs. The emblem, which fixed the Kendall attitude in their minds, was the drawing by their grandfather, Henry Kendall Jr., which he produced as a "fancy" for the river entrance of Rosherville on the Thames, a modest development. The drawing of the Shining City was exhibited in 1851 at the Royal Academy and later in the English section of the Paris Salon where Baudelaire was taken by it (Fitzgerald 25–6). Titled "A Composition," it influenced Baudelaire's writing of "Reve parisien" which appeared in the 1861 edition of *Les Fleurs du Mal* (Davidow "Biography" 15–17). For Charlotte and Anne, this picture of marble staircases, monuments, fleets at anchor, and tiny people dwarfed by golden gates, was the family New Jerusalem.

Perhaps this shining city is the site where Charlotte's artistic values were born. As Bachelard remarks, "One must go beyond logic in order to experience what is large in what is small (*Space* 150). Mew's poem, "Not for that City" speaks of the dilemma of finding a place in which to confront eternity. For the persona, it is a staircase seen from afar—a marble staircase in her New Jerusalem. This silent rising form with "the grace of a curved line is not a simple Bergsonian movement with well placed inflexions. Nor is it merely a time that unreels. It is also habitable space harmoniously constituted" (Bachelard *Space* 145). The Kendall fancy helped develop a taste for what was only attainable through the imagination. How often would Charlotte and Anne wish themselves into the picture? The frustrations of their reality as opposed to the freedom of the imagination gave them a thirst for the unattainable. The girls' pre-lapsarian fantasy developed at the Mew farm at Newfairlee on the Isle of Wight. It was their family Eden. The elegiac tone of most of Mew's poems can be attributed to the slow realization that Charlotte and Anne would never reach the New Jerusalem; the family Eden was lost when their youngest sister, Freda, was sent there to Whitelands Mental Hospital.

Declining fortunes and tales of the past when the family was notable have driven many a Victorian writer or artist toward trying for a fame which will restore the family honor. The multiple ironies of the Kendall fall from grace were not lost on Charlotte Mew. The hubristic attitude that habitat uplifts, if it has been designed by the pure-hearted, dogmatic amateur, was shown to be a foolish sham by *fin de siècle* political and social realities. As we shall see, the Mew girls did try, in the genteel way of distressed gentlewomen, to redress the failing family fortunes, but their efforts were constantly hampered by their mother, who believed that all the family attention should be focused on her desire for an ever more prestigious, fashionable address.

This same attitude from the mother would plague Anna Wickham's first attempts to publish her poetry. While Wickham's father wanted her to be a poet, her mother wanted her to make a good marriage so she could live at an acceptable address. A parental obsession with notions about homes, houses, living spaces, and what they represent, then, fueled both Mew and

Wickham's writing. They were not comfortable in the structures where they became the angel in the house. For them, the most important shelter would be the configuration of their art.

What sort of painter or illustrator could Charlotte's sister Anne Mew have become if she had discarded the genteel Victorian sensibility inculcated by her mother? Bram Dijkstra comments,

> if a woman proved her ability to do what the famous male painters [. . .] were doing, she could be dismissed as a 'typical female imitator,' whereas if she ventured into uncharted realms of visual expression her productions could be seen as incompetent, while similar experiments of male artists might be regarded as daring innovations. (208)

Both Anne and Charlotte were afraid of becoming professionals in their fields. What this circumstance created in Charlotte is a writer who both desires fame and abhors it because the attention such fame brings to the family is not commendable. If the place of publication can be viewed as a (publishing) *house*, then beginning her career in *The Yellow Book* was too scandalous a site for a family that a mere forty years earlier had been writing about reredoses, stained glass, and the importance of a properly spiritual setting for the sacraments. However, much of Mew's poetry evolves directly from her Kendall background, of propriety and property, as is seen most obviously in her long dramatic monologue, "Madeleine in Church." The speaker, a divorced, self-identified "rip," confesses in a tumultuous vernacular to a little plaster saint. Madeleine feels at home in church, so her prayer is rhetorically unselfconscious, chatty, and intimate. Madeleine's ironic, ambiguous voice leaves the reader in no doubt about Mew's attitude toward her forbearers. While she despises the macrocosm, there are microcosms within it that speak worlds to her—a lit candle, a little porteress, the gold and crimson lancet windows—and she longs for an absolute and unreflective faith. Like Bachelard after them, Mew and her persona prefer to see the immense in the miniature. By focusing on the intimate details of a cathedral instead of its flying buttresses, Mew, as Merrin puts it, "both tells and does not tell." [She] "plays the power of withholding against the power of revelation" (213).

As if the steady diminishing of the family fortunes were not enough to bear, the family also suffered a typically Victorian, but no less terrible for that, loss of its members. Fred and Anna Maria Mew had seven children: Henry Herne (b. 1865), Frederick George Webb (b. 1867), Charlotte Mary (b. 1869), Richard Cobham (b. 1871), Caroline Frances Anne (b. 1872), Daniel Kendall (b. 1875), who was renamed Christopher Barnes when he was a few months old, and the "afterthought," Freda Kendall (b. 1879) (Fitzgerald 16). Of these children only Henry, Charlotte, Anne, and Freda lived to be adults. Anna Maria Mew, described by Fitzgerald as a "tiny, pretty, silly young woman who grew, in time, to be a very silly old one," had seven confinements in fourteen years (13). While that was typical and even normal for a Victorian family, what was not was the acrimony surrounding the naming of the children and the sense of guilt and blame attached to their deaths. Anna Maria was determined that the sons should be named as Kendalls and Fred thought that the Mews should also be honored.

The renaming of Daniel Kendall to Christopher Barnes was a pyrrhic victory for Fred because the child died of convulsions shortly after receiving his new name. At the time the unsettled emotions of the nursing mother were thought to cause convulsions. Fred's namesake child had died on a family outing when he was two months old, and the same year as Christopher Barnes died, so did five-year-old Richard Cobham of scarlet fever (Fitzgerald 16–17). It is no wonder that many years later Charlotte would write poems with titles such as "Expecto Resurrectionem." "To a Child in Death" contains a plaintive line lamenting that the rest of the family would not know what to do with the summer "meant for you." At least the grief of death can be shared. The further trials of the Mew family could not.

Fred Mew's status in the Kendall firm was directly related to the mental state of Kendall junior's son, Edward Herne, who never joined in a partnership with his father even though he had completed his training. Throughout his life, he had no occupation of any kind and could never be trusted with his own affairs. In the expansive servant-filled Victorian household of the Kendalls, Edward Herne always had someone to look after him, but when the Mew's eldest son, Henry Herne, began to exhibit signs of instability and mental breakdown, the Mews had no choice but to have him confined, with a private nurse, to Peckham Hospital. He was diagnosed with *dementia praecox*, which we call schizophrenia or bi-polar disorder, and never returned to his family. Henry, on whom Fred and his grandfather, H.E. Kendall junior, had placed such high hopes, died in Peckham Hospital of pneumonia at the age of thirty-five (Fitzgerald 43, 75).

An equally devastating blow fell on the Mews in the late 1890s when Freda also began to show signs of mental illness. As with Henry, there was a parallel in the Kendall family. Anna Maria Mew's unmarried sister, Mary Lenora, was described as, in the euphemism of the times, "not strong in her wits," and it was her mother's fear that she might fall under the spell of an unscrupulous person who would leave her penniless. Yet Mary Lenora Kendall's family had the means to keep her at home and protected throughout her life. At her death in 1902, another trust was set up for her feckless brother Edward Herne, Anna Maria Mew received some jewelry and furniture, and Charlotte and Anne each about twenty pounds per year more from the income on two small house properties. Freda had to be sent to the asylum on the Isle of Wight, where she lived until 1958 (Fitzgerald 43, 81, note 253). By the late 1890s Charlotte Mew's family was fractured beyond repair. Yet it is curious that the Kendall family could remain intact, harboring its eccentrics in the home while the Mew family was rent asunder

just a few years later. What cultural and social factors caused the differ-
ences between the treatment of Edward Herne and Mary Lenora Kendall
and Henry and Freda Mew?

In *A Social History of Madness*, Roy Porter points out a rarely stated
fact: "Even the mad are men of their times" (5). Victorian England made
madness big business. It is a sickening irony of circumstance that Kendall
and Mew made a significant profit from their designs for the County
Asylums of Essex, Sussex, and Dorset. Porter states that in 1800 around
5,000 people were confined in asylums; by 1900 this figure had leaped to
100,000 (20). A theory that accounts for this huge increase mentions the
contemporary pundits who advertised that society was degenerating, as
witnessed by the depraved writings of the decadents, the *poètes maudits*.
However, a more realistic explanation is that the middle-class fetish for
propriety and property changed the concept of home as sanctuary to one
of home as exhibition of morality. Coupled with Darwinian ideas of the
survival of the fittest, the belief that the more rational a society grew, the
more prominently the irrational or mad stood out, led to a more refined
classification of varieties of madness. Life-long confinement became the
norm rather than the exception. The mad were sent to the edges of civi-
lization: to the suburbs. Asylums, hospitals, prisons, and cemeteries were
large-scale habitats situated away from the heart of the city because the
passions housed in these structures disrupted the good citizens' stability.

And, Porter adds, the Waterloo of psychiatry was schizophrenia. The
German psychiatrist Emil Kraepelin depicted the sufferer of *dementia prae-
cox* as a person who had renounced his humanity, abandoned any desire to
engage in human social intercourse, and slipped into an autistic, solipsistic
world (20–1). In some ways, Mew's poetry can be viewed as an attempt to
speak for these unspeakables. With all hopes for the continuation of the
architectural firm collapsing, the Mews did not have the servants needed to
take full care of their two schizophrenics. By the late 1800s several new
theories about the causes of mental illness made it more imperative to send
the mentally ill away where they could not be a constant visible reminder
of a family defect. Also, the circumstance of having a couple of eccentrics
who need constant care in a family, is a very different matter from having
two people who have so totally withdrawn that they can not function at
all. Upper class or upper middle-class families could absorb some aberrant
behavior; a family clinging to its last shreds of respectability could not. By
the time Henry Herne and Freda were diagnosed, the firm of Kendall and
Mew was a mere façade. With no one to pass the business to, Fred Mew
lost all interest. However, the charade of respectability, gentility, and an
upper middle-class lifestyle had to be maintained for Anna Maria's sake.
Charlotte Mew lived the rest of her life with the horror and shame of having
two siblings who had to be sent away and kept away so that her mother
could maintain a precarious social status in an abode that reflected the status.

Shortly after Freda's breakdown, Charlotte and Anne made a pact that they would never marry. They vowed to each other that they would not have children who might become schizophrenics. They knew of Francis Galton's *Natural Inheritance* (1889) and the research laboratory he set up in 1894 in University College. His belief is that the improvement of society depends upon genetic politics. Galton baldly states in the conclusion of *Natural Inheritance*, "The value of a good stock to the well-being of future generations is therefore obvious" (198). For Charlotte, this decision might not have been as hard as it was for Anne, but both women loved children, and the guilt and anguish caused by their inheritance must have deeply grieved them.

One of Charlotte's most powerful poems, "On the Asylum Road," has an arresting image of the "clouded glass" panes, "darkly stained" that obliterate the light in the house of our "brother-shadows." The poem ends "Our windows, too, are clouded glass/To them, yes, every pane!" (*CPP* 19–20). Those locked away by their madness saw the speaker's eyes as nothing but dark panes or clouded pain that reflects yet absorbs their anguish. The line could also be interpreted to mean that the normal household's windows, through which the family views society and is viewed by it, are rendered opaque when schizophrenia blinds its victims. It is also significant that she calls the insane "brother-shadows," since Charlotte was the designated replacement for Henry in the family hierarchy.

As Porter notes, "private madhouses had always been deeply concerned to keep those who were out of their mind out of sight, and secretiveness was to dominate the nineteenth-century public asylum." A trade in lunacy grew up, and what distinguished the private asylum from its eighteenth-century counterpart was its seclusion and secrecy (31, 167). In a lawyer's letter to the Bedford Estate, which owned the lease on the Mew's second home, 9 Gordon Street, Bloomsbury, Freda is described euphemistically as very delicate (Fitzgerald 184). As close as Alida Monro became to Charlotte in her later years, still she was not told about Freda or Henry: "[. . .] only after Charlotte's death did I hear from an intimate friend that they had gone out of their minds many years before and were both in asylums" (*ix*).

It was bad enough to have the taint of madness in the family, but to have to worry about the possible drying-up of sufficient funds to keep Henry and Freda in their expensive private hospitals must have been torture for Charlotte and Anne, because neither one had any idea of what to do to earn money. The disgrace of having to send either of their siblings to a county asylum, and the equally horrible thought that it might have to be one that their grandfather and father built, must have tormented them. It is no wonder that Charlotte did not tell Alida Monro or any of her other literary acquaintances (except May Sinclair, who Charlotte thought would be the most sympathetic), about her siblings' condition. And it is no wonder that Alida Monro describes Charlotte's temperament as "naturally keyed very low" (*ix*).

With the financial burden of Henry and Freda's private nurses and asylum fees, and Fred's lack of income, Charlotte and Anne were desperate about the future, so they undertook the earning of a living for the family in the ways available to distressed gentlewomen. Even though their mother had inherited almost four thousand pounds from her grandfather, Thomas Cobham, and her mother, this money was all invested in an annuity that realized three hundred pounds per year for her. This was to be spent, according to the terms of her mother's will, as if she were not married. A spiteful wife, determined to punish a husband for his part in inflicting the world's ills upon her, could make domestic life utterly miserable. That is what, in a lady-like way, Mrs. Mew did. She established herself in the role of chronic invalid; Fred lost all interest in life.

So Charlotte wrote and Anne painted. Anne painted fire-screens and renovated seventeenth-century furniture for antique dealers; she had been trained at the Royal Female School of Art, founded in 1843 to cater to the daughters of professional men who were unexpectedly forced to earn a living. Anne specialized in bird and flower painting hoping to exhibit, teach, or paint on commission. To her mother's satisfaction, she "would still have the prestige of an amateur," even though it was the elder male Kendall's clinging to the attitudes of the amateur that destroyed the firm (Fitzgerald 49).

The chasm between the amateur and the professional also dogged Anna Wickham's family, causing the same problems in her writing that it caused in Charlotte Mew's. In both families, the daughter who should have been a son was expected to step into the traditional role of the eldest son, and enhance the family reputation, if not fortune. In the Mew family, it was left to Lotti to uphold the family honor, maintain an outwardly stable front in spite of her parents' fractured marriage, and to resurrect the family name through her own artistic accomplishments. Mew shares with Wickham an ambivalence toward this destiny that she expresses in the poem "Fame" in which the persona places herself "among the crowd/Where no one fits the singer to the song" but longs for the opportunity to take instead of fame, "One little dream, no matter how small, how wild." This dream is "A frail, dead, new-born lamb, ghostly and pitiful and white,/A blot upon the night,/The moon's dropped child!" (*CPP* 2–3). Wild dreams, cosmic error, the mysteries with which nature blots our copybook and the dead are Mew's dominant motifs. In this poem the reader can clearly see Mew's ambivalence toward her art. The dream song of the poem, the lamb, reflects the death of hope for redemption through art. A poem becomes merely a blot dropped in the night.

As is also the case with Wickham, Mew had to contend with circumstances that date back to her great-grandparents and grandparents. It is not only these circumstances that shaped her into the writer she became, but also they constituted a burden on her life that she wrote from and against. While it may be easy to see that Mew's themes arise from her early experiences, as indeed what writer's do not, it might not be as apparent that her style is also affected by the particular circumstances of her riven family. A thorough investigation of Mew's background and influences shows that even within specific poems, the tensions between tone and voice cause a disjunction, a literary schizophrenia, which is directly explained by biography. Mew's dramatic monologues often are spoken by voices usually mute. This voice is rarely her own, the voice of one expected to play the role of the Victorian dutiful daughter; instead, Mew's dramatic monologues are spoken by those for whom silence has become the only waking option. Many times this voice is male. These disparate, silenced—but speaking— voices, and their sometimes halting, sometimes galloping rhythms are Mew's contributions to modern poetry. Her manipulation of the ballad stanza, a favorite form of children's verse, charts Mew's dissatisfaction with her role as the child/angel in the house. As Merrin notes, she flexibly increases or decreases accents, compacts rhyme and makes effective use of incremental repetition to mark the oscillation of her persona's unquiet mind.

In contrast, Anna Wickham's poems are written from the persona of "Anna Wickham: Freewoman and Poet." This difference in voice is both a class and generation difference—the difference between the dandy and the bohemian. However, a location that Mew and Wickham share is the actual site of many of their poems. Many modernists are urban poets, and while the split between modernists and Georgians is often couched in terms of urban versus rural, both Mew and Wickham, although they lived in London, situate some of their poems in the suburbs. The suburb is a logical landscape for women poets. It combines the features of both city and country, yet it is neither. Its central feature is the home "irradiated by the light of a pastoral imagination. It could seem a country of peace and innocence where life was kind and duty natural" (Houghton 344). Mew and Wickham's poetry both exposes the hypocrisy of this view, and reveals its truth. The suburb is city and country condensed and sanitized. A miniature manicured version of either, the suburb is a place where values become condensed and intensified. Bachelard argues that miniature sites are "the refuges of greatness" (*Space* 155).

During the time of Thomas Hardy and Fred Mew's architectural apprenticeships, between the mid-1840s and the early 1860s, several architectural trends created a need for eager, intelligent young men, even if they were "countrified, and sadly lacking in worldly experience and social assurance"(Seymour-Smith 61). The booming population required places to live, go to school, and worship, so it pushed the boundaries of London ever and ever outward. These suburbs are the location of much that changed the direction of English arts during the Victorian era. Perhaps it is the avant-garde's sneers about the stultifying effects of a suburban existence which cause those already on the margins for other reasons to situate their work in such a supposedly barren locale.

Charlotte Mew's poetry, however, also does illuminate the countryside of southern England and the Isle of Wight, where the children of the Mew family spent all their summers. Their mother summered at No. 6 Codrington Place, Kemp Town, Brighton, with Mary Lenora Kendall, her witless sister, and their mother (Fitzgerald 22). The Brighton connection came about because of Mrs. Mew's aunt's marriage to Thomas Cubitt's brother Lewis, who had been a pupil of H. E. Kendall, Sr. When the architect Thomas Read Kemp became overextended in his grandiose scheme which has given Brighton much of its Georgian sweep, Thomas Cubitt stepped in and completed the project in the same manner as his development of the London area of Belgravia (Dixon 256, 59). The Kendalls, because of their Cubitt connection, became one of the Brighton families of distinction, and it is significant that neither her husband nor her children joined Anna Maria Kendall Mew for the Brighton season. "Ma," as she came to be called in later years, divorced herself early on from a family tainted by her husband's genes. The irony is, of course, that Kendall genes were the faulty ones. If Charlotte Mew had gone to Brighton as a child, she might have grown up to be a novelist instead of a poet, and her readers might have been treated to a dissection of Brighton society in the manner of Jane Austen, George Eliot, or Ivy Compton-Burnett. In Brighton, the Kendalls associated with Dickens, and possibly with Dicken's good friend and illustrator, George Cruikshank (Davidow "Biography" 15).

So it is lucky for admirers of Mew's poetry that Fred Mew won the battle of summer holidays. Proper Victorian children released from the confines of the attic nursery could hardly bear the excitement. For a high-strung and sensitive child like Lotti, it was intoxicating, provoking outbursts of outrageous behavior, even though the Mew's formidable nanny, Elizabeth Goodman, an upstanding North-country, Evangelical treasure selected by Anna Maria herself from the Kendall household, always came along to keep order. Once when Charlotte Mew jumped up on the driver's seat of the wagonette hired to take them to Newfairlee, the Mew family farm, and Elizabeth Goodman rapped her knuckles with her parasol, Lotti grabbed it and broke it in two (Fitzgerald 14, 22). For Mew, these times on the Isle of Wight were the highlights of a magical childhood, which informs the central themes of her work. Poems such as "Ken," "The Changeling," and most certainly "Saturday Market" are full of the images of Newport and the Isle of Wight countryside, as well as the specters of insanity and, in "The Changeling," the childish desire for fairy genes. Even if Charlotte Mew loved her family, she also wished to be released from her obligations to it. As the changeling persona cries, "I shall grow up, but never grow old,/I shall always, always be very cold,/I shall never come back again!" (*CPP* 14).

One of the most vivid images for Mew is that of a dead rat seen on the farm track. This rat appears in one of her last poems, "The Trees Are Down." "I remember thinking: alive or dead, a rat was a god-forsaken thing/But at least, in May, even a rat should be alive" (*CPP* 48), and again in the unfinished short story, "Aglae:"

> And the earliest morning we found it [our rat] again by the window but prostrate and dying though not yet dead. Its [His] ears one saw were very delicate, brown and of a texture not the same as its [his] body, finer, creased—One might have said—a leaf. (CPP 330)

In both the poem and the story, the rat and a tree are conflated. Mew subscribes to the belief that men are trees walking ("Men and Trees" *CPP* 388). In the deaths of trees and rats, she believes, we see our own deaths. Describing death in terms of trees and rats is also a way for the survivor to explore the guilt the living feel, without having to resort to explicit references to human mortality.

It was not only from her own experiences that Charlotte Mew drew her country images. She also had a store of tales from Elizabeth Goodman, the nanny, whose influence on the Mew children colored the rest of their lives. For one thing, Goodman lived with the Mews from the day they were married until she died at the age of sixty-nine in 1893, when Charlotte was twenty-four. Mew's essay, "An Old Servant," reveals her love for the woman who raised her and from whom she received many of her personality traits. "[A]s fixed a part of the universe as the bath (cruelly cold in winter)," Goodman retained a child-like desire for play and treats. At sixty-five she wished to "skate and slide and snowball with the best of us," and she delighted in the Christmas annuals which she had the children read to her, gorging on "a whirl of highwaymen and elopements." These entertainments made a change from her regular reading of the Bible and *Ally Sloper's Weekly*, a popular cheap comic paper. However, she felt that both smoking and writing poetry were prime causes of brain injury and she would dispose of both ashes and ink-splotched manuscripts "with a gesture of indiscriminate disgust" (*CPP* 401–06).

For many years Goodman's favorite bedtime reading for the children was *Line Upon Line, or a Second Series of the Earliest Religious instruction the Infant Mind is Capable of Receiving, with verses illustrative of the subject, by the Author of The Peep of Day* (1837) (Fitzgerald note 252). Between that, the readings of Proverbs in the Bible, and daily prayers, which included the minute detailing of "our trespasses," a tense submission to God's will was inculcated in the Mew children. As well, they were taught to "waste not, want not," daily practicing small household economies designed to prepare them for a time when they too might have to scheme over a half pound of cheese, and learn to drink weak tea, contriving to turn the collars and cuffs of a blouse with plenty of life left in it (*CPP* 404).

The need to learn these economies of life was blamed on Fred Mew and his lack of starch. Anna Maria was of course protected from these exigencies because, it was agreed, she had suffered enough. Indeed, Lotti barely had time to enjoy her school years before the family began to rely on her in the late 1880s as the master of the house because her parents had become the children. With Elizabeth Goodman's help, Charlotte managed the family affairs. But it was at school that Charlotte Mew was to receive her most important understanding of her true nature.

The third world of the Mew children was the world of school. Both Charlotte, in 1879 at age ten, and Anne were sent to the Gower Street School under the direction of headmistress Lucy Harrison. The editor of *Spenser for Home and School* (1883), Harrison favored a curriculum strong on service to those less fortunate (she was an enthusiastic supporter of Octavia Hill's settlement houses for the working poor), and on readings from her favorite authors—Shakespeare, Dante, Blake, Wordsworth, the Brontës, the Rossettis, the Brownings, Coventry Patmore, and Alice Meynell. Fitzgerald specifically mentions Alice Meynell's *Preludes* (1895) which contains "To a Daisy" whose persona longs for the day when a daisy will grow over her grave so that she might then "drink from in beneath a spring" and with the same view as God's be able to penetrate the mystery that the daisy represents. Of the influence on Mew of the ideas in Coventry Patmore's *Angel in the House* it is sufficient to mention that just as Patmore depended on his daughter, Emily, so Fred Mew depended on Charlotte. In the same way, Geoffrey Harper, Anna Wickham's father, would put the burden of his ideas about intellectual companionship onto his daughter when his wife seemed uninterested. Also, as Davidow notes, there are echoes of Patmore's poem, "Toys" in Mew's sonnet, "A Farewell" ("Biography" 174).

Lucy Harrison's impact on Charlotte Mew should not be underestimated. Harrison's attitude that poetry is the way that we can express the emotionally inexpressible passed to Lotti. Miss Harrison inculcated in Charlotte Mew a passion for poetry as a way to express her unruly emotions. Because Mew had to leave the stimulating confines of Harrison's influence before she was ready to do so, in some sense, Mew remained a perpetual adolescent, always pining for the mentor-student relationship. Harrison's influence extended even to Mew's last poetic action.

In 1928, after the death of Anne, Charlotte changed her will to stipulate that she be buried in the same grave as Anne under the inscription, "Cast down the seed of weeping and attend" from Dante's *Purgatorio* Canto XXXI (line 46). In this verse Beatrice is advising Dante to master his feelings so that he can finally learn how her death might instruct him about the transitory nature of earth's delights. The canto continues:

> You never saw in Nature or in Art
> a beauty like the beauty of my form,

which clothed me once and now is turned to dust;
and if that perfect beauty disappeared
when I departed from the world, how could
another mortal object lure your love? (331)

When Anne died, "perfect beauty disappeared" so Charlotte had no recourse but to join her. In the family sense, Anne was the great love of Charlotte's life. When all else disappointed Lotti, Anne was always there to soothe and calm her frenetic spirits. As Steven Mintz argues, the sense of sibling solidarity was a symbol of a connection to a past whose values the siblings no longer espoused; sibling bonds represented a harmony of interests not marred by issues of physicality (151). It would not be inappropriate to say that Anne and Charlotte were married to each other, and after Fred's death in 1898, their mother and her parrot WEK, Willie Edward Kendall, became their children. In this marriage within a marriage (of their parents), Anne was the wife and Charlotte the husband. But this is not to imply that Anne and Charlotte had any kind of physical relationship.

Although much of what Suzanne Raitt says in "Charlotte Mew's Queer Death" opens interesting possibilities for Mew scholarship, her notion that a comment by Alida Monro perhaps implies a more than sisterly attachment between Anne and Charlotte is not probable. Raitt is correct when she remarks that Anne was the love of Charlotte's life, and that Charlotte probably killed herself because she felt she could not live without Anne. Moreover, Raitt's contention that Mew's death is a kind of "coming out," a statement of personal identity and closure, does fit with what is known of Mew's personality. Raitt rightly notices that Mew anticipates a "queer aesthetic" in her themes of desire thwarted and loss suffered; Mew loved women but would never have labeled herself an *invert*, the term used to describe a lesbian in the early twentieth century (72–74).

Nicholas Shrimpton describes Charlotte Mew's sexual orientation best when he says, "her sexual inclinations were almost certainly chastely lesbian" (21). Mew's crushes on the writers Ella D'Arcy and May Sinclair follow the pattern of her feelings for Miss Harrison. Love like this is not to be physically consummated; instead, it brings the loved ones together in times of sorrow, with personal sacrifices played out in small gestures or understandings between them. This is a love of idealized self-control and (as the lover hopes) mutual spiritual seeking. The lover constructs a fantasy world, and the world of literature provides a sufficiently remote, but also sufficiently emotional connection. Letters become the means of communication, as they were for Miss Harrison and her fellow teacher, Amy Greener. The only way for this relationship to end is for the object of devotion to ridicule the devotee.

Miss Harrison's intense emotional attachment to uplifting prose and poetry found a ready heart and ear in Lotti. At a crucial time—the time

Victor Turner calls betwixt and between—Mew became enamored of Miss Harrison. Lotti wished to be like Miss Harrison in every way, and although Lotti was not allowed to wear tailored jackets and waistcoats as her idol did, the Mews did allow her to cut her hair short, in Miss Harrison's style (Fitzgerald 33). In 1882 when Lotti was thirteen, Miss Harrison, suffering from overwork and strain, retired from the Gower Street School to rooms in Hampstead from which she could work on her never published history of England. Hearing the news, Lotti, in a paroxysm of grief, began banging her head against the wall, and she refused to stop grieving until she was accepted as a boarder at Miss Harrison's. One can imagine a stern Miss Harrison admonishing Lotti to buck up, capping her reprimand with an apt quotation: "Cast down the seeds of weeping and attend!"

Lotti was in the throws of a rave or gonage (gone on). According to Martha Vicinus, "sexuality found expression [. . .] through a disciplined love," often focused on a teacher. Non-fulfillment and the sacrifice of personal feelings combined with bodily self-control became the means of expressing an individual self (187–89). As long as Lotti did not give way to her feelings as she had when she first heard the news of Miss Harrison's retirement, then she would be allowed to have her rave. Such a passion was also passionately self-involved because it could not ever be demonstrated in public by overtly sexual acts. The devotee could only fill hot water bottles, clean blackboards, or keep the valued mistress supplied with pen-wipers. Vicinus states that such situations created lives lived through symbolic acts and conversations where each nuance and varied tone is hoarded to be mulled over in the silence and solitude of night (190–91). What better training could a writer have?

Lotti would walk to Hampstead for evening lectures in English literature, and best of all, Miss Harrison's company over tea, the evening meal, and breakfast. Her crush on Miss Harrison lasted until Miss Harrison's final retirement in 1886 to a cottage in Yorkshire, which she later shared with Amy Greener who had taken over the Gower Street School. After Amy Greener gave up her position at Gower Street in 1895, they remained companions and fellow staff members of the Mount School, Yorkshire, where Miss Harrison served as headmistress, until 1902 (Greener 20–55).[4]

Lotti's love for Miss Harrison was a love for the mind that introduced her to the works that could begin to help her understand her own complicated psyche and provide a way for her to channel the feelings that overwhelmed her. As much as Lotti relied on Elizabeth Goodman as the moral compass of the home front, Goodman's taste in reading was very narrow, so naturally a dynamic teacher like Miss Harrison would make a lasting impression. Having an intellectual as well as an emotional mentor was important for Mew. She was able to accomplish her best work when she was influenced by such attachments. Later, the adult Mew's passion for literature would turn into an acceptable means to make money and, more importantly, to escape the dull horrors that overtook the Mew household in the late 1880s. A charismatic teacher can have a major influence on a child. Charlotte Mew imbibed many of Harrison's emotional and intellectual attitudes along with the plain teas and lectures on English literature. Lucy Harrison's often-voiced stance was that marriage never held any attraction for her. She loved the freedom and independence that she had as a child in a family in which both Anglicanism and Quakerism mingled harmoniously, and in which Lucy was allowed room to get herself into scrapes and freely exercise her imagination. She often told the Gower Street girls about her childhood pranks and repeated the poems recited by her mother during the children's hour before bedtime (Greener 4–7, 24–25). Perhaps it is Harrison's idyllic picture of Victorian childhood and her free and easy romping that prompted Lotti's high spirits and her regard for the idea of motherhood. Certainly she never saw examples of either in her own family.

What Charlotte Mew learned from her association with Lucy Harrison and her fellow students at the Gower Street School was a love for an individual intellectual life outside the bounds of family. She also found a literary mother whose serious and passionate response to literature shaped Mew's own vocation. As well, Mew learned a way to love that did not necessarily involve physical contact, but could possibly lead to the penetration of the private intellectual or emotional, rather than physical, space of the loved one. A large part of the pleasure of loving for the adult Charlotte Mew was the remoteness or even absence of the love object. "Without gratification, countless fantasies could be constructed, a seemingly continuous web of self-examination, self-inspection, self-fulfillment" (Vicinus 191). Not only does this type of love enable a writer to work through the relationship totally *in print*, but it also enabled Mew to articulate her feelings for her schizophrenic siblings.

By 1886 Charlotte Mew's formal schooling was over, although Warner does say in passing that she sometimes attended lectures at University College, London and by 1891 had obtained a ticket for the British Museum Reading Room ("Introduction" *Collected and Selected ix*). Mew got the rest of her education there. She collected material for articles on Mary Stuart, Emily Brontë, and one titled "The Governess in Fiction" (*CPP* viii).[5] It is tempting to speculate about the years between 1886 and 1894 when her first short story, "Passed," was published in *The Yellow Book* (*CPP* vii). However, what is known about the Mew family fortunes and Charlotte's responsibilities toward her family can account for this gap. Charlotte Mew, in the manner of so many unmarried middle-class Victorian women became stuck "betwixt and between," fulfilling the role of the angel in the house in place of the absent mother. Since Anna Maria Kendall Mew's delicacy prevented her from taking any household responsibility, Charlotte ran the house. Like many another New Woman of the era, she was a mixture of new and old attitudes, tailoring her actions and stances to fit household needs.[6]

In 1888 the Mews moved to a larger more expensive house because, when Henry Kendall, Anna Maria's father, died in 1885, her mother and unmarried aunt, Mary Lenora Kendall, moved to their Brighton home permanently, so it was felt that the London remnants of the family needed a better address. Nine Gordon Square in Bloomsbury was the house they settled on, partly because Thomas Cubitt had built it, and therefore Anna Maria felt they would be keeping up the connection. Shortly thereafter the Mew son, Henry Herne, was diagnosed with *dementia praecox*. The firm of Kendall and Mew's last commission had been in 1885. In the early 1890s Freda Mew also was diagnosed as a schizophrenic. In 1893 faithful Elizabeth Goodman, who shared the running of the household with Charlotte, died as a result of blood poisoning she contracted from puncturing her hand with a sewing needle (Fitzgerald 41–54). Fred Mew must have somehow conveyed the state of family affairs to Charlotte, because by the late 1880s she began to take her scribbled manuscripts more seriously. Elizabeth Goodman no longer tried to sweep them into her dustpan.

Charlotte Mew's decision to become a woman of letters coincided with the heyday of English periodicals. *Tit-Bits* might have seemed a bit too low-brow for her, but new magazines like *The Strand*, which first appeared in 1891, and older more respectable periodicals like *Cornhill*, the *Saturday Review*, and *The Spectator* beckoned with the idea that "there was money to be made in literature" (Altick 279). Mew's first assay in the "curious experience" genre of personal essay, which she had carefully sent out to a distressed gentlewoman lady typewriter, was "The Minnow Fishers." According to Warner, this story was published in a revised form in *Outlook* 31 January 1903 ("A Note on the Text" *Collected and Selected xxii*). A short piece about "three minute and very shabby anglers" who ignored the fourth of their number when he fell in the canal at Maida Vale, it is narrated by "my friend, John Hilton," obviously a gentleman of leisure who had been indulging in "after-dinner patter" on the elevating influence of Sport. This is the kind of story her grandfather and great-grandfather would have delighted in; yet when Mew tells it, she strips it of the condescending moralistic tone they might have used.

Instead it becomes a bleak, ironic commentary on late Victorian poverty, both moral and physical. Of the many ironies in the piece, not the least is the specter of poverty, which was hovering over the Mews. A tiny person herself, Mew must have identified with the minnow fishers, who are minnows (or sprats), barely big enough to hold their bits of "twig and twine." The drowned infant, or "rescued atom," is described unsentimentally as "a crimson airball, a gruesome penny toy," presaging Mew's later stillborn lamb from "Fame" and the red, dead thing of "Saturday Market." His rescue by a passing carpenter and the gentleman, John Hilton, did not deflect the other boys from their "sport." As Mew puts it:

> They kept on. You can't imagine anything quite so relentless and remote
> as the way they kept on, those three remorseless specks, intent, oblivious,
> aloof; three tiny profiles and three spindly lines as calm and obdurate as
> Fate. They might have stood for it; one felt at last that they were not to be
> disturbed; that there was something mystical, symbolic, in their complete
> detachment from our distant and unnecessary violence. (CPP 306)

Here the irony is that the return to life of the drowning victim is labeled
"unnecessary violence." When one of the silent fisher-mites betrays his
chum by revealing his relationship to the resuscitated child, "the injured
relative bestowed on his betrayer a vindictive cuff" while blaming his part-
ners for the disaster by claiming that "*they* brought 'im out." The sur-
vivor's guilt is revealed by his violence and refusal to accept blame. The
epigraph from Richard Jeffries, "To be calm without mental fear is the
ideal of nature," adds to the irony, especially when the Mew family trou-
bles are considered. The gentlemanly Hilton has enough fellow-feeling to
aid in the rescue of the child and follow along to see that the brother does
begin to take him home, but not enough to go with the boys to see what
he might do about the underlying causes of their destitution.

To the reader who knows the family history, it is obvious that Mew
could have been writing about the loss of members of her family, those
drowning in their descent into madness. There is no evidence of Henry
Herne and Freda having been sent away for short periods of time, but they
might have been, and the violent emotions that these brief hopes for
"resuscitation" engendered in the Mews must have been very painful. The
key phrase, "*they* brought 'im out," resonates because the words are an
attempt on the victim's brother's own part to release himself from blame
for the accident, but it also begs the question of "who put him *in*"; in other
words, how did he fall into the canal?

It is tempting to read this piece as an allegory for the upheavals experi-
enced by the Mew family and the dread that mental illness might strike
again, or the self-revulsion and guilt experienced by the survivors of disas-
ters who let loved ones "slip away." In "The Minnow Fishers" Mew
implies that the revived child would be better off dead, a notion that must
have occurred to her about her own brother and sister. Like her character
John Hilton, Mew can go only so far in following her siblings toward the
madhouse. By the late nineteenth century, "The therapeutics of maximum
environmental control [. . .] seemed to demand the minimalization of con-
tact between the sufferer and society" (Porter 31). As Warner notes in
"Mary Magdalene and the Bride," "Mew's characteristic note is negation.
[. . .] One aspect of negation is Mew's exaggerated lament for youth, often
not in the usual sense of regret at mortality" (95).

Mew's attitude is close to Richard Jeffries' talking Reed in *Wood Magic*
(1881), which says:

I don't know why. [. . .] There is no why at all. We have been listening to
the Brook [. . .] for ever so many thousands of years, and though the
Brook has been talking and singing all that time, I never heard him ask
why about anything [. . .] nor does the sun, nor the stars [. . .] so that I
am quite sure there is no why at all. (95)

The unpublished manuscript, "A Country Book," a brief treatment of
his themes, confirms Mew's interest in Jeffries (Davidow 166). Mew echoes
Jeffries' notions about the "why" of things in her most powerful poem
about the family, "The Quiet House." If Charlotte Mew were one for
whom "family ties meant everything" as Alida Monro reports, then her
sardonic picture of family ties in "The Minnow Fishers" can be looked at
as a necessary release of feelings and an antidote to middle-class Victorian
sentimentality about the ill and the poor. And it can be read as a gloss of
Jeffries' "there is no why at all," which, even though it appears in a senti-
mental instructional novel for children, contains a bleak assessment of the
state of the world; this attitude is more in tune with Mew's modern sensi-
bility.

"The Minnow Fishers" also introduces a characteristic style that Mew
refines in each successive piece. While changing the specific circumstances
of every poem and prose piece, she is determined to speak for those who
can't or won't, speak for themselves. "In the long run, the development of
segregation through the madhouse system [. . .] served to silence the mad
[. . .] to render their voices inaudible to most and unintelligible to others,
little inclined to listen" (Porter 31). This does not imply that all Mew's per-
sonae are mentally ill or unstable. It merely suggests that she likes to speak
for the silenced, whomever they may be. Her attitude is evident in her
championing of Emily Brontë, silenced by her sister Charlotte's meddling
discovery of her poetry, and in her poetic brinksmanship. In many poems
Mew brings her characters to the edge of an hysterical relinquishing of self-
control—to the point of madness, but not beyond.

CHAPTER THREE

Charlotte Mary Mew 1904–1913
"Yet, to leave Fame, still with such eyes and that bright hair!"[1]

Henry Harland, the editor of *The Yellow Book,* accepted Charlotte Mew's story, "Passed" for the second issue. Fitzgerald implies that Mew read the first issue to see what sort of work the editor wanted before trying her talents at something he might take. Certainly "Passed" is very different from "The Minnow Fishers" in style and tone. Instead of detached irony, the reader is confronted with the clichés of *fin de siècle* subjects. In "Passed" Mew is responding to what Cunningham calls "The portrayal of a new type of heroine [which] would almost inevitably entail a more frank approach to sexuality, and would open vast new areas of female psychology and behavior" (17).

However, if one were to read "Passed" as the staking out of an artistic space, either ignoring or accepting Mew's use of current clichés as a blatant ploy to assure publication, then the story might open itself up in a new way. All of Mew's work is concerned with fashioning an architecture of the soul. The soul house is a body, of course, but by what route does the soul lead the body to home? Where does one locate the angel in the house, and what angel, and what house? These are the questions that Mew's work continuously asks. In "Passed" she situates the search between "the heavy walls of a partially demolished prison" which serve as a landmark for a "church in the district, newly built by an infallible architect" (*CPP* 65). In this telling architectural reference, Mew identifies the narrator with the Kendall preference for Gothic architecture and indulges in sarcasm at the family's expense. Between the falling prison and new church, the narrator walks along "[a] row of cramped houses, with the unpardonable bow window, projecting squalor into prominence" (*CPP* 65). As Dixon notes, in the mid-nineteenth century "The bay window also became increasingly popular in all types of houses and all styles of architecture," specifically in London's burgeoning inner-suburban, modest, terrace housing built during the 1860s to 1900; it was Ruskin who advocated the "delightfulness" of the bow window (61–62). The narrator of "Passed" states that the bow window reveals and projects the squalor beneath the portentous walls of the half-torn away prison which stand as a "silent curse" to the myriad "diseased and dirty children" whose leers and "maddening requirements" bounce off the prison walls along with their mother's exasperated cry. She ends this scene by commenting, "These shelters struck my thought as travesties—perhaps they were not—of the grand place called home . [. . .] What withheld from them, as poverty and sin could not, a title to the sacred name?" (CPP 65–66). The answer seems to be that these buildings were architecturally unsuited for the type of activity they contained.

Charlotte Mew's grandfather and great-grandfather believed that architecture would influence social progress. Given beautiful homes and beautiful churches, people would naturally respond, bettering their social situation because their physical surroundings, the very walls that enfolded them, were urging them to it. What the narrator of "Passed" comments upon is the failure of the ideals espoused by the Ecclesiological Society in The Ecclesiologist. The church does not meet the speaker's exacting standards, either. It has a forbidding exterior and ugly details, which the narrator equates with the architect's "complacent eccentricity." Here, Mew may be snidely commenting on the movement by which Victorian churchmen hoped to emulate their medieval forbearers. Mew realized, as perhaps her maternal ancestors did not, that the sea of faith was withdrawing, and that all the new urban "cathedrals" with their beautiful stained glass, roodscreens, and soaring Gothic arches could not redeem and uplift the lives of the poor. As the persona of "Madeleine in Church" comments:

> Here, in darkness, where this plaster saint
>   Stands nearer than God stands to our distress,
> And one small candle shines, but not so faint
>   As the far lights of everlastingness
> I'd rather kneel than over there, in open day
>   Where Christ is hanging, rather pray
> To something more like my own clay,
>   Not too divine. [. . .]

She continues twenty-eight lines later, "I, too, would ask him to remember me/If there were any other Paradise beyond this earth that I could see" (CPP 22–23).

The open square, which contains the Gothic details of an old stone pump, irregular lamps, and broken iron fences, does lift the narrator's spirits. When the narrator of "Passed" moves "outside," she meets a prostitute who looks like a medieval saint, and who, mistaking the narrator for one of her own, asks not unkindly, "'who I was a shoving of'" (CPP 66). In the open spaces of the urban cityscape the old ideals are irredeemably blurred.

Whore and (plaster) saint, Mary Magdalen and innocent (m)other Mary, seem one and the same. Here, a middle-class girl can be teased by a whore and seem to enjoy it.

Perhaps if whore can mistake heroine for her own kind, then the rigid Victorian demarcations between types of women are false. This cheerful, saint-like whore is contrasted with the more hypocritical sexuality of a picture in a shop window, which showed a bare-bosomed girl at prayer. Such a "personification of pseudo-purity was sensually diverting and consequently marketable" (*CPP* 67). The narrator, trying to divert the reader with ironic social criticism, gives herself away. She is the type of girl pictured, and the reader discovers that she hates her own pseudo-purity and marketability. Alternatively, she desires both the medieval saint/whore, and the girl pictured at her prayers. The realization that she does drives her to a betrayal in the second half of the story.

The last part of the story concerns two impoverished sisters, one of whom the narrator encounters in the ugly church, and the other of whom is dead in their garret, "down some blind alley." The narrator allows herself to be dragged through the "concert of hoarse yells and haggling whines" of the children they hustled out of their way in a mad dash to the dead girl. In this, the first instance of her art to be published, Mew reveals almost all of her subsequent themes. The completely silent house in which the girls inhabit the top floor is like the Mews' house, including the children's attic nursery, in Doughty Street. The girls themselves, "These deserted beings," "must have first fronted the world from a sumptuous stage" (*CPP* 69). The unknown girl clings to the narrator in a tight swoon while the narrator confronts her own realization of Death by gazing at the girl's dead sister. The story implies that the dead girl, or perhaps the live one, or both, had been ruined by a club-man or even a nobleman; while the swooning girl mumbles about a "recently wrung promise," the narrator sinks into a waking dream where all her family turn into monsters. They bind her in an icy prison.

When the girl she met at the church wakes and asks her to stay and help, the narrator flings her away and flees, but not before she has realized that the "indefensible bow-window" and the prurience of the picture of the praying girl have caused her to lose her faith in prayer. The prison, the shop, the church, the bow-windowed house, and the ice-cold garret have betrayed the souls housed in them. Form and function never mesh. At the same time, the narrator is afraid of and attracted to the other girl's heart, which "throbbed painfully close to mine." She protests too much, gratuitously stating, "The proximity was distasteful. An alien presence has ever repelled me. I should have pitied the girl keenly perhaps a few more feet away." The rough syntax of this last sentence betrays the sexual anxiety of the writer, as well as that of the narrator. Yet the narrator lingers over a description of the girl's hair, which came undone and flowed over her shoulder, emitting a faint fragrance "like a subtle and seductive sprite hiding itself with fairy cunning in the tangled maze" (*CPP* 69–70). In this passage, form just escapes perverting function, if the reader subscribes to the Victorian belief that a woman's function is to love, marry, and bear the children of a man. But of course, Mew's unconscious purpose is to meld angel and fallen Magdalen to create a new woman who is both saint and whore, or neither. It is no wonder that Henry Harland gladly accepted this story for *The Yellow Book*. He probably could see, more than Mew herself could, what it said.

In "Passed" a creative dam broke and it is as if Mew felt that she would have no other opportunity to express the thoughts that obsessed her. So instead of ending the story here, Mew sends the narrator back into the church the next day, after she had spent a fruitless morning trying to find the two sisters of the night before. Saying, "Some dramatic instinct impelled me to reenter," instead of encountering the specters of the first pair of sisters, she observes another pair. One is normal, but the other's "ceaseless imbecile grimaces chilled my blood" until she saw the older sister kiss and stroke the younger one to quiet her. This scene renews the narrator's determination to find the first pair of sisters and she spends the rest of the day searching fruitlessly.

While it seems yet again that the story might end here, it does not. In spite of the sentence, "Fate deals honestly with all," Mew continues the plot, advancing the time from before Christmas to late spring. The narrator seems to have forgotten the whole disgraceful and embarrassing episode until she is caught in the wrong part of town at the wrong hour. What she sees are high-class prostitutes and kept women, and, while the narrator is "not inapprehensive of a certain grandeur in the scene, [. . .] It was Virtue's very splendid Dance of Death" (*CPP* 77). Of course she meets the girl who dragged her out of the church. She is shopping for expensive jewelry with her paramour. The narrator, holding her hands out in supplication (in unconscious imitation of the praying-girl picture), wordlessly begs for mercy only to be met with cold stares, and a "laugh mounting to a cry." The narrator wonders, "Did it proceed from some defeated angel? or the woman's mouth? or mine? God knows!" (*CPP* 78).

In spite of its excesses "Passed" does make an impact. Its real theme, the theme that "The Minnow Fishers" hero refuses to acknowledge, is that of guilt. But it is the women who feel guilt, not the men. Finally Mew was able to work out in her own way the charge that Miss Harrison had laid on her when she passed on the idea that literature can express the inexpressible. The houses, and the bodies, of men have failed to protect women from the turmoil within them. In changing the name of the story from "Violets" to "Passed" Mew surpasses what she had been taught. The evocative range of the word "passed" coupled with its homonym "past," puts Mew into the ranks of the moderns for whom each word must carry many meanings and for whom time is a major theme. A third emphasis of "passed" illustrates the narrator's (and author's) passing beyond the bounds of conventional middle-class behavior into a realm that was to destroy *The Yellow Book* when the magazine became linked in the public's mind, through Aubrey Beardsley, with Oscar Wilde. The modern persona has "passed" beyond Victorian convention. The final meaning of "passed" indicates that Mew realizes the bankruptcy of Kendall architectural and social ideals. That Mew would deliberately pick out the current literary clichés and subvert them to her own ends is also a modern tactic.

The issue of *The Yellow Book* that contained "Passed" also featured Henry James's "The Coxon Fund" and John Davidson's poem, "Thirty Bob a Week" (Fitzgerald 62). Like "Passed," "Thirty Bob a Week" is a hurrying-through-the mean-streets evocation of urban life, but from a male point-of-view. Since Mew has not left much indication of which of her contemporaries interested or influenced her, the critic's resource must be the magazines in which she was published or the works that Amy Greener mentions as favorites of Lucy Harrison's. It would be safe to say that Mew read every piece in this particular issue of *The Yellow Book*. Another modern poet, one who does specifically acknowledge his debt to Davidson's poem, T. S. Eliot, said that "Thirty Bob a Week" was the one poem from the nineties that had the most effect on him. Peter Ackroyd calls the genre "urban romance," which characteristically depicts a dramatic persona, world-weary, yet eloquent, wandering in a prison of numbing duty. This persona is both morbid and extremely self-conscious. In France, Baudelaire was the master of the type (33).

From her Yellow Book connection with Ella D'Arcy, Henry Harland's office help and a contributor herself, Mew learned for the first time of the excitements of reading Flaubert, Rimbaud, and Baudelaire (Fitzgerald 65–6). Her interest in French writers spurred her own writing efforts, as they did Eliot's. Warner suggests that Mew, like Eliot, might have been influenced by the rhyming free verse of Jules Laforgue (*Selected xix*). In spite of their similarities, this parallel development between Eliot and Mew has only briefly been explored. There are several correspondences between the poems of Charlotte Mew and the early poems of T.S. Eliot. The connection is perhaps most obvious between Mew's "Madeleine in Church," which she was writing in 1913, and Eliot's "The Waste Land" which appeared in the October issue of *Criterion* in England and the November issue of the *Dial* in America in 1922 (Ackroyd 125–6). "Madeleine in Church" first appeared in *The Farmer's Bride* (1916) with sixteen other poems, including "The Fete," which was first published by Pound in *The Egoist* in 1914.

John Newton makes a good case for Eliot's debt to Mew. He cites Eliot's famous line from "The Waste Land," "I will show you fear in a handful of dust," beside Mew's "Why this is awful, this is fear. [. . .] No, not quite dead, while this cries out in me,/But nearly very soon to be/A handful of forgotten dust" from "Madeleine in Church." While these dust images might also have come from Donne, Tennyson, or Conrad, Newton correctly notes that the conflation of dust and fear occur only in Mew and Eliot. Even more telling is Newton's equation of Mew's line from "In Nunhead Cemetery," "I am scared, I am staying with you tonight," spoken by a "thirty-bob-a-weeker" who is lapsing into insanity beside the grave of his dead fiancée, with Eliot's "My nerves are bad tonight. Yes, bad. Stay with me," from the Game of Chess section of "The Waste Land" ("Another" 18). The third correspondence noticed by Newton is between the famous beginning lines of "The Waste Land" and Mew's beginning for "The Quiet House," perhaps her best-known poem. It contains the following lines:

> Red is the strangest pain to bear;
> In Spring the leaves on the budding trees;
> In Summer the roses are worse than these,
> More terrible than they are sweet:
> A rose can stab you across the street
> Deeper than any knife. [. . .] (*CPP* 18)

Newton feels that Mew's persona is "mixing/Memory and desire." He also notes that Eliot's line could possibly be mixing Mew's cadences and flowers with Tennyson's "Is it then regret for buried time/That keenlier in April wakes" from *In Memoriam* ("Another" 18).

Newton has furthered his investigation of Mew's poems with thorough notations in his *Charlotte Mew: Complete Poems* and in "Charlotte Mew's Place in the Future of English Poetry." In both, he advances the case that Mew is the forgotten genius of early twentieth century English literature. He attributes the neglect to the "shameful gender reason" agreeing with Dowson that women poets have never been considered the equal of men, and he reiterates his belief that the most probable sources for both Mew and Eliot are Donne, Tennyson, and Conrad ("Preface" *xi*, 110, 113, 115). Day and Wisker discuss the similarities and differences between Eliot's "Love Song of J. Alfred Prufrock" and Mew's "Madeleine in Church." They focus on the issue of the rhythmic structure of the expression of personal voice. Concluding that Mew's prosody "escapes the constraints of traditional verse while preserving a sense of self from the encroachments of modernist aesthetics," they also mention the differences between Eliot's and Mew's use of imagery, claiming that Eliot's draws attention to European literary tradition while Mew's achieves resonance through her use of the image of the child (74–75).

In terms of personal connections, Mew and Eliot were both friendly with May Sinclair; Pound published them both; they both knew the Aldingtons. In fact, H.D. wrote a favorable review of *The Farmer's Bride* for a 1916 issue of *The Egoist*. Eliot became the assistant poetry editor in June 1917 (Ackroyd 82–83). The place where they were most likely to actually meet was at the Poetry Bookshop. However, neither mentioned the other's work. A careful search through the poetry would possibly turn up several more correspondences between Eliot and Mew. Certainly their mutual gifts of dramatic impersonation should be studied together and even linked to the multiple uses of language which James Joyce and Dorothy Richardson were concurrently exploring.

Monro printed *The Farmer's Bride* but not before he was forced to change printers because his usual printer's compositor would not set up "Madeline in Church." The compositor cited its blasphemy as his reason. Another problem with "Madeleine in Church" concerned its line lengths. The war caused paper shortages and Monro was trying to make do with what he had. Mew's insistence that the long lines in "Madeleine" not be run-on caused the final book to be an awkward quarto page (Alida Monro *xvi*).

A Prufrock-like man, a man like E. M. Forster's Leonard Bast in *Howard's End*, and Virginia Woolf's Septimus Smith from *Mrs. Dalloway* is the persona of "In Nunhead Cemetery," another poem from *The Farmer's Bride*. As the persona says, he used to be a "cheap, stale chap [. . .] Before I saw the things you made me see" (*CPP* 9). This character descends into madness as he stands by the grave of his beloved, and his stream-of-consciousness juxtaposition of incongruous images to delineate both his love and his insanity, reminds readers of these more familiar angst-ridden men. Yet until very recently Mew was not ever mentioned in articles and books that treat the works of these other modernists.

Unfortunately for her career, "Passed" was the only publication Mew had for five years, although Mary Davidow claims that two poems published under the name "Charles Catty" in an 1896 number of *The Yellow Book* are by Mew ("Biography" 66). Warner refutes this saying, "Mew did not contribute [. . .] as Charles Catty—poet and bank official" ("Introduction" *Selected* x). As soon as she became a New Woman, hobnobbing with the writers of John Lane's Keynotes series, she had "The China Bowl," a long local color piece set in Cornwall, rejected by Henry Harland because he said it was too long for *The Yellow Book*.[2] "The China Bowl" was produced as a BBC play after Mew's death (*CPP* 419). In either 1912 or 1913, Mew had rewritten it as a one-act, hoping to get it to the stage and make some money from it, but it was never produced. Fitzgerald makes an unfavorable comparison between Mew's play (she claims that Mew completely ruined the story), and J.M. Synge's "Riders to the Sea," while noting that "The China Bowl" had been written eight years earlier than Synge's play (68, 112). Henry Harland suggested that it be printed in a short story collection he was getting together for John Lane. Before anything definite could be settled on, the Wilde scandal broke, and Charlotte severed all ties with that crowd, except for Ella D'Arcy. Mew's personality was a combination of daring and conventionality. In this instance, conventionality won, as it also did in each instance where she could have broken away from her family and become a New Woman in a more substantial way than mere personal style.

Other unfortunate checks to her career occurred at this same time. Fred Mew became ill, and after his death from stomach cancer in 1898, despite the fact that he left two thousand pounds, Charlotte decided that the only way the family would be able to afford to stay in Bloomsbury would be to take in a lodger who would rent the top two floors for one hundred pounds per year on a long-term lease. Luckily, the Mews found a decorous widow who agreed to their terms (Fitzgerald 67–73).

Although other New Women were openly making changes in their previous living arrangements, some living in clubs for single working women, and some, like Virginia and Vanessa Stephen just around the corner in Gordon Square, opening their house to a stream of intellectual friends, Charlotte and Anne could not manage that type of freedom. Mrs. Mew's *amour propre* could not be disturbed. She must not be moved away from the few friends who still called. In fact, Mrs. Mew was not to know about the lodger at all. Only laboring families took in lodgers; for a middle-class family to do so was a terrible disgrace. Alida Monro comments:

> When I first knew Charlotte, the top half of their house was let to some people, but it was a long time before this was disclosed to me in confidence, as it was felt that such a circumstance was a matter of which to be deeply ashamed. Her mother [. . .] was treated very much as if she were a naughty child . [. . .] Charlotte would always say [. . .] that family ties meant everything to her; but it is probable that she adored the idea of a mother rather than the woman herself, for there was little in common between them. (*ix*)

For almost twenty years, until 1922, when the lease on the Gordon Street house expired, Charlotte and Anne pretended that there was no one else in the house. So as not to disturb their mother's sense of her social position, they also pretended that their work was mere hobby. If Henry and Freda had been well, then the need to conserve money for their expensive incarcerations would not have existed. If Anna Maria had "recovered" from her invalid state, Charlotte and Anne might not have had to work so hard to keep her in expensive nostrums.

It is no wonder that Charlotte Mew wrote of the resuscitation of the drowned child as "unnecessary violence"; it is also no wonder that she was consumed by guilt because she wished for her siblings' (and perhaps her mother's) deaths. Certainly, as the reader can see from her work, she had no easy faith in the religion of her forbearers to sustain her in dealing with the tribulations of her family. The persona of "Madeleine in Church" speaks for her creator when she says, "He [Christ] has never shared with me my haunted house beneath the trees/Of Eden and Calvary, with its ghosts that have not any eyes for tears" (*CPP* 28). When her brother, Henry Herne Mew, died in Peckham Hospital in March of 1901, the responsibility (and expense) of his care ended. However, for the sisters, his death was not easier to accept because he had been insane for the last twenty-odd years. In fact, it might have been harder.

The male persona of "In Nunhead Cemetery" says, "There was nothing we could not do, you said/And you went, and I let you go!" (*CPP* 10). Henry Mew was buried in Nunhead Cemetery, and it is almost as if his voice is blended with Charlotte's in the words of this poem. It begins:

> It is the clay that makes the earth stick to his spade;
>> He fills in holes like this year after year;
> The others have gone; they were tired, and half afraid
>> But I would rather be standing here;
> There is nowhere else to go. I have seen this place
>> From the windows of the train that's going past
> Against the sky. This is rain on my face—
>> It was raining here when I saw it last.
> There is something horrible about a flower;
>> This, broken in my hand, is one of those
> He threw in just now: it will not live another hour;
>> There are thousands more: you do not miss a rose. (*CPP* 8)

It is difficult to tell from the syntax if the speaker is the actual mourner or the soul of the dead woman speaking to her coffin-bound, earthly body.

What is apparent is the ironic location of the ideal home: the grave in a suburban cemetery. Perhaps Mew learned this trick of speaking "up from the grave" from Alice Meynell's "To A Daisy." The theme of the poem, revealed as the persona descends into madness, is the anger and guilt felt by the living when they confront the dead. It is also about the impotent fury felt by the survivor who cries:

> Now I will burn you back, I will burn you through,
>> Though I am damned for it we two will lie
>> And burn, here where the starlings fly
>> To these white stones from the wet sky—;
>
>> Dear, you will say this is not I—
>> It would not be you, it would not be you! (*CPP* 10)

Here the speaker hallucinates, in the first indications of his madness, that his thwarted desire will be able to resurrect his fiancée. If the speaker is the soul of the dead girl, then it would rather decay with the body of its beloved self, than ascend into heaven. But the creature that is revived by that passion would not be the gentle one who transformed "The cheap stale chap I used to be/Before I saw the things you made me see" (*CPP* 9). The Henry Mew who died was not the same brother who liked the lions in Trafalgar Square and who compared the gulls at Westminster to old sea-captains' souls (*CPP* 11). Charlotte Mew the poet is a much different woman than Lotti, the angel in the house.

Perhaps to assuage her guilty feelings and certainly to keep up the social obligations of a middle-class unmarried woman, Charlotte followed the prescriptions of Lucy Harrison and engaged in social work. Her work with Miss Paget's Girls' Club at 26 Cartwright Gardens may account for the gaps of several years when she published nothing. When Miss Harrison had first come to London, she had been involved with the Octavia Hill set-tlement-houses in which middle or upper-class women would settle in an impoverished area of a large city to help its residents. One of the most pop-ular projects for the settlement-house workers was a girls' club. Most clubs were connected to the Federation of Working Girls Clubs; catering to thir-teen-to-eighteen-year-olds, the clubs offered lectures, sewing, dancing, music, gymnastics, and refreshments four or five nights a week. Charlotte helped with the music and dancing. She visited the neighboring houses to help settle disputes about rent, doctor's orders and the like (Vicinus 211–33). Whether she also read poetry and inspired in certain girls the ado-ration she herself had felt for Miss Harrison, we do not know.

After Fred Mew's death, any source of money was desperately needed. Anne began working for a guild of decorative artists and Charlotte placed her writing in a much more respectable magazine than *The Yellow Book*. She became a regular contributor to *Temple Bar*, in which "The China Bowl" appeared in two parts in 1899. Between 1899 and 1905, Mew pub-lished either twelve or thirteen items—short stories, feature articles, and poems in this staid periodical (*CPP* vii–viii).[3] The only remnants of New Womanhood that remained for her were her relationship with Ella D'Arcy, and her personal style, which imitated that of Miss Lucy Harrison. Fitzgerald states that Charlotte fell in love with Ella, but, as I have stated in the previous chapter, Mew's kind of love was restricted to an adolescent longing for a spiritual or intellectual rapport, even though it might be fueled by physical attraction.

Ella D'Arcy was a woman who attempted to live off her writing and translations. She would go to the Continent, which was cheaper than London, when she ran low on funds. Her relationship to John Lane, editor of the Bodley Head publishing company's Keynotes series, was an on-again-off-again one; he did not take her to America in 1895. Since the Wilde scandal, Ella D'Arcy had been in the Channel Islands or on the Continent "trying to save money." In April 1902, after having spent June of 1901 in Brittany at a convent with five old school friends from Miss Harrison's, Charlotte went to Paris. She stayed there until June. Although

Fitzgerald makes a case for Charlotte Mew's strong emotions during this time, citing her letters to friends which contain lines such as "'it is a queer uncertain mind this of mine—and claims are being made on it at the moment which I find difficult to meet,'" it is impossible to know the intimate details of any relationship between Ella D'Arcy and Mew (77–82). As Warner sensibly notes, these comments could just as well refer to family matters, which were always on Mew's mind when she spent time away ("Introduction" *Selected* xi).

Certainly Fitzgerald is employing too much poetic license when she says of those months, "When Charlotte left Paris, she felt as though she had been spat upon. She had made a fool of herself, but she had acted from the heart, without calculation as to what kind of woman Ella was, though that was not hard to find out" (84, 86). Perhaps D'Arcy made an off-hand or cutting remark about Mew's writing. That would have created enough humiliation in Mew's mind to end the relationship. What *is* telling about the relationship appears in the stories Mew published in *Temple Bar* between September 1901 and May 1903. These four stories, "Some Ways of Love," "In the Cure's Garden," "An Open Door," and "A White Night" are about varieties of renunciation. The first and the last stories have leading female characters named Ella.

In "Some Ways of Love," Lady Ella Hopedene sends her younger suitor, Captain Henley, off to fight in the Boer War. He takes this to mean that she is trifling with him, but he holds himself to his promise to her, even though he has also fallen in love with a young girl, Mildred Playfair, on the voyage back to England. Henley is set to tell Lady Ella of his betrayal, but her first words to him show that she has been in love with him all along. She also tells him she is dying and has no more than a year to live. He promises her that they will remain in a platonic love relationship until her death. When he asks the girl from the shipboard romance to wait for him, she declines. Henley's name reminds the reader of W. E. Henley's poem, "Invictus." "I am the master of my fate/I am the captain of my soul" intones the persona, but ironically Mew's Henley is neither. His fate and mistress is Ella Hopedene, or "Ella—Hope—denied—died," in a kind of emotional acrostic message from Charlotte Mew to Ella D'Arcy. The names "Hopedene" and "Playfair" contrast the women's attitudes, and play fair could also be taken as a message to D'Arcy. This story, while it negates the possibility of physical love, emphasizes the rapport that Henley feels with Lady Ella at the moment of Playfair's spurning. He hears an echo of her voice saying, "We were neither of us made to turn our backs upon what lies before us" (*CPP* 113). At the end of the story, the reader assumes that Henley will keep his pledge to Ella Hopedene. This story was published in September 1901, before Charlotte Mew traveled to Paris in April of 1902.

The two middle stories both treat the emotional toll extracted from one who gives up love for spiritual or social ideals. But it is the final story of this quartet, which is the most interesting in its treatment of women's renunciation. "A White Night" tells the story of a nameless Spanish woman who is buried alive beneath the crucifix in a small cloister, which joined the nave of a larger structure. 'The narrator, Cameron, his honeymooning sister Ella King, and her new husband, become locked in this space. Unwilling witnesses to the event, they nonetheless remain silent as monks chant the Mass for the Dead and lower the woman into her tomb. After the monks leave, although the men try to rescue the sacrificial woman, they are not able to; the British Consul, when appealed to, suggests a hasty return to England. However, Cameron cherishes his feelings of being able to wait with the victim, in a type of soul bondage with her, to help her "play it as she pleased." After acknowledging that his sister Ella would never get over the experience, he muses:

> She hasn't ever understood, or quite forgiven me my attitude of temporary detachment. She refuses to admit that, after all, what one is pleased to call reality is merely the intensity of one's illusion. My illusion was intense.
> 'Oh, for you,' she says, and with a touch of bitterness, 'it was a spectacle. The woman didn't really count.' (CPP 159)

Cameron believes that the spectacular elements of this tale didn't really count for the victim either, because she was fulfilling, "not dishonourably," the "traditions of her kind." Here, Mew identifies most strongly with Cameron's, not Ella King's, attitude. Mew also identifies with the woman's sacrifice, even if later feminist critics have declared that she does not. Showalter praises this story, calling it the feminist counterpart to Conrad's *Heart of Darkness* and even more frightening than "The Yellow Wallpaper" ("Introduction" *Daughters x*).

If we grant both Fitzgerald and Warner their suggestion that in Mew's work the events of her life were subject to reversals, inversions, and negations, then the stories in this group say a good deal about her relationship with Ella D'Arcy. What Mew was prepared to give was the selfless devotion of an Amy Greener for a Lucy Harrison if D'Arcy would play fair within the traditions of this kind of relationship. Mew was ready to stand by and help D'Arcy "play it [life] as she pleased." If D'Arcy wished to engage in hopeless love affairs with men, then Mew would be ready to help her pick up the pieces when they ended. Mew would sacrifice *her* emotions on the altar of her beloved's more conventional ones. As Warner comments, "Many of her poems intimate the tensions of a strongly emotional nature submitting to restraints in which although there is some element of choice, the mind or conscience dictates a negative" ("Mary Magdalene and the Bride" 95). Yet after a mere two months in Paris, the intense illusion of the sacrificial woman ended; although they corresponded, Charlotte Mew never saw Ella D'Arcy again.

When Charlotte Mew's tenure as a regular writer for *Temple Bar* ended in 1905 because the magazine ceased publication, she was at a loss for something to do. The household's need for money was as great as ever, so Charlotte embarked upon a project which was dear to her heart. She began work on an introduction to what she planned as the first edition of Emily Brontë's complete poems. This project grew out of an essay she had published in *Temple Bar* (1904), but no publisher accepted her proposal since there were other editors working on the same project. Still, this essay serves as a turning point because it marks Mew's first published venture into the realms of poetry. While some of the nursery scribbles that Elizabeth Goodman swept up and burned might have been poems, so far Charlotte had not published any. In 1909 *The Nation*, edited by H.W. Massingham, accepted her poem "Resquiescat," which was also printed at the end of the posthumous *The Rambling Sailor* (*CPP* vi).

While Mew acknowledges reading both Elizabeth Barrett Browning and Christina Rossetti, calling them in "The Poems of Emily Brontë," "[t]he two most prominent women poets of the century," Mew's own poetry is tuned to a much different pitch than Browning's, Rossetti's, or Brontë's (*CPP* 365). "Resquiescat," for instance, begins abruptly in the middle of an interior dialogue with the dead:

Your birds that call from tree to tree
Just overhead, and whirl and dart,
Your breeze fresh-blowing from the sea,
And your sea singing on, Sweetheart.

Your salt scent on the thin sharp air
Of this grey dawn's first drowsy hours,
While on the grass shines everywhere
The yellow starlight of your flowers.

At the road's end your strip of blue
Beyond that line of naked trees-
Strange that we should remember you
As if you would remember these!

The poem continues with five more stanzas about how the dead Sweetheart wants to wake to the earth just as it is, "As if your spirit [. . .] were not free/Of Spring's wild magic" (*CPP* 51–52). While it is easy to see that this poem might be a lament for one of Mew's siblings, or an (emotionally) dead friend, no critic has made the connection between this poem and what Mew writes of Emily Brontë. Mew's Emily is a pagan, for whom the earth is the only recipient of passion, of an ever-unsatisfied desire, and for whom death (a return to earth) is the one benign power, though Nature cares nothing for the humans who love it. In "Resquiescat" the phrase "half-haunted joy" echoes Mew's description of Brontë's "Remembrance," which Mew calls "the spectacle of surviving life stationed stern and unswaying before the *spectacle of murdered joy*" (*CPP* 365, my italics). As well, this idea elaborates on one Alice Meynell explores in "To a Daisy" where the best view of nature is from death, as a corpse looking up and around from God's side.

> Slight as thou art, thou art enough to hide,
> Like all created things, secrets from me,
> And stand a barrier to eternity.
> And I, how can I praise thee well and wide
>
> From where I dwell—upon the hither side?
> Thou little veil for so great a mystery,
> When shall I penetrate all things and thee,
> And then look back? For this I must abide,
>
> Till thou shalt grow and fold and be unfurled
> Literally between me and the world.
> Then I shall drink from in beneath a spring,
>
> And from a poet's side shall read his book.
> O daisy mine, what will it be to look
> From God's side even of such a simple thing? (*Preludes* 70)

Here it is well to remember that for the Victorians the daisy was one of God's hieroglyphics, emblem of man's inward light, which is the presence of God in his heart (Vicinus 174). This poem also expresses the desire of all writers to have some kind of communion with dead writers that they think of as kindred spirits. The questions they have for their creative models can only be satisfactorily answered when they "drink from in beneath a spring/And from a poet's side shall read his book." The idea that a person's consciousness could remain alive in her dead and buried body haunted both Mew's work and her own psyche.

Mew's identification with the poetic spirit of Emily Brontë can be seen in telling phrases from "The Poems of Emily Brontë." "It is said that her genius was masculine, but surely it was purely spiritual [. . .] freed from any accident of sex," a "love-song of a woman who never loved" and "the note of pure passion is predominant, a passion [. . .] unappropriated by sex— the passion of angels, of spirits" (*CPP* 358, 365, 363). These fragments illuminate as much about the life and belief of Charlotte Mew as they do about Emily Brontë. Just as sister Charlotte's meddling ended the poetry of

Emily, so did Ella D'Arcy's comments on "Resquiescat" prevent Charlotte Mew from publishing any other poem for three more years. Fitzgerald quotes a letter written in 1914 to Mrs. Dawson Scott in which Mew recalls rereading old letters of Ella's which praise "Resquiescat" as being "realer and more beautiful" than anything by either Brontë sister, even though Mew feels that Ella always spat on anything she (Mew) wrote (96). This kind of praise, even if it were meant sincerely, always had the effect of silencing Mew, especially if it came from one for whom Mew had once felt an intimacy. The same withdrawal happens between Mew and May Sinclair a few years later. Like Emily Brontë, Charlotte Mew felt seared by friends' (or family's) attentions; like Emily Brontë, to disguise her own self, Mew often spoke through a masculine voice.

The poem that brought Mew to the attention of the world is "The Farmer's Bride." On February 3, 1912, it was published in *The Nation.*

Three Summers since I chose a maid,
Too young maybe—but more's to do
At harvest-time than bide and woo.
    When us was wed she turned afraid
Of love and me and all things human;
Like the shut of a winter's day.
Her smile went out, and 'twasn't a woman—
    More like a little frightened fay.
    One night, in the Fall, she runned away.

"Out 'mong the sheep, her be," they said,
'Should properly have been abed;
 But sure enough she wasn't there
 Lying awake with her wide brown stare.
So over seven-acre field and up-along across the down
We chased her, flying like a hare
Before our lanterns. To Church-Town
      All in a shiver and a scare
We caught her, fetched her home at last
      And turned the key upon her, fast.

She does the work about the house
As well as most, but like a mouse;
      Happy enough to chat and play
      With birds and rabbits and such as they,
      So long as men-folk keep away.

"Not near, not near!" her eyes beseech
When one of us comes within reach.
          The women say that beasts in stall
          Look round like children at her call.
          I've hardly heard her speak at all.

Shy as a leveret, swift as he,
Straight and slight as a young larch tree,
Sweet as the first wild violets, she,
To her wild self. But what to me?

The short days shorten and the oaks are brown,
          The blue smoke rises to the low grey sky,
One leaf in the still air falls slowly down,
          A magpie's spotted feathers lie
On the black earth spread white with rime,
The berries redden up to Christmas-time.
          What's Christmas-time without there be
          Some other in the house than we!

          She sleeps up in the attic there
          Alone, poor maid. 'Tis but a stair
Betwixt us. Oh! My God! the down,
The soft young down of her, the brown,
The brown of her—her eyes, her hair, her hair! (*CPP* 1–2)

In this poem, as she did in "Passed," Charlotte Mew writes as if she will never write another poem. However, here the excess is restrained more than it is in "Passed." Yet all her favorite themes and images appear. The leaf standing in for a dead something, the contrasting colors of white and red to signify intense frozen and burning emotion, and most importantly, the undone hair, all signify penetrations into the private rooms of the heart. Just as the farmer is on the brink of invasion, an invasion of a solitude, and thereby a freedom, almost unearthly, so the poet Mew stands as a voyeur at her own poetic windows, always desiring, but always outside the house. Is Mew's desire here, like T.S. Eliot's in many of his early poems, to escape from emotions that threaten to destroy her? Certainly his style is much like hers. As Ackroyd remarks, "His [Eliot's] natural instinct was to write poetry which was as close to fiction as possible—to depict externals, to anatomize social life by a process of selection and concentration" (51). Eliot confesses in a letter to Richard Aldington that he suffers from *aboulie,* a withdrawal into negative coldness, which saps his ability to do anything (Ackroyd 115). This may have been one of Mew's problems as well.

"The Farmer's Bride" caught the attention of its readers. Alida Monro confesses that it electrified her, so much so that she immediately memorized it (*vii*). It caused Mrs. Catherine Dawson Scott, a determined collector of poets and the founder of International PEN, to work very hard to add Mew to her stable of writers. Dawson Scott, who was known as Sappho because that was the title of her first published work, sponsored readings at a poetry circle in her home. It was after attending one of these that Charlotte wrote "Fame."

If Charlotte Mew and Anna Wickham ever met, it would have been either at one of Dawson Scott's affairs or in the offices of the Poetry Bookshop. While neither directly mentions the poetry of the other, both shared an attitude toward public displays of their poetry and attempts to collect them as celebrities. Wickham once wore a woollen jumper to dinner at Dawson Scott's just because she knew Edith Sitwell would turn up in brocade (R.D. Smith 22). Mrs. Sappho called Mew's ways rough and often rude, the actions of a young soul neither quite boy or quite girl. This is a highly unusual description of a forty-four-year-old spinster, but it might be an accurate depiction of a dandy suffering from *aboulie* or from the strains of having to be the angel in the house. Davidow uses the word "intensity" to describe Mew's philosophy of life. She pairs it with Walter Pater's theories developed in "New Cyrenaicism" from *Marius the Epicurian,* and remarks that to display "intensity" one must costume oneself. And even though Mew felt she had to sever ties to *The Yellow Book,* she could still show solidarity with Wilde by dressing as a dandy ("Biography" 60).

Mrs. Sappho urged her two friends, Charlotte Mew, and the much better known and more successful May Sinclair, to read each other's work and to meet (Fitzgerald 115). Mew's relationship with May Sinclair, beginning in 1913, signals her last burst of creative energy. In many ways, Sinclair's championing of Mew's poetry is the most significant literary relationship Mew had, next to the one that developed between Mew and Thomas Hardy. And while some critics might be tempted to read the following as a comment on their emotional relationship, it perhaps is the most important critical advice Mew ever received. In a May 14, 1914 letter to Mew, Sinclair says, "[b]etter to take things simply and never go back on them, or analyse them [. . .]" (qtd. in Davidow "Biography": 107–08).

Charlotte Mary Mew 1913–1928
"But I mean to go through the door without fear"[1]

The nature of the relationship between May Sinclair and Charlotte Mew has caused more questions in the minds of critics than the meager clues about it provide them with answers. May Sinclair's encouragement to innovative modern writers such as Ezra Pound, T.S. Eliot, Rebecca West, and Dorothy Richardson, to name just a few, has been extensively documented elsewhere. With Mrs. Sappho, Charlotte Mew could enjoy literary teas and readings, as well as relax with the Dawson Scott children. Mrs. Sappho's awe at Mew's talent enabled Mew to keep a necessary emotional distance. May Sinclair's patronage, however, had the possibility of becoming a true literary friendship where each party feeds off the mind and emotions of the other for the greater benefit of their art. To a certain extent this did happen between Sinclair and Mew.

Much has been written about May Sinclair's interest in and use of William James's term "stream of consciousness," which she employed in "The Novels of Dorothy Richardson," a review published first in *The Egoist* (April 1918) to describe the prose of Dorothy Richardson. But Sinclair must have been thinking about this term much earlier, perhaps even as early as the beginning of her association with Charlotte Mew in 1913. This year also marks the start of Sinclair's work toward the founding of the Medico-Psychological Clinic of London where psychoanalysis as a treatment for mental disorders would be available. Sinclair spent five hundred pounds and a considerable amount of time and energy on this project (Zegger 58). Sinclair's personal and professional interest in the workings of the human mind might have frightened Mew because of her family history, but it must also have attracted her. Sinclair's purpose was to get the ideas of Freud and Jung into the popular consciousness, and she succeeded. Any theory that would explain, treat, or in general ameliorate the condition of the mad would have been fascinating to Charlotte Mew.

Since her days at Cheltenham Ladies College (1881–82), Sinclair had been interested in T. H. Green's philosophy of Idealism. Briefly, this philosophy espoused a society that would assist individuals to realize the divine within, so that they might work unselfishly toward a higher good. Sinclair wrote two books, *A Defence of Idealism* (1917) and *The New Idealism* (1922), explaining her beliefs. Consciousness, both spiritual and psychological, was of utmost importance to the individual who, of her own free will, sacrifices her own desires for the good of the whole. Further, with her study of the new science of psychology, Sinclair felt that the high-minded rhetoric of Idealism could be joined to a Naturalistic view of biological and cultural determinism through the bridge of psychology. Once these three disciplines were joined and the positive aspects of their revelations disseminated, then humankind could begin to sublimate its baser impulses and to work toward the higher good. Sublimation, in Sinclair's words, is "a turning and passing of desire from a less worthy or fitting object to fix it on one more worthy or fitting" (qtd. in Brown: 14). As well, she believed that the renunciation of desire is perhaps achievable through a quasi-mystical, or truly mystical experience. For the woman artist, this experience is felt through the influence of Nature on her psyche. Suzanne Raitt's analysis of Sinclair and Mew's relationship emphasizes Sinclair's dedication to the theories of sublimation as the driving force behind civilization and culture. Raitt cites Sinclair's unpublished book, *The Way of Sublimation*, which Sinclair was working on at the time of her last letters to Mew in August, 1916, as Sinclair's working-through of the dangerous emotions their friendship aroused. "Sinclair's reaction to the growing psychoanalytic visibility of women's desire, and to the intensity of her friendship with Charlotte Mew, was to formulate an aesthetic which foreclosed upon the possibility of sexual pleasure" (7). Sinclair's philosophy set up sexuality as the enemy of creative freedom.

If Sinclair discussed these ideas with Mew over tea, Mew must have been dazzled by how well they applied to her own experience of life and love. In Mew's "The Farmer's Bride" Sinclair would have heard the living voice of a fictional character who embodied the theories that Sinclair herself had been grappling with and trying to express in both prose and fiction for many years. "The Farmer's Bride" is a perfect artistic rendering of the liminal zone where the passions of May Sinclair and Charlotte Mew abided. Their desires could neither be fully satisfied, nor fully sublimated. Mew is like her farmer, caught forever on the stair below the beloved's room, yearning for "[t]he brown of her." This cry could not be called sublimation, but it does represent the disciplined passion, which is never consummated. Mew's passionate poetry threatened Sinclair's artistic equilibrium, so she had to retreat from the temptations of its demands. The way to do so was to devise a theory, which excused her retreat, focusing on artistic rather than personal grounds for it. In theory Sinclair stood for the eradication of sexual hypocrisy, thereby dispelling the harmful effects of repression of desire. In practice she remained committed to sublimation as the path to artistic freedom.

A realization that they shared a fascination for the austere ecstasy present in the poetry of Emily Brontë would have increased the developing rapport. Sinclair wrote a series of introductions to the Everyman editions of the Brontë novels reissued between 1907 and 1914 as well as a critical biography, *The Three Brontës*, in 1912. Further, she published a novel, *The Three Sisters* (1914), a thinly disguised account of the Brontës' life, which Sinclair uses to critique Victorian patriarchal values, especially family and religious ones (Brown 14–15). Perhaps Sinclair had even read Mew's essay on the poetry of Emily Brontë; their ideas on the source and inspiration for the poems and *Wuthering Heights* are remarkably similar. Both describe Emily's style as asexual, cerebral, and as elemental as Nature herself. May Sinclair's passion for the Brontë sisters' work evolved together with her interest in psychoanalysis. She made several interesting connections between the penchant for the self-conscious interiority of modern narrators and the novels of Charlotte and Emily Brontë. In writing about the Brontës, she focused on their feminism, their psychology of passion, their truthful rendering of male/female relationships, and their intensely realized depiction of the "'kingdom of the inner life.'" A cogent point about Charlotte's development as a novelist reaching fruition after she had read and absorbed the passion of Emily's *Wuthering Heights* states that *Villette* could only have been written after Charlotte saw the power of Emily's daring to be herself and letting herself go (Zeigger 66–68).

At every point, Sinclair's intellectual interests mirrored and even surpassed Mew's. The thrill of finding someone with so many literary points-of-view in common with oneself is intoxicating. Charlotte Mew, raised in a typical Victorian household, held the conventional Victorian viewpoint that "[p]assionate intimacy between people of the same sex was unselfconscious and widespread, but did not necessarily involve sexual relations" (Reynolds B5). Sinclair, raised in an equally typical family, had to make a living for herself because her ship-owner alcoholic father ruined the family business. During the course of her mother's life, May, as the only daughter, was expected to remain at home in genteel poverty. Their lives were saddened by the deaths of four of her five brothers, and her father (Zegger 16–17). Out of the shambles of her home life, Sinclair made a reputation for herself as one of the most respected writers of her day. The great effort that this cost her left no energy for emotional entanglements. Yet it must have seemed to Mew that the more Sinclair revealed about her interests and background, the more ideal a soul mate she became. Without attributing a source for the information, Fitzgerald claims that May eventually got Charlotte to talk about her sad, and, at least to Charlotte, shameful family history, something she never did with anyone else.

However, the friends differed in their ultimate commitment to their art. Sinclair's art and philosophy were life. For Mew they were perhaps a means to express the agonies of life, but life meant love above work. Because she retained the Kendall mistrust of professionals in art, Mew remained an amateur. Alida Monro comments, "Also I think she was afflicted with a certain dilettante outlook, perhaps the result of her education [. . .] and also [a result of] her mother's attitude to a daughter with a career" (xx). Amateurs, as is the case with Anna Wickham's parents, always lose against professionals. One of Anna Wickham's problems with publication of her work is the uncertainty she felt about this amateur/professional divide. Certainly Mew lost more than she gained in both her public and private relationship with May Sinclair. Sinclair was more of a rebel, active in the suffragist movement, a volunteer with the Motor Field Ambulance Corps who braved the front with the Belgian Red Cross, and a vocal champion of writers like Ezra Pound and D.H. Lawrence. She protested the suppression of _The Rainbow_ in 1915 (Zegger 17, 43, 82).

Just at the point when Sinclair could have been the major force behind Mew's circulation among the avant-garde in London poetry circles, there occurred a permanent emotional split. Alida Monro, who might not have known the whole story, but who heard a version of it from Mew's side, comments on the Sinclair/Mew relationship: "Among people who appreciated her work was May Sinclair, now [in the 1950s] almost forgotten, with whom she had a _very complete friendship_ [my italics] until something she heard about Miss Sinclair destroyed it forever" (xv). Whatever Mew's emotional revelations were, they served as grist for Sinclair's implacable artistic mill. Yet her artistic productions connected to Charlotte Mew show that Sinclair was not as immune to emotion as she liked to think. An undated Sinclair poem, "_La Morte_," found copied on paper headed 9 Gordon Street (the Mews' address), shows just how much Sinclair must have been affected by Mew. That Charlotte read it as a personal message is understandable. While May Sinclair always wanted to keep her emotional self a strictly authorial one, Mew could not help confusing the personal with the authorial, because she often did just that in her own work. The text of "_La Morte_" is as follows:

Qu'avez-vous fait de vos beaux jours, ma chère,
Les jours qui sont passés,
Et de vos joies, Les âpres, Les amères,
Qu'avez-vous fait?

Du petit corps, si tendre, si frileux,
Des bras qui se tordaient,
Du petit coeur malin et les yeux
Qui ont tant pleurés?

De l'âme sauvage, qui se tourne et se brise
(Ma pauvre bien-aimée!)
De la petite âme fuyante, fragile, exquise—
Qu'avez-vous fait?
O mon enfant, tout ce que tu as souffert
Tu ne saurais jamais—
Et moi, je ne donnerais mon enfer
D'être ce que tu es. (qtd. in Fitzgerald: 132)

This poem must have been written sometime in the summer of 1914. Sinclair would not have given this poem to Mew if she had thought that Mew would take it as a declaration of love. Because she had heard Mew read dramatic monologues in a variety of voices, perhaps she assumed that Mew would see this poem as written from a voice separate from Sinclair's own. However, Mew was much too clever a poet herself to be fooled, and Sinclair was not a good enough poet to disguise her own voice. An equally telling piece is Sinclair's short story, "The Pin-prick" published in *Harper's* February 1915 issue.

As Mew did in her fictions, in "The Pin-prick" Sinclair employs a number of inversions and diversions, which become transparent when the underlying circumstances are understood. The story's focus is "poor May Blissett" a starving artist, whose friend Frances Archdale suggests that she take a studio in the same building as Frances's fiancée. It is interesting that the Charlotte Mew figure is named "May" and that she is a painter, as was Anne Mew. May seems like a ghost in the building; the narrator (Frances's fiancée) describes her as an exquisite little person whose subtlety seemed mysterious and at times malign. The description of May Blissett which precedes this conclusion is a perfect description of Charlotte Mew. The physical description fits Charlotte's "broad-browed, broad-cheeked, and suddenly pointed face, very dark crinkly hair," and "the tiny scale of the whole phenomenon" (392). Further, the fictional May's family circumstances also mirror Charlotte's, as well as Sinclair's own. May is described as having lost all her family, which had lost all its money, and "her father had gone mad—mad as a hatter" (394). Lest she seem too blatantly biographical, Sinclair added a failed marriage, a dead child, and a drowned lover to the long list of May Blissett's woes. The climax of the story comes when Blissett stays too long at tea with Frances. Frances is also entertaining Daisy Valentine, who wants to confide in Frances about her romantic entanglements. The names of these main characters are particularly telling. "May" asks permission for "bliss" while "frank" Frances, entangled with a different emblematic love sign, indicated by "daisy" and "valentine," ignores her. During tea, they are rude to May, so she leaves. The same night Blissett commits suicide by suffocating herself with disinfectant sulphur candles.

All through the story, the narrator and Frances have been assuring themselves that May's self-possession is "immune" and "hardly human" with a "beneficent, tender, supernaturally lucid" subtlety. This is to protect them from the emotional inroads she is making on them, just as Sinclair felt the need to protect her artistic freedom with her theories of sublimation. But at the end, blaming herself for May's death, Frances admits that she had been afraid of Blissett's loneliness. The following is perhaps as close to an apology to Mew as Sinclair could get: "She had been afraid that it [May's loneliness] would cling, that it would get in her way. She had compelled her to suppress it. She had driven it in, and the thing was poisonous." A few sentences later Frances continues, "She wouldn't have done it if she'd known we did care. It was the very essence of her despair that she had thought we didn't" (397). Is it merely coincidence or a macabre joke that in 1928, long after Sinclair's rebuff, but shortly after Anne's death, and Thomas Hardy's death, when she is alone and ill in a nursing home, Charlotte Mew kills herself by drinking a disinfectant? It might have suited Mew's *petit coeur malin* to turn Sinclair's fiction into fact.

"The Pin-prick" appears only about six months after Mew made some sort of emotional declaration, embarrassing herself to the point where she felt she could no longer be friends with May Sinclair, although Sinclair continued to write her until August, 1916. But perhaps Mew did get the last (literary) word when she says in "*Ne Me Tangito*," which appeared in the posthumous *The Rambling Sailor*:

> Odd, You should fear the touch,
> The first that I was ever ready to let go,
> I, that have not cared much
> For any toy I could not break and throw
> To the four winds when I had done with it. You need not fear the touch,
> Blindest of all the things I have cared for very much
> In the whole gay, unbearable, amazing show.
>
> True—for a moment—no, dull heart, you were too small,
> Thinking to hide the ugly doubt behind that hurried puzzled little smile:
> Only the shade, was it, you saw? but the shade of something vile:
> Oddest of all! (*CPP* 43)

While Angela Leighton rightfully points out the similarities between this poem and Christina Rossetti's sonnet "On the Wing," citing the title's allusion to Christ's admonition to Mary Magdalen, still its theme of renunciation fits it to Mew's relationship with Sinclair (282–83). Particularly telling is the end of the poem where, in the persona's dream, the beloved suddenly appears on her bare breast, tugging at her heart with "tiny fingers [. . .] no more afraid." As can happen in dreams, things we long for become conflated; the beloved turns into a baby at the breast, "The child for which I had not looked or ever cared,/Of whom, before, I had never dreamed" (*CPP* 43). This is not only, as Leighton claims, Christ reborn as Mary Magdalen's child, but rather it can also be the "moon's dropped child," "frail, [and] dead," from Mew's "Fame." This is the little dream the persona takes "To our tossed bed" when she abjures Fame. If it is Christ, then he is a dead lamb; if it is Sinclair, then the emotion she engenders is "A blot upon the night." Charlotte Mew's desires could neither be fully sublimated nor satisfied, and the gesture she made toward May Sinclair has caused critics to read her work in the light of a label manufactured many years after the events that precipitated it.

Fitzgerald seems to confirm Mew's approach to Sinclair when she cites Mrs. Sappho's diary entry for July of 1914, "'Charlotte is evidently a pervert. Are all geniuses perverts?'" Another diary entry has May Sinclair gossiping about the event with Mrs. Sappho, implying that she told Mew not to bother wasting such a perfectly good passion (133–34). Sinclair's discussion of her intimacy with Mew would have seemed to Mew to be the ultimate betrayal. The nature of Mew's revelation of feeling has, unfortunately, been turned into the stuff of farce. Not only are there Mrs. Sappho's diary entries, but also there is an article by T.E.M. Boll explaining the mystery about Charlotte Mew and May Sinclair's relationship.

In this article, Professor Boll says that he received a letter from Rebecca West, which enclosed another letter from the novelist Gladys B. Stern. This undated letter recalls a story May Sinclair told them "'in her neat precise voice'" of how Mew wildly chased Sinclair into her bedroom. Sinclair continued, saying that she had to "'leap the bed five times.'" Stern reminds West that they realized "'with a thrill of horror'" that five times would have trapped Sinclair between the bed and the wall (453). It is well to remember that in 1914 or 1915 when this incident supposedly occurred, Sinclair was fifty years old, and Mew six years younger. Still, Boll tediously works out how it must be true, citing Sinclair's well-documented athletic ability and her "unflawed gift for devoted friendship" which moved Stern and West to write to him. In reply, Davidow proposes the theory that Mew was enamored of Thomas Hardy, castigating Boll for his "eagerness to save Miss Sinclair from criticism for her obvious indiscretion" ("A Reply" 298–99). Davidow rightly notices the wording of Stern's letter which says that she is reminding West of a little incident about *May Sinclair* [my italics] ("A Reply" 297). Readers should decide for themselves the import of these revelations and defenses. There are two suggestive facts to ponder: Charlotte Mew saved her letters from Sinclair; Sinclair destroyed her letters from Mew (Boll 453) and a newspaper photograph of Sinclair from 1924 was found with the letters Mew saved (Warner "New Light" 46).

Sinclair's artistic affinity for Charlotte Mew's work arose because both women were interested in how writers depict interiority, especially the mental musings of people *in extremis*. Because its themes parallel her own, Mew wrote to Sinclair about her fiction in 1913; Sinclair's novel, *The Combined Maze*, is about an Oxford Street clerk, Rannie Ransome, whose "higher feelings" are aroused by his experiences in co-educational gymnastics classes at the Marleybone Polytechnic. Yet Ransome sacrifices these feelings because he does the decent thing for Violet Usher, the sexually experienced working girl who sets her sights on him. The novel also explores the friendship between Violet and Rannie's childhood friend, a girl who loves him selflessly throughout her life (Raitt 4, Zegger 51). Mew's poem "The Farmer's Bride" intrigued Sinclair. Sinclair's generosity included sharing Mew's poems with Pound, who also liked them. He sent them, along with some by John Masefield, to Harriet Monroe's *Poetry* because she paid well, but she rejected them. Perhaps Mew got caught and lost in Pound's literary one-upmanship games, which he was playing out at the time between *The Egoist* and *Poetry*. But as Fitzgerald so succinctly puts it, "Pound, however, was a connoisseur of metamorphosis, of speaking through and being spoken though, and, what was more, he understood the broken rhythm [of Mew's poem 'The Fete']" (127). Just how much he understood the freedoms and limitations of this form can be seen in his correspondence with Eliot over revisions of "The Waste Land."

In 1913, Pound was the temporary poetry editor of the *Egoist*, and he printed "The Fete" in 1914 in the same issue as part of the serialization of Joyce's *Portrait of the Artist as a Young Man*. This poem is told from the viewpoint of an adolescent boy remembering when he lost his innocence, and perhaps even his virginity, with the trapeze artist from a traveling circus. In one hundred and fifty-eight lines the persona reveals his split nature about the act. Calling it "the enchanted thing," he switches back and forth between himself, super ego and id, as "I" and "you": "I" wants to cry a confession on his mother's breast while "There was not anything you did not dare—" In the end of the poem, the two parts of the self are united again, but the world will never be the same. "The stalks are cruelly broken where we trod,/There had been violets there,/I shall not care/As I used to do when I see the bracken burn" (*CPP* 2–7).

"The Forest Road," another long dramatic monologue, seems almost a continuation of the same voice. It is a poem that repays close reading although Fitzgerald calls it "almost impossible to follow" and Mrs. Sappho's physician husband felt that Charlotte was revealing her own insanity in such a deeply realized piece (124). The persona explores an intense relationship with a woman, imagining her dead, lying on a cliff, yet still in some way alive to the speaker because of

Fold after fold of all the loveliness
That wraps you round, and makes you, lying here,

The passionate fragrance that roses are.

But death would spare the glory of your head

In the long sweetness of the hair that does not die:

The spray would leap to it in every storm,

The scent of the unsilenced sea would linger on

In these dark waves, and round the Silence that was you-

Only the nesting gulls would hear-but there would still be whispers in your hair. [. . .] (*CPP* 21)

It is in this poem that Mew first introduces the idea of the torn out heart. In some of her poems it is joined to the heart of the lover; in others, like the poem "Saturday Market," it is murdered, or thrown away. In "The Forest Road" near the end of the poem the persona says:

I cannot strike your lonely hands. Yes, I have struck your heart,

It did not come so near. Then lie you there

Dear and wild heart behind this quivering snow

With two red stains on it: and I will strike and tear

Mine out, and scatter it to yours. [. . .] (*CPP* 22)

All Mew's poems are about memory and desire; they speak of "the smell of dust, the scent of all the roses in the world/, the sea, the Spring,/The beat of drums, the pad of hoofs, music, the dream, the dream, the Enchanted Thing" ("The Fete" *CPP* 6). "The Fete" contains images and phrases that have echoes in Eliot's "Burnt Norton" (1936) in "the dust on a bowl of rose-leaves" (Eliot *Complete* 118). And his "Go, go, go, said the bird" is much like Mew's "The building birds had sung 'Soon, soon'" (Eliot *Complete* 118, Mew *CPP* 7). While these similarities are suggestive, they do not prove anything. Eliot's well-documented aversion to the feminization of poetry would have prevented him from acknowledging any debt to Mew. However, I agree with Newton, and Day and Wisker, that the correspondences should at least be explored in the hopes that they would revive a well-deserved interest in Mew's poetry. As the above passages from "The Forest Road" show, Mew's use of line-length, rhythm, and diction confirm that she is a modern poet. Davidow's characterization of Mew's style is apt. Intensity and compression, a deceptive surface simplicity, a tortured restlessness of spirit, a rare individual treatment of the metrical arrangement approaching the organic rhythm of the human emotions underlying the poetic content, and a multitude of private allusions characterize her poetry. ("Biography" 262)

Mew's personal emotional appeal to May Sinclair, while it ruined the possibility of further friendship between them, did produce a swath of fine poems. "Fame" and "*Pecheresse*" were accepted for publication in *New Weekly* in 1914, but in April of that year Charlotte had to cut short her solitary vacation in Dieppe when she got news of Anne's illness from over-work (Fitzgerald 130). Just when it seemed that her overwhelming emotional attachment to a mentor and constant family troubles would once again curtail the publication of her work, Mew received a letter from Alida Klementaski (Monro), secretary of the Poetry Bookshop, inviting her to submit "a number of poems that could be got together to form a book" (*vii*). Without Alida Monro's prompting, Charlotte Mew probably would not have gathered together her work and submitted it to a publisher.

This invitation came just in time. Under Sinclair's influence, Mew was talking about writing a novel; she had been reading the Russians and Conrad's *Chance* and felt she might be able to contrive something like the introspective, self-absorbed narrators she was encountering in these works. "The Wheat" published posthumously in *Time and Tide* in 1954 is her most fully realized fictional rendering of this favorite persona (Warner "Introduction" *Selected xvi*). As much as she might have disparaged her mother's need to maintain her social connections, Mew herself needed her social and artistic ones to sustain her own faith in her productions. An added goad to publication was the sisters' decision that Anne should quit her outside work because it was threatening her health. From now on, Anne would give lessons and take commissions from the home. Charlotte Mew did not have the stamina for the sustained daily grind of novel writing. She also was not an obsessive organizer like May Sinclair. In fact, Mew's energies were needed in the home and during the war she increased her volunteer work; she wrote little after 1916 (Alida Monro *xx*).

Alida did not have to work very hard to persuade Harold Monro that Mew was a poet worthy of publication by the Poetry Bookshop. The story of Monro's major contributions to the development of modern poetry is told in Joy Grant's *Harold Monro and the Poetry Bookshop* (1967). This book chronicles the ins and outs of Monro's involvement with *The Poetry Review*, *Poetry and Drama*, and the extremely successful Georgian Poetry anthologies, which he edited with Edward Marsh. In 1913 he opened the Poetry Bookshop at 35 Devonshire Street, Theobolds Road, near the British Museum, and Mew's home. However, it was on the slummy side of Theobolds Road, and interested parties like Osbert Sitwell felt they had to run the gantlet of jeering street urchins to get to it (Grant 61–2). Not that its location would have daunted Charlotte Mew; she had been visiting these environs for several years through her volunteer work. Along with providing a space for poets to buy the latest works of fellow writers, the Poetry Bookshop also published individual poems in illustrated rhyme-sheets, chapbooks, and broadsides. But perhaps its most important contributions to the history of modern poetry were the readings held on Tuesday and Thursday evenings, beginning from its inception in 1913 and continuing for another twenty-three years (75).

Unlike Ezra Pound, Harold Monro disliked poetic schools. Monro had an affinity for the reticent writer. As he sarcastically remarks in *Some Contemporary Poets* (1920), to be a successful modern poet one must

> [. . .] be sharply trained on the main chance. It will be well for him soon to attach himself to some group. Thus he may strengthen his position socially, besides intellectually, and be saved the trouble of reading. The Group will pass remarks on books it has *not* read, of which he will pick out the cleverest for his own use. The Group also will teach him quickly to talk extremely cleverly about modern painting. And it will publish a periodical, or anthology, in which his poems will be printed. (11)

He continues that the successful modern poet must have an insatiable instinct and drive for self-advertisement. Fortunately for poets like Charlotte Mew who had no instinct for self-promotion, Monro encouraged publication; he and Alida read their works at the evening readings if they chose not to do so themselves. In spite of being gratified by the effects of her readings of her poems at Mrs. Sappho's gatherings, Mew was too shy to read at the Poetry Bookshop. When Mew began her association with the Poetry Bookshop, she was almost fifty years old. The young enthusiasts she encountered there must have seemed just as strange to her as she did to them. Still, it is a tribute to her work, and to Monro's genuine love for poetry in many forms, that on one occasion her poetry was read beside the work of John Masefield, James Joyce, Eleanor Farjeon, D.H. Lawrence, Walter de la Mare, Harold Monro, and Anna Wickham (Grant 85). While Wickham is cited by Grant as one of the poets who did read her own work on several occasions, there is no record that either she or Mew attended this particular reading, although they may have, and may have met.

Although Fitzgerald claims that one thousand copies of Mew's *The Farmer's Bride* were printed, she does not give a specific source for this figure. Perhaps she extrapolated from the Mew letter to Monro that commiserates with him about the 850 remainders with which he is saddled (qtd. in Davidow "Biography": 321), but these could be assorted remainders from several different poets. Both Alida Monro and Joy Grant say that five hundred copies were run, which was a risk in wartime, and since the usual run was half that, it touchingly shows the Monros' faith in Mew's work. Monro praises her poetry in *Some Contemporary Poets*, saying that it reflects the magic of her personality and that it is natural, free of artifice, and full of the force of her imagination, which most moves the reader when it makes no apparent effort to do so (78–82). His words are still the most accurate summation of Mew's impact.

The copies sold slowly, but the friendship that developed between Alida and Charlotte was warm. It contained none of the sexual and emotional tensions that plagued Mew's association with Ella D'Arcy and May Sinclair. This personal and literary friendship sustained Mew for the rest of her life. In fact, on the day before she killed herself, it was to Alida Monro that she gave her most prized possession, a copy of her poem, "*Fin de Fete*," transcribed by Thomas Hardy. Florence Hardy had given the poem to Mew after his death. Sydney Cockerell found it on Hardy's desk at Max Gate on January 11, 1928, the day of his death (Davidow "Shadow" 437).

The entrance of Sydney Cockerell and Thomas Hardy into her life in 1918 must have seemed incredible to Mew. Cockerell, who was the Curator of the Fitzwilliam Museum in Cambridge, had been brought to one of the Poetry Bookshop readings. Meeting him, Alida thought he seemed just the sort to really take to *The Farmer's Bride*. At the same time, Monro suggested to Edward Marsh that he include Mew in *Georgian Poetry IV*, and he began querying Macmillan in New York about the possibility of an American edition of *The Farmer's Bride* (Fitzgerald 164–65). While Marsh and Macmillan declined, Cockerell was enthusiastic. He sent copies of the chapbook to W.S. Blunt, T.E. Lawrence, Siegfried Sassoon, A.E. Housman, and most importantly, Thomas Hardy. Eventually, Cockerell introduced her work to Hugh Walpole, Robert Bridges, and Ottoline Morrell, who invited her to visit (Warner "Introduction" *CPP xi–xii*). Sassoon even considered her a mentor, writing to Edith Sitwell on March 28, 1928, of Mew's death:

> And we have her magnificent poetry. I am curious to see whether anyone will write about her. If they *don't*, we must, some time, make an effort to get her work properly recognized.
>
> I have heard Virginia Woolf speak admiringly of her—but—query— is Bloomsbury a generous-minded locality? (Berg Collection NYPL)

Woolf did call Mew the greatest living poetess in a 1924 letter to Vita Sackville-West, but Sassoon is correct in his interpretation of Bloomsbury as not generous in its championship of writers outside the group. Woolf's attitude casually brushes aside her praise of Mew, almost as if it is not important. In her first written reference to Mew's work, she mentions to R.C. Trevelyan that "I have got Charlotte Mew's book, and I think her very good and interesting and unlike anyone else." Yet in the next sentence she rails against bookstores for not having his translation of *Ajax*. In the letter to Sackville-West, Mew is added as a postscript, along with a list of other writers, merely to demonstrate that Woolf is getting to know London's literary set (*Letters Vol. II* 419, *Vol. III* 140–41).

Still, in a very short time from the publication of *The Farmer's Bride*, Mew was becoming a name. That Thomas Hardy was interested in her poems gave them an undeniable *cachet*. He paid her the great honor of inviting her for a weekend at Max Gate in December 1918. Various Hardy biographers have described this meeting. Robert Gittings emphasizes the rapport that Mew and Florence Hardy developed, and says of her impact on Hardy himself, "He had seen signs of genius in Charlotte Mew, and acknowledged them by catching an echo of her 'queer original' voice" in the lines of "Nobody Comes" (194, 203). Michael Millgate says that Mew's shabby plain looks did not appeal to Hardy as she was not his type of woman at all, but he does acknowledge that Hardy was impressed with her conversation and her poetry. Hardy remained, for the rest of his life, "deeply interested in her work and her welfare" (525). During this visit Mew read "Saturday Market," a poem written from her recollections of Newfairlee on the Isle of Wight, but which also includes her own outrageous touch. "Saturday Market" is one of the eleven additional poems that were included in the 1921 Poetry Bookshop reissue of *The Farmer's Bride.*

The poem is about a woman who traverses the market with a "red dead thing" wrapped in her shawl. Most critics have taken the thing to be a dead child whose out-of-wedlock birth has driven the woman insane, but I believe this to be a restrictively literal reading. The "red, dead thing" could also be her heart, metaphorically standing for her passion, which has been exposed in the marketplace by some unknown action. This reading is strengthened by the phrase "you, in the house on the down with a hole in your breast" which occurs near the end of the poem. Even though the spectacle has caused "grinning from end to end" of the market, finally "When a murder is over and done why show it?/In Saturday Market nobody cares" (*CPP* 33). Now the poem becomes an indirect reference to Sinclair's discussion of the Mew/Sinclair relationship with Mrs. Sappho and Rebecca West who then broadcast it in "the marketplace." The object could also be the persona's work, given Mew's anxiety about public dissemination of her poetry. Some recent critics have noted that "Saturday Market" shares technique and tone with Christine Rossetti's "Goblin Market." Probably the most important aspect of "Goblin Market's" effect on Mew is its validation of the bond between sisters. This theme, while not overtly stated in any of Mew's poems, resonates through many of her finest pieces where the speaker addresses a "you" or speaks of "we." The end of "Goblin Market" has Laura advising her children and Lizzie's that there is no friend like a sister. One of Charlotte's most important reasons for writing was to ease the financial burden so that Anne might not have to work so hard.

Between 1918 and 1922 life would have been tolerable, and perhaps even good, for Charlotte Mew. She published "Sea Love" in the first issue of Monro's *The Monthly Chapbook* in July of 1919, and the new edition of *The Farmer's Bride* appeared in 1921; in America, Macmillan brought out the same book under the title *Saturday Market.* Louis Untermeyer, who also championed Anna Wickham's verses, touted it enthusiastically. He calls Mew a "cameo cut in steel" (340). Fitzgerald's father, *Punch's* EVOE, for the series "In Search of a Bard" wrote an omnibus parody of her work. This long poem, "The Circus Clown," appeared in the August 24, 1921 issue. EVOE prefaces his poem with the following comments:

> I have written these verses because I have been reminded that there have been a lot of poets in this series, but no poetess, if one may use the word.

The subject I have chosen is perhaps not quite so heartrending as those
which CHARLOTTE MEW, the authoress of *The Farmer's Bride*, would
select, but I have tried to make up for this by sheer intensity of treatment.
(146)

While this parody contains digs at "The Fete," "The Forest Road," and
"The Quiet House," there are no echoes of "The Farmer's Bride," the poem
that is Mew's most famous. Another poem that he might have chosen to
parody, "Madeleine in Church," is also curiously ignored. "Madeleine" is
the poem most appealing to feminist critics because of its complex repre-
sentation of a certain type of new woman.

Critics who have discussed "Madeleine in Church" include Virginia
Moore, Linda Mizejewski, Val Warner, Gary Day and Gina Wisker, and
Angela Leighton. This dramatic monologue, over two hundred lines long,
stands as a bridge between the over-worked Victorian "fallen Magdalen"
poem and the modern, introspective, disjointed *angst* of "The Love Song of
J. Alfred Prufrock." Bell notes that many of Mew's poems derive their con-
text from the debates current in her time. She continues, "[not] only did the
re-establishment of the sexual woman by sympathetic characters engage
directly with the purity campaigning of Christabel Pankhurst and the
Women's Social and Political Union but it contradicted the increasingly
unsympathetic treatment [. . .] by male writers from the 1890s onward"
(16). "Madeleine" is Mew's most successful attempt to write poetry in the
feminine voice; it is no wonder that May Sinclair was astounded by it. She
later championed Dorothy Richardson's use of the "feminine sentence,"
but she first heard it in Charlotte Mew's poetry.

Not only is "Madeleine" spoken by a new voice, but it is also a more
realistic treatment of the worn-out dichotomy between the fallen and the
virtuous woman. While Mizejewski mentions its debt to Rossetti's "Jenny"
and Swinburne's "Stella Maris," it is Leighton who traces the development
of women's "fallen women" poems, showing Mew's place in this tradition.
Madeleine is a sensual woman afraid of growing old. In her sojourn in the
church, she contemplates Mary Magdalen's relationship to Christ, con-
cluding "She was a sinner, we are what we are: the spirit afterwards, but
first, the touch." This line recalls Madeleine's own confession that even
"black shadows on green lawns and red carnations burning in the sun" reg-
ister an acutely sexual response in her. Her body was so much her soul that
"my own hands about me anywhere—/The sight of my own face (for it was
lovely then) even the scent of my own hair" swept her into ecstasy. Self-love
of this kind might have seemed to Mew to be the only release available for
queer desire. Mew's sensual response to a woman's body has to be encrypt-
ed as long as she continues to be seen as the angel in the house. Madeleine
rejects the forgiveness and religious comfort symbolized by Christ on the
cross saying, "Then safe, safe are we? in the shelter of His everlasting
wings—/I do not envy Him his victories. His arms are full of broken
things" (*CPP* 23–26).

The history of the Victorian Magdalen poem, written by women, is detailed in Hickok's *Representations of Women: Nineteenth-Century British Women's Poetry*. She does not include Mew's poem in this text, but does give a comprehensive overview of the treatment of the fallen woman in the poetry of Caroline Norton, Sara Coleridge, Adelaide Proctor, Mary Robinson, E. Nesbit, Amy Levy, and Augusta Webster ("The Fallen Woman" 92–116). Although there are no clues as to whether or not Mew might have read any of these writers' works, the final poem mentioned by Hickok, Alice Meynell's "A Study" is from *Preludes*, which also contains the sonnet "To a Daisy," so we can be fairly certain that Mew had read this sample of the genre.

"A Study" (in three monologues, with interruptions), is an introspective rendering of the subject. The speaker of this dramatic monologue is allowed merely a glimpse of the illegitimate son she bore long ago. He leaves for America to start a new life because he could not prosper in England as a bastard. But the point of this poem really has little to do with conventional morality. "A Study" takes as its theme the joy that even a heart-stricken woman can experience. This joy comes in "feasts [that] broke in upon my fasts;/And innocent distractions and desires/Surprised me" (*Preludes* 82). Nature itself becomes her child and at the end of the poem, she is "Thrilled with a west wind sowing stars." Two lines later "[s]he heard the fitful sheep-bells in the glen/Move like a child's thoughts. Then she felt the earth/Lonely in space. And all things suddenly/ Shook with her tears"(*Preludes* 83–84). This fallen woman poem, instead of ending with a child's death, or the Magdalen's death, as so many of the aforementioned women's poems do, ends with an affirmation of a union with her lost child through Nature.

In this piece Meynell functions as a direct line from the Romanticism of Emily Brontë to Charlotte Mew's Madeleine, who is set on fire by the colors and smells of this world and returns in her imagination to the small girl in the Convent school who responds to the earthly image of Christ's scarred, hurt hands—his humanity, rather than his divinity. Madeleine does not ask for forgiveness for her waywardness; instead, she merely wants the human Jesus to notice her. "Or, if, for once, He would only speak" (*CPP* 28). The poem ends here because Mew's modern woman knows that he never will speak to her.

Hers is not the easy sentimentality of the Victorian reformed prostitute who has "heard the word of the Lord" to become saved when all her sins are washed away "in the blood of the Lamb." Instead, Madeleine situates herself in the darkness on the boundary, in the liminal space of "this plaster saint" whose one candle shines brighter than the faint hope of everlasting life. Because this saint might have once been a sinner too, having had "one short stroll about the town," his taint brings him closer to the persona's own need for someone who can make her forget that she is "very soon to be/A handful of forgotten dust" (*CPP* 26).

Leighton is mistaken when she calls Mew's phrases "the vocabulary of guilt," meaning the sexual guilt of the prostitute. Madeleine is not a prostitute; she is a modern woman who has had a series of marriages and affairs. She has affection for the men she uses to remind herself that she is alive and desirable. Toward the end of the poem Madeleine realizes that "it is the dream in us that neither life nor death nor any other thing can take away" (CPP 27). As Bachelard states, "[. . .] psychologically speaking, limbo is not a myth" (Reverie 109) and it is only when soul and mind are united through reverie that we are able to create, because then, when we dream, we benefit from the union of the two (Reverie 104–05). For Mew, the dream is her poetry. Although Leighton insists that Mew's poem is the remnant of an outmoded Victorian tradition, and that her prostitute poems "have a lurid colorfulness which betrays their lack of moral conviction," she can not help but admit that "Madeleine," "written in a colloquially wandering meter, ranging from two feet to twelve [. . .] shows Mew at her most inventive and modern" (284–85). The following lines signal Mew's challenge to her contemporaries:

If there were fifty heavens God could not give us back the child who went or
  never came;
Here, on our little patch of this great earth, the sun of any darkened day,
Not one of all the starry buds hung on the hawthorne trees of last year's May,
  No shadow from the sloping fields of yesterday;
For every hour they slant across the hedge a different way,
  The shadows are never the same. (CPP 25)

Again, as in previous passages of this poem, readers have taken Mew's meaning literally and speculated about Madeleine's abortion or lost child, or even equated these lines with Charlotte and Anne's decision not to marry or have children. However, these lines can also be read as a poetic challenge to the patriarchal male voice. Women must write in their own voice, not in the voice of one hoping for a child, a poem from the male muse. Instead, women write from the shadows, the liminal zone, where the voices are never the same.

While Mew had some success with her poems, the household began to fall apart. In 1922 when the lease of Gordon Street expired, the sisters were forced to house-hunt for a place that would be affordable and suit Ma. They felt they could not move her far; her physical frailty precluded a place with many stairs, but the only place that would suit and that they could barely afford were the upper two floors of 86 Delancy Street, at the northern end of Regent's Park. The place was rented with the purpose of maintaining a good address for Anna Maria Mew, even though she was too frail to visit or to have visitors. Less than a year later, old Mrs. Mew fell and broke her hip, and in 1923, she died and her three hundred pound annuity expired with her. At this point, Sydney Cockerell arranged, with the help of Thomas Hardy, Walter de la Mare, and John Masefield, for Charlotte to receive a Civil List pension of seventy-five pounds per year (Alida Monro *xv*).

For two years, 1924 to 1925, Charlotte and Anne Mew's lives were a bit easier. Although they still struggled with the rent of Delancy Street and Anne's 6 Hogarth Studios, 64 Charlotte Street, just off Fitzroy Street, where she had maintained an artist's *atelier* since 1909, they were also able to travel, visit friends in the country, and even spend the summer and fall of 1926 outside Chichester. By 1926 they had given up Delancy Street and were prepared to camp out in the studio on their return to London. The change had been precipitated by Anne's growing ill health. Anne spent most of 1926 in nursing-homes, and early in 1927 was diagnosed with inoperable liver cancer. Charlotte nursed Anne around-the-clock, only returning to the studio infrequently to sleep. There was no more time to write poems. Anne's lingering death occupied half of 1927; when she died in June, Charlotte returned to the jumbled mess of their belongings, which had been piled into the studio willy-nilly. In this terrible time, Charlotte preferred to see only those old school friends from the days at Miss Harrison's (Fitzgerald 197–208).

Raitt opens a somewhat neglected aspect of cultural criticism in "Charlotte Mew's Queer Death" when she correctly stresses the overwhelming love Charlotte had for Anne. Raitt reads Mew's suicide as an emotional coming out that unequivocally names Anne as the focal point of Charlotte's love. Raitt argues, with Sedgewick, that sibling love might be "one of the growing host of candidates for the appellation 'queer'". The affective bond between siblings is an emotional standpoint that has yet to be widely explored as an approach to the works of women writers (73). Raitt positions Mew's work on the borders between life and death; in other words, in the liminal zone that I mention as crucial to an understanding of both Mew and Wickham.

After Anne's death, Charlotte Mew became one of the eccentrics mentioned by Sally Fiber in *The Fitzroy: The Autobiography of a London Tavern*. Living in the neighborhood of the tavern as she did, perhaps Mew encountered Anna Wickham, who frequented the Fitzroy with a group that included T.E. Hulme. If so, neither recorded the event. She had become May Blissett from Sinclair's prescient short story, creeping quietly up the stairs, keeping to herself in the pubs where she ordered the cheapest meal, probably only one a day. There, she smoked her innumerable cigarettes in silence, her pork-pie hat crammed straight down over her white hair. Although there is no date on her poem "Rooms," it sums up Mew's mental state:

> I remember rooms that have had their part
>
> In the steady slowing down of the heart.
>
> The room in Paris, the room at Geneva,

> The little damp room with the seaweed smell,
>
> And that ceaseless maddening sound of the tide—
>
> Rooms where for good or for ill—things died.
>
> But there is the room where we (two) lie dead,
>
> Though every morning we seem to wake and might just as well
>
> > seem to sleep again
>
> As we shall somewhere in the other quieter, dustier bed
>
> Out there in the sun—in the rain. (*CPP* 38)

She began to worry that she had buried Anne alive because she had not ordered the doctors to cut her artery when they pronounced death. She feared that the soot covering everything in the studio was a transmitter of cancer germs. While these fears seem unfounded, perhaps they do signal the onset of the family *dementia* as Warner suggests; Warner also mentions that a letter from Sidney Cockerell intimates that Charlotte had tried to kill herself by ingesting bleach in November of 1923, the year her mother died ("Introduction" *Selected xvii, xviii*). In January 1928 Thomas Hardy died. Shortly after, her uncle Edward Herne Kendall died and Fitzgerald claims that he left Charlotte eight thousand pounds. However, Warner notes that Fitzgerald does not provide a source for this information. Mew's estate, valued at a little over eight thousand pounds, included over three thousand pounds inherited from Anne six months before ("New Light" 47). In spite of the anxiety caused by having to maintain Freda's asylum stay indefinitely, the Mew sisters were not as poverty-stricken as some have claimed. Still, when financial worries were eased, there was no one with whom to share the irony of this event. Charlotte changed her will so that she could be buried in the same grave as Anne. The estate was willed to Freda with some small bequests to friends like the painter, Katherine Righton. Her nerves were such that the doctor recommended a nursing home. On March 24, 1928, Mew drank half a bottle of Lysol, and died (Alida Monro *xii*). She died because she did not care to go on living without Anne. As she says in "From A Window,"

> Up here, with June, the sycamore throws
>
> Across the window a whispering screen;
>
> I shall miss the sycamore more, I suppose,
>
> Than anything else on this earth that is out in green.
>
> But I mean to go through the door without fear,
>
> Not caring much what happens here
>
> > When I'm away:-
>
> How green the screen is across the panes
>
> Or who goes laughing along the lanes
>
> With my old lover all the summer day. (*CPP* 37)

One of her writer friends, Osbert Sitwell, wrote a long, moving elegy that gives a vivid picture of Mew in her prime. Claiming that her conversation contained both "high-kicks" and "home-truths," Sitwell says she used words as weapons, but he adds, "[h]ow few/The things we knew/About Miss Mew!" (171–180). He concludes that no one can fathom the grand accidents, and colossal struggles that went on inside her tiny body. Yet, the frank sensuality present in many of Mew's poems, like "The Farmer's Bride" and "Madeleine in Church," opens the way for other poets—H.D. and Anna Wickham, for instance, to further verbal exploration of women's desire. That some did so in outmoded traditional verse forms, as Schenk contends, does not detract from or negate the innovative content of this work. There is a need for a careful technical exploration of Mew and Wickham's prosody to determine exactly whether or not this verse is indeed outmoded, or if it is an early innovative use of "stream-of-consciousness" and the feminine sentence. Several critics have noted that Mew's use of what Brad Leithauser calls "the risking of monotony through the piling up of a single rhyme" influenced the poetry of Marianne Moore (3–4). John Newton boldly calls her the "lost genius" of modern English poetry and compares her work favorably to Hardy's and Eliot's. "Mew could have helped to teach poets [. . .] how to be powerfully direct, passionate [. . .] lean and vigorous" in simple, pure English ("Place" 46). If we choose to leave the poems of Charlotte Mew out of our literary heritage, we are leaving out an original. We need her work to remind us of all the rooms that echo with the "steady slowing down of the heart" caused by life's unexpected cruelties.

Anna Wickham 1883–1904
"Where in this wilderness shall I find my path?"[1]

The story of Anna Wickham's fight to become a "free woman *and* poet" [my italics] must begin with the story of her mother, Alice Whelan Harper, one of those remarkable New Women who emerged as a force for political, social, and intellectual change in the late nineteenth century. The impact of her personality and will blasts through the words written about her by Wickham and R.D. Smith. Smith's summation of Alice Whelan is that she "seemed to transcend all class barriers, *being more a force of nature* than a social being" [my italics] (11). Her relationship with her husband, Geoffrey Harper, as it is told by their daughter, could have been an excellent example for Gilbert and Gubar's *No Man's Land: Sexchanges*, but unfortunately they do not even mention Wickham or her work in this volume. Whereas both R.D. Smith and Anna Wickham herself privilege Geoffrey Harper's ancestry in their accounts of Wickham's life, a feminist scholar can see that the matrilineal line is actually much more important in the development of Anna Wickham, free woman and poet.

The first mystery concerning Wickham's mother, Alice Whelan, is never discussed straightforwardly by either Wickham in "Fragment" or R.D. Smith in his biographical sketch of Wickham. Both talk at great length about the artist George Cruikshank's involvement with the Whelan family, but neither speculates that Cruikshank may be the father of one or all of the children of Martha Whelan, mother of Alice and grandmother of Anna Wickham. I shall make the case that there is a strong possibility that he was their father, and that indirectly his influence on the poetic life of Anna Wickham is significant because he is the person who gave the Whelan family their treasured text, *The Ingoldsby Legends*. This text, passed down from Alice Whelan Harper to Anna Wickham, was both women's first book. As such, its poetics made a lasting impression.

The Whelans can best be characterized as poor bohemians. Wickham frankly states that her grandmother, Martha Burnell Whelan, was a woman "of problematic origin" who "had been adopted and lived in Belgium" until "something happened" when she was fifteen, and she was sent to live with her mother in London, where she married Michael Whelan, an Irish plumber. R.D. Smith later characterizes Martha's mother, Joanna Bournelli, as an illiterate "lady's maid at the Belgian Court" whose husband, a courier, died two months after Martha's birth. Continues Smith, "Inevitably, in the common romantic habit, the family hinted at royal bastardy" because, supposedly, Martha's godfather was the King of the Belgians (10). Yet the story continues that when the courier died, Joanna Buornelli (Anglicized to Burnell) came to England and married a shoemaker, leaving the infant Martha in Belgium; later, Joanna died in a workhouse ("Fragment" 67). Was Buornelli, or Burnell, the name of the courier, or of the shoemaker, or are they the same? Is the whole story a romantic mask to hide Martha Whelan's past from her children? Martha apparently never capitalized on her ties to the Belgian royal family, or to her adoptive family in Belgium, when she was destitute.

Widowed at twenty with three children, Helen, George and Alice, she became a charwoman, house sitter, and an artist's model whose association with George Cruikshank[2] enabled her to support her family. "Mid-Victorian pictures seem full of her head and hands and feet." She was painted by Frank Potter[3], who lived in the same building, 401 Camden Road, in a picture that hangs in the Louvre. Wickham's mother, Edith Alice Whelan, is featured in Potter's "A Music Lesson" and "A Quiet Corner: Miss E.A. Whelan" and other portraits in the Tate. Alice's half-sister, Annie (the result of Martha Whelan's relationship with a Welsh gentleman, a painter named Lister, who moved to New Zealand instead of making an "honest woman" out of Martha), "is still to be seen smirking out of pictures of the period" ("Fragment" 68–69).

For a time, Helen and Alice Whelan were even artists of a sort. They held jobs as "black-boarderers"(girl factory hands who painted the black boarders on fine linen stationery designed for the businesses catering to the vogue in extensive bereavement correspondence), before they both became certified board-school teachers. To their mother Martha, in her quest for respectability, the opening of the Board School for London in 1870 seemed the best chance for her girls to rise above the class into which they had been born. However, it is my opinion that Alice's most significant job was as secretary to Edward Bibbins Aveling[4], whom Wickham describes as "the atheist lecturer," an habitue of number 401 ("Fragment" 70). Whereas Wickham attributes her mother's adult suicide attempts (and Alice's cruelties to her husband and daughter) to being left locked out of the house while Martha, Helen, and George attended the funeral of Michael Whelan (which was paid for by George Cruikshank), I believe that her relationship with Aveling also must be considered. Alice Whelan's melancholy, hysteria, and fear of abandonment, as well as her choice of careers and the development of her talents, were fostered by an unscrupulous *roué*. These emotional stances, or poses, were passed on to her daughter.

Clearly, Wickham's mother dominated every aspect of her life, and when Wickham is telling the family tales, handed down from Alice, we hear a contrapuntal song that incorporates some curious phrasings, glossing-overs, and missed notes. To be able to understand Wickham's life of art, we must first investigate Alice Harper's art of life. Sometimes the silences speak with more force than the words. However, before the silence that envelops Alice Whelan's relationship with Edward Aveling is explored, we should return to her mother, Martha Whelan, who was one of George Cruikshank's models.

The question must be asked. Are Helen, George, and Alice Whelan the children of George Cruikshank, or the children of Michael Whelan, who "sang charmingly, and left a treasure of beautiful folk stories as the only inheritance" ("Fragment" 67). Wickham tells us that Whelan died of tuberculosis, but, while seven out of eight of his family died from the same disease, none of his children did. Is this because Martha's skills as a house-keeper and provider were so good, or is it because their father was really George Cruikshank? The later answer seems most likely when we consider for whom George Whelan, the only son, is named. Also, Cruikshank's children with Attree were remarkably vigorous. In an era when high infant mortality was the norm, ten of the eleven Cruikshank/Attree children lived to adulthood. Robert Patton's *George Cruikshank's Life, Times, and Art* is a comprehensive evaluation of the artist. Here, he details Cruikshank's professional and personal ups and downs; his harebrained schemes to make money put him always at the brink of bankruptcy, but as Patton remarks, Cruikshank "never stopped giving and lending more than he owed" (422). Cruikshank was especially generous and helpful to appeals generated through his work for the Temperance movement. A "reformed" rake and alcoholic, Cruikshank never stinted in his efforts to help the "deserving" poor (350). Perhaps he never stopped "giving" his strong constitution and *joie de vivre*, either.

It seems probable that Wickham's grandmother herself was illegitimate. It seems probable that Martha's mother, Joanna Buornelli/Burnell, far from being a lady's maid at the Belgian Court, was instead a seamstress, who may have worked for a member of the court on occasion. She left the family some samples of beautiful needlework and must have taught Martha well, because Wickham reports that Martha "always had a sense of quality in clothes, so the children's pinafores were of fine diaper, and spotlessly white" and that she supplemented the income from modeling by making chenille hair-nets and "endless miles" of tatting ("Fragment" 68). The simplest story is that Joanna had an affair with a man connected to the court. We have to wonder: was he a "courtier" or as Wickham says, a "courier"? Is this a typographical error, or Wickham's way of letting her reader know that she understands the dropped notes of her mother and grandmother's discourses? A courtier would surely have been noble; a courier could have been anyone, even a shoemaker.

Whatever her origins were, Martha Whelan knew what stories to tell to give her children heart. Her *beau ideal* for herself and for her daughters was a "gentleman." Her story was that she was the daughter of a "gentleman," and she revealed in a dramatic death-bed confession that her last child was the product of a liaison with a "gentleman" painter, even though she was, or so Wickham claims for her, "too steadfast to keep her family by the easy way of whoring" ("Fragment" 68). Careful readers of Wickham's autobiography are left to wonder whether Wickham is being ironic or naive about her grandmother's past liaisons. Both Martha Whelan's and Alice Harper's stories are the real-life versions of fallen Magdalen tales. It was not until her granddaughter, Edith Alice Mary Harper (Anna Wickham) married Patrick Hepburn, gentleman solicitor, whose family traced its origins back to "the Stuarts, the Tudors and Charlemagne" ("Fragment" 135) that Martha Whelan's fantasies for her descendants became the reality for at least one of them. Wickham's aunt Helen's chance to marry quality died when Frank Huddlestone Potter died in 1887, and her mother Alice's marriage to Geoffrey Harper, a worker in a piano manufacturing factory, and later a piano tuner and salesman, was disappointing to both the Whelan and Harper families.

Why, if both sides of the family disapproved of the marriage, did Alice and Geoffrey persist? Alice was pregnant and "Geoffrey satisfied her sensationalism by the insistence and hurry with which he made an honest woman of her" ("Fragment" 76). But Wickham does not supply the date of her parent's marriage. This omission, coupled with the discrepancies surrounding Wickham's birth date and added to other suggestive phrases in the account of her mother's early years, points to a reason that Alice Whelan might have married Geoffrey Harper, even though she did not love him. The only gentlemen callers at the Whelans around this time were the artist, Potter, and Edward Aveling, and, by this time, Helen and Frank Potter might have reached an understanding, even if they were not officially engaged. "Aveling took the girls about with him, notably to fine feasts at the Holborn Restaurant" and he employed Alice as his secretary. He also got Alice a job of reader of verses to accompany *tableaux vivants* of scenes from the life of Mary, Queen of Scots, in the theater of the Royal Polytechnic in Regent Street ("Fragment" 70). Apparently Alice was very good at dramatic reading; she was the leading lady in the local dramatic society. "She did [. . .] so well that the theater critic of the *Illustrated London News* [called] her the new Siddons" ("Fragment" 70). While Alice collected a group of stage-door johnnies, including Geoffrey Harper, Wickham writes, "Helen had only the devotion of Frank Potter, and the not altogether creditable attentions of Dr. Aveling. Frank Potter and Dr.

Aveling were gentlemen at any rate" ("Fragment" 74). Here, with her insistence on belittling her own father, Wickham is speaking in the voice of her grandmother and her aunt Helen, both of whom despised Geoffrey Harper for his intellectual enthusiasms and uncouth manners.

Alice Whelan followed her mother's pattern of freedom in her dealings with men. No one ever said that Alice was the child of George Cruikshank, but she may have suspected that she was. She may have given in to Aveling's attentions, knowing that, like her mother before her, she could find someone from among the less gentlemanly stage-door hangers-on to marry her if Aveling would not. Alice Whelan, who taught in the London schools with many young intellectuals, thought of herself as one of the New Women. As such she would have believed that women should enjoy the same opportunities as men, but, as did Eleanor Marx and Olive Schreiner, she ultimately suffered from the "huge gap between socialist-feminist theory and the realities of women's lives" (Showalter *Sexual Anarchy* 53).

Edward B. Aveling may have appeared to be a gentleman to Alice's mother who seemed to have a touching faith in the honor of gentlemen, in spite of her own experiences. However, as Warren Smith relates, he was characterized by George Bernard Shaw as a man with "absolutely no conscience in his private life [. . .] though no woman seemed able to resist him" (74). Did Alice Whelan tell her story of Geoffrey Harper's ardor for a quick marriage as a way to mask an intimate relationship to Aveling? Aveling's notorious association with Eleanor Marx began in 1882, around the time Alice Whelan and Geoffrey Harper married.

The child, named William Harper, was stillborn six months after the marriage, and according to her account in "Fragment," Anna Wickham was born a year after the stillbirth. During labor, Alice Harper suffered an epileptic fit, so the baby was set aside on top of a chest of drawers and given up for dead while the midwife worked to save the mother. Luckily the infant Anna cried and "so set out on my difficult way." Wickham believes that her brother's birth and death charted the course of her life "for my father made me a substitute for his dead son" ("Fragment" 77–78), but perhaps Geoffrey's love for his daughter was strong because he felt surer of her paternity.

The second mystery, of the several mysteries in Wickham's "Fragments," surrounds the year of her birth. Although most reference sources (including R.D. Smith) list her birth year as 1884, several list it as 1883. Margaret Newlin's essay includes a portion of a letter that Wickham wrote to Louis Untermeyer on June 10, 1920, in which Wickham states that her birth year was 1883 (284). Edith Alice Mary Harper (Anna Wickham) was born in Wimbledon, Surrey; she moved with her parents to Australia in 1889 when she was six, and did not return to England until she was twenty-one, in 1904 or, as R.D. Smith lists it, 1905 (13). The biographical problems arise because Wickham does not supply any dates in her 1935 "Fragment of an Autobiography: Prelude to a Spring Clean" and Smith seems not to have checked the public records. I accept the 1883 date as the correct one.

There are several explanations for the birth year discrepancy. Wickham may have told Smith and her sons that she was born in 1884 to shield her mother's reputation. At the same time, Wickham reveals in "Fragment" that Alice Whelan was pregnant when she married Geoffrey Harper. There is no indication that Wickham wrote "Fragment" with an eye toward publication. Rather, she seems most intent on "attempting to order the house" and on telling the truth of her family background and her life as a wife and mother as she sees it. Perhaps the misery and mystery of Anna's brother's birth changed her life because Alice Whelan Harper was constantly comparing Geoffrey Harper to Edward Aveling, and finding Geoffrey wanting. Geoffrey Harper was the eternal amateur, an artist *manqué*, who loved to talk politics and philosophy, but who was never able to write the great work of literature he longed to produce. His best gift to his daughter was to pass along his enthusiasms and to remain steadfast in his conviction that she would someday become a poet.

Edward Aveling, like George Cruikshank, was a different proposition altogether. Aveling rose to prominence in the Secular Movement as interim editor of the movement's magazine, *The Freethinker*[5], while the editor, G.W. Foote, was in jail for blasphemous libel. By the early 1880s he was known, as Warren Smith succinctly puts it, to be "unstable politically and a libertine personally. He was as repulsive to many men as he was unaccountably appealing to a series of women" (68). He was a lecturer at London Hospital, a science teacher at King's College, London University, and the main scientific contributor to the Secularist journal, *The National Reformer*. Aveling frequented the Reading Room of the British Museum, had a passion for amateur theatrics, and "serious pretentions [sic] as a poet and playwright" (74). While tutoring the daughters of Charles Bradlaugh, the editor of *The National Reformer*, he first met Annie Besant. In separate articles, both Lewis Feuer and Havelock Ellis imply that Aveling had an affair with Besant.[6]

Although Wickham's autobiography is silent about her mother's later life, R.D. Smith mentions "Alice's later escapades and exploits that took in the U.S.A., Mrs. Annie Besant, [and] a new 'religion' to whose 'community' she invited Geoffrey as a disciple" (12) long after Geoffrey and Alice had gone their separate ways. Perhaps this new religion is the Fellowship of the New Life, which established a colony in the Adirondacks of New York (W.S. Smith 133).

It is conceivable that Alice Whelan met Annie Besant, and perhaps even Eleanor Marx, through her association with Aveling. She and Helen might have gone to the lectures delivered by Aveling and Besant at the Hall of Science. Both Alice Whelan and Annie Besant attended lectures given by

T.H. Huxley, although Besant's studies with him proceeded far beyond Alice's attendance at his Board School lectures on Physiology (Nethercot 177–79). Interestingly, Wickham says that Alice's connection (however tenuous) with T.H. Huxley was one of the main reasons that Geoffrey Harper became so infatuated with her. She had studied with the great man who was his idol ("Fragment" 72).

Alice would have admired Mrs. Besant for her efforts on behalf of working-class women and public education; she would have admired Eleanor Marx for her Ibsenism. Both Alice Whelan and Eleanor Marx were London board-school teachers in the late 1870s and early 1880s ("Fragment" 69–70, W.S. Smith 79). Presumably they knew each other. Alice Whelan aspired to the intellectual status of Besant and Marx, and she craved dramatic situations like the ones that surrounded the public appearances and speeches of Annie Besant.[7] Several years into her married life, when Alice realized that a Mrs. Besant-style of life was slipping away from her, she "fell from one attack of hysterio-epilepsy to another" because Geoffrey "irritated her so much" ("Fragment" 78). Wickham writes all around her parents' incompatibility, attributing it to class antagonism, money mismanagement, lack of ambition, and feelings of social inferiority. Yet she never states that it might have stemmed from Geoffrey's inability to accept Alice's intellectual aspirations as on a par with his own, or from his fear that she would leave him if a better prospect came along.

Wickham does, however, document her mother's relationship to Geoffrey Harper's friend, George Riddell, later Lord Riddell, founder and editor of the tabloid *News of the World*, saying, "there is some reason to think that he knew her too well." When he was near the end of his life, he told Wickham that he had learned everything he knew about women from Alice Harper, and, in fact, that it was Alice's hysterical reaction on hearing of a gruesome murder which gave him the idea for his newspaper ("Fragment" 81–2). Later in "Fragment" Wickham dates her own alienation from her Harper relations to the aspersions they cast on her mother, hinting that Anna had "inherited her [Alice's] inchastity" because of the way Anna "let her hair down" when she sang (122).

The best clue to Aveling's relationship to Alice Whelan and why it suddenly ended can be found in *The First Five Lives of Annie Besant* in which we learn that while Aveling was conducting his affair with Annie Besant, and beginning his relationship with Eleanor Marx, he was publishing some revealing poetry in the pages of a general monthly magazine, *Progress*, which he had also taken over for the period that G.W. Foote was incarcerated. One poem, "From the South," deals with a love triangle in which the "male lover righteously upbraided and rejected his sweetheart who had not been honest either with him or with her husband-to-be" (206). Nethercot rather weakly describes this poem as one of the many Aveling wrote to express his feelings about the love triangle he was experiencing with Besant

and Marx; however, neither Besant nor Marx *had* a husband-to-be. But
Alice Whelan had Geoffrey Harper. While Geoffrey Harper was a hand-
some and personable young man of good solid yeoman stock, he was
always a disappointment to his wife. In "Fragment" Wickham devotes
twelve pages to the genealogy of Geoffrey Harper, and places it in Chapter
I, privileging the paternal heritage because it was the more respectable and
professionally artistic (two of her Harper aunts attended the Royal
Academy of Music), although she does concede that the "folk of real dis-
tinction of birth" who were drawn to the Harpers carried with them an
attitude of "polite patronage" ("Fragment" 64–65).

After she was married to Patrick Hepburn, Wickham's mother's family's
more intimate relationships with the gentry and the London heretics would
have seemed to Wickham to be impolite patronage that must be hushed-up.
Wickham's embarrassment about her antecedents could be the reason for
her obfuscation about certain dates in her family history. In "Fragment"
Wickham complains that she has been trying to put "things away in loath-
some sets of drawers" so that "everything will be splendidly clean." But she
also laments that once she has done this there will be nothing left for her
but suicide because once everything is clean, she will be "finished" (52).
She means this statement both literally and metaphorically. Burdened by
the demands of ancestry, huswifery, and motherhood (which she loved),
Wickham felt that her artistic life was a failure. That did not keep her from
wanting to be a success at being the angel in the house for all her jobs as
daughter, wife, mother, and artist. However, she concluded that "women of
my kind are a mistake" and "the story of my failure should be known"
(52–53). The writing of "Fragment" comes during a period of her life when
she was anxious to clean up, but this kind of honest psychological cleans-
ing can be deadly, as she herself acknowledges. Her determination to tell in
prose the truth about her own and her parents' marriages signals the end
of her poetry. The sensitivity to minute class distinctions that marred
Wickham's life began early.

The Harpers and the Whelans intersected through their mutual acquain-
tance with another family, the Reeders. The younger members of all three
families participated in the productions of the local drama society.
Unfortunately, the Reeders had first met the Whelans when Wickham's
grandmother, Martha, was at her poorest; she had been their charwoman
for a time, while her Harper grandfather, Edwin, had been the organist at
the Reeder's church. The fact that James Reeder drew for *Punch* so
impressed Geoffrey Harper that when he sent Wickham back to England
to make her name as a singer and poet, he shouted as the boat pulled away
from the dock, "*Punch*, Anne, *Punch*," as if to say that a poem in *Punch*
would signify that she had made a name for herself in London's literary cir-
cles. Today, *Punch* is a bit of a joke. In *A.A.Milne: The Man Behind
Winnie-the-Pooh*, Ann Thwaite recalls how excited Milne was to be asked

to join the staff. "It is difficult for us now to realize just what a pre-eminent place *Punch* held at this period" (91). Of course, Milne's goal was both more attainable, and more reasonable than Harper's wish for his daughter. Milne was the editor of *Granta* at Cambridge, a *protégé* of H.G. Wells, and a man with an independent income (91–103).

In late 1884 or early 1885, after nearly three years of marriage, Alice Whelan had had enough of Geoffrey Harper's ambition to have "empty hours for dreams and a quiet room in which to write about them" ("Fragment" 77). She rented a furnished room in London and shortly after sailed to Australia, taking her eighteen-month-old girl with her. The Harper gossip was that she worked her passage as the ship captain's mistress; when the ship reached Sydney, she had contracted pneumonia, was placed in a public hospital, and Anna "in some charitable institution" until Geoffrey was notified. By this time Alice was recovered and had a job, so she refused his offer of money for the passage back, but accepted reconciliation. Still, as Wickham grimly relates, "Our absence had done nothing to improve my parents' relationship with one another." Wickham became the pawn in Alice and Geoffrey's marital game; by the age of four she was "already very sorry for my father and glad to find so easy a means (writing and reciting poetry) of pleasing him" ("Fragment" 80).

A love for hymns was one wellspring for the creative vision she shared with her father and his father, the church organist. Years later, when Wickham met D.H. Lawrence, their mutual love for hymn-singing and their similar family backgrounds created a sympathy for each other's work. This love for hymn-singing even inspired her pen-name. It was joyous, dueling singing that gave Edith Alice Mary Harper her *nom-de-plume*. In "Fragment" Wickham tells the story:

> One Sunday night, walking on Wickham Terrace [in Brisbane, Australia] we came to a point equidistant between the Church of England and the Presbyterian Church. Hymns were blaring out of both. My father put his arms around me, begging me with great tenderness to promise him that I would be a poet when I grew up. I gave him my word, and when my first set of verses was printed in the honourable company of Verhaeren and Maurice Hewlett I signed them 'Wickham' in memory of that curious and very emotional pact. (102)

To placate her mother, Wickham says that she played the part of the repentant bad child to appease Alice's dramatic rage ("Fragment" 80). Wickham became the angel in the house, the child whom both parents loved, even if they could not love each other. She was the focus of their prayers and dreams, carrying the load of both Alice's and Geoffrey's failure and guilt. Their combined thwarted dreams give Wickham her talismanic "Freewoman and poet" designation, which she flaunted as a badge of herself even as her choices as an adult placed her into a position where she could be neither.

When Geoffrey Harper was proud of the Australian poet Brunton Stephen's response to Wickham's juvenilia, "'She will be a poet on a condition you can hardly wish her since you are her father: she will be a poet if she has pain enough'" ("Fragment" 101), Alice became jealous. Frightened at the implied necessity of pain, she mocked Geoffrey's delight in Wickham's work, calling it ridiculous and exploitative of a talent that he himself did not possess. Wickham's summation of her parents' war over her nascent development is succinct:

> As my mother had failed my father in not supplying him with the com-
> plementary energy to enable him to be a novelist or the tranquility he
> needed to make some use of his studies, so my father had been repelled by
> the great natural dramatic force of my mother. He always wanted to dis-
> cipline it, to teach it. [. . .] She was maddened at the implied criticism. She
> had no faith whatever in books, learning only in the school of experience:
> she learned everything about her acting from life. If my father had given
> her the same quality of unquestioning sympathy he gave me, she would
> have felt in some way liberated. ("Fragment" 101)

The geographical cure did not work to heal the Harper's marriage. The early years in Australia were briefly harmonious, but during most of their life together, Geoffrey and Alice suffered in mutual antagonism. Their frequent separations and noisy reconciliations kept Wickham's emotions always on edge. When Alice found herself unemployed with no outlet for her restless energies, she would "go on a sort of hysterical debauch," taking laudanum, chloral, and on one memorable occasion, a whole "bottle of Stephen's ink" and "a strong solution of bromide of potassium" ("Fragment" 96, 113–14). After her suicide attempts, she was full of nervous energy. Alice's behavior could be attributed to manic depression or bipolar disorder. However, she was not, as far as we know from Wickham's writing, ever sent to an asylum. It must have distressed Wickham tremendously when she herself was, and for far less reason. Once Alice opened a Physiognomist and character-reading-by-the-face business in which, as Madame Reprah, she was wildly successful. Her ability to fall into a trance, revert to her childhood, and converse with the long-dead artists for whom she had once modeled, attracted the interest of W.T. Stead.[8] Alice, at various times, was the first woman to sell life insurance in Australia, the director of elocution for the school system of New South Wales, and a Mrs. Besant-like fund-raiser for orphan children. Her fund-raising concerts, for which Anna provided the scripts and musical scores, were such a success that students from all over Sydney desired either Alice or Anna as teachers; soon, they were making over twelve hundred pounds a year and it was decided that Anna should return to England to "make a success in one or more of the arts" ("Fragment" 117–18).

But of course Geoffrey Harper, who had "read Walter Pater and knew about style," had no notion of what constituted poetic success at the time

Anna Wickham presented her *verse libre* to Harold Monro at his Poetry Bookshop in 1912 or 1913 ("Fragment" 6, 18, 71, 86). Alice Harper's notions of performance were also *passé* by the time she sent her daughter back to England to make her artistic mark. Even though all firsthand accounts by people who heard Wickham sing acknowledge that she had an unusually beautiful timbre and style, her voice was untrained and nothing in her childhood musical or literary precocity had given her the discipline she needed to become a successful singer or writer. She also lacked a sustained formal education. Disappointed in their own adult lives, and nostalgic for the late Victorian intellectual and spiritual ferment that they had experienced in their youth, the Harpers sent their talented daughter on a quixotic quest "back to the future" in 1904.

Anna Wickham 1904–1947
"I married a man of the Croydon class"[1]

In Australia Anna Wickham was educated haphazardly; because of her parent's peripatetic life, she attended a series of public schools in the outback of north Queensland, a convent school in Brisbane, public schools in Sydney, and finally Sydney High School for Girls from which she graduated at sixteen. However, as she notes in the autobiography, "I was only a passably good student; the condition of our life, the quarrels, the boarding-house, did not give me much opportunity for concentrated work, and I was naturally inaccurate" ("Fragment" 110–11). The bald phrase "the condition of our life" sums up a melodramatic story, which is yet typical of a certain class of late-Victorians. Her father's frustrated literary ambitions for himself, and her mother's emotional ups-and-downs as both a performance artist and the economic mainstay of the family caused them to alternately spoil and ignore the young Anna Wickham. Sending her to England may have seemed a way to demonstrate that they had indeed produced a daughter who was a work of art, but there is a difference between being a living work of art and making a living, or a name for oneself, by working at an art.

R.D. Smith sums up Wickham's poetic stance by referring to W.B. Yeats's idea that it is out of the quarrel with ourselves that we make poetry. While Smith is correct, he neglects to mention the importance of the first part of Yeats's aphorism. Out of the quarrel with others we make rhetoric: this phrase neatly sums up the Harpers' impulse. In their quarrel with each other, and against the world, they fashioned their offspring into their defense, their rhetoric, their angel, or as Smith calls it, propaganda (1). Their urge to objectify Wickham resulted (as some critics would assert that it has in all major artists) in areas of insecurity and crippling tensions in her writing.

Anna sailed to England full of inchoate desire, but no real inner ambition. She "knew that somehow I had to get my parents into the news, fortify their self-respect with grand contacts and successful exploits" ("Fragment" 120). Her father advised her that there was plenty of room at the top (*"Punch*, Anne, *Punch"*), and her mother said that she wanted her to enter into some interesting love relationships. With little but these enigmatic pronouncements and a weekly allowance of four pounds, Wickham arrived in London. The only friend she had was a professional cellist, May Mukle, whom she had met in Sydney. May's feminist opinions had encouraged Anna to think that she would be able to form an artistic life with Mukle as her mentor; instead, Mukle's sisters felt that a Harper (the families had been musical rivals) could not enhance May's burgeoning career, so they laughed at Wickham's *naiveté* and "made me feel like a rejected lover" ("Fragment" 123). Shortly before Anna arrived, May had formed a new friendship with the ballad singer Carmen Hill, so Wickham's notion of being a rejected lover was probably not off the mark. She felt like an intruder into a relationship she did not understand.

At the same time, because the demands of her voice teacher were driving her to nervous prostration, she auditioned for Beerbohm Tree's Academy of Acting. Her success in his advanced class restored some of Wickham's self-confidence. Attending a lecture by George Bernard Shaw on "The Economics of Art," she met William Ray, a freelance reporter. While still living with the unfriendly Mukles, Wickham quickly became Ray's daily companion. She claims that she helped him get his first full-time reporting job with the *New York Sun* by infiltrating a Russian revolutionary group and passing the movement's news on to him. However, Wickham's relationship with Ray got off to a bad start. He knew (and scorned) her Whelan aunts from his days as a secretary for the London Board of Education, and he was not an intellectual. She characterizes him as a would-be snob who, as he asked her to marry him, also told her he could introduce her to a rich man, implying that she should marry for money and keep him on the side. He accepted her help in his work, but then she showed him the scripts of her plays for children, which she and her mother had successfully produced in Australia. Wanting him to find contacts in Fleet Street who might get the plays published, she was hurt when he snubbed them as rubbish ("Fragment" 124–28).

Meanwhile, Wickham's singing improved to the point where she felt confident enough to apply to the Conservatoire in Paris. Her London voice coach, Randaegger, compared her to another great Australian singer, Nellie Melba, and reduced her fees. At this juncture in her life, Ray introduced Wickham to her future husband, the solicitor Patrick Hepburn, who had just inherited one of the oldest law firms in the city and sixty thousand pounds. Wickham tells us that the practice provided him with twelve hundred pounds per year, and he had four hundred a year in private income. His passions were the architecture of Romanesque churches, astronomy, and "prodigies of endurance" in hiking, swimming, and cycling ("Fragment" 125–33).

Anyone looking at photographs of the young Anna Wickham can under-
stand the pull of her beauty. She was six feet tall, with thick dark hair, dark
eyes, and a voluptuous body. The love triangle that she created, with her-
self at its apex, gave Wickham a feeling of control, and fulfilled her moth-
er's spoken desires. With two interesting men fascinated by her, she could
move to Paris, develop her voice, live *la vie de bohême* and forget about
writing as a career. On his first visit to Paris, William Ray pushed for a
more physical relationship; Wickham gave in. As soon as she did, she was
assailed by guilt and fear. She felt unfaithful to her parents, terribly afraid
of "being the mother of a bastard," and, recalling her mother's tales of
birth pangs and the stillborn brother, Wickham succumbed to the emo-
tional excesses that her mother always exhibited before momentous
changes in her life. On the verge of artistic success (just as Alice Whelan
[the new Siddons] had been when she decided to marry Geoffrey Harper),
Wickham haunted churches, praying at the shrine of the Virgin, and each
time tearfully took a farewell "of my mother's portrait before William
joined me" ("Fragment" 132).

In the midst of this turmoil, Wickham agreed that Patrick Hepburn's sis-
ter Ellen could come to live with her. Ellen Hepburn, with her upper-middle-
class standards of propriety and deportment, took Anna to buy woolen
underwear, and criticized the way she ate. Justifiably or not, Wickham
blames the resultant loss of *joie de vivre* for her failure to be accepted at
the Conservatoire. At the same time, Wickham learned that Patrick
Hepburn had been financing William Ray's trips to Paris. In these two
roundabout ways he declared his love for her. Wickham believed that
Patrick loved her chastely, more for her intellect, her talent, and her beau-
ty, than for the use he could get out of her body; so, just as her studies with
the "most sought after teacher in the world," Jean de Reszke, began to
develop "the best voice [he] had ever had from England," she left Paris to
marry Patrick Hepburn in the autumn of 1906 (R.D. Smith 15). She got
pregnant on the honeymoon in spite of the twenty-two books they took
with them, and the twenty-two Romanesque churches they photographed
in twenty-two different towns ("Fragment" 142).

They were happy together until Alice Harper returned to England.
Dramatically, Wickham states, "Into this paradise my mother broke like an
avenger" crying "Anne, oh, Anne [. . .] from the rail of the steamer, strain-
ing towards me, her eyes full of the most devastating emotion." Summing
up Alice Harper's mixed emotions of jealousy, spite, and sorrow over
Anna's abandonment of her artistic ambitions, Wickham says her mother
raised hell and Patrick removed Mrs. Harper from the house, but not
before Alice had further humiliated her daughter by asking her new son-in-
law to "repay the three or four hundred pounds she had spent on my jour-
ney to England and my musical education." Then, to get Wickham's mind
off her mother's incivilities, Patrick took her hiking and sailing, but the

boat capsized, precipitating premature labor. Their daughter lived for only a few minutes ("Fragment" 144).

Before the year ended, Wickham was miscarrying a second pregnancy; the miscarriage was apparently brought on by another strenuous walking tour with Patrick. Alice Harper was on her way back to Australia, sending a breezy "Luck in Thirds!" cable to her daughter. This turned out to be true, but only because Wickham refused to travel with her husband this time. Instead she went to Margate, where she worked on her voice and her songs. Her first two sons, James and John, were born in 1907 and 1909. For some time after, Wickham functioned as a turn-of-the-century super mom, joining the School for Mothers movement, "thrusting my son into the company of the offspring of scavengers and coalheavers" and "filling a cab with new saucepans to deliver them at the tenements" ("Fragment" 146–48).

Yet to live out the dream of her grandmother, Anna Wickham had to disguise or hide her poet's soul. Women of the Hepburns' class did not draw attention to themselves through any sort of public display. Hepburn women were supposed to be typical suburban matrons. And when Wickham again began to try to get her name in the news as her parents had urged, her husband protested. "Three years after my marriage, my domestic happiness was in ruins [. . .]; the shades of the prison house began to close in on me" ("Fragment" 51). Her most famous anti-suburban, feminist protest poem comes out of this period in her life.

> Nervous Prostration
>
> I married a man of the Croydon class
> When I was twenty-two.
> And I vex him, and he bores me
> Til we don't know what to do!
> It isn't good form in the Croydon class
> To say you love your wife,
> So I spend my days with the tradesmen's books
> And pray for the end of life.
>
> In green fields are blossoming trees
> And a golden wealth of gorse,
> And young birds sing for joy of worms:
> It's perfectly clear, of course,
> That it wouldn't be taste in the Croydon class
> To sing over dinner or tea:
> But I sometimes wish the gentleman
> Would turn and talk to me!

But every man of the Croydon class
Lives in terror of joy and speech,
"Words are betrayers," "Joys are brief"
The maxims their wise ones teach.
And for all my labour of love and life
I shall be clothed and fed,
And they'll give me an orderly funeral
When I'm still enough to be dead.

I married a man of the Croydon class
When I was twenty-two.
And I vex him, and he bores me
Till we don't know what to do!
And as I sit in his ordered house,
I feel I must sob or shriek,
To force a man of the Croydon class
To live, or to love, or to speak! (*Selected* 20)

This is the poem she taunts her husband with by reciting it at the top of her considerable voice when he locks her out of the house after a fight about her writing. In "I & My Genius" Wickham describes the struggle: " [. . .] he burst out of the house and beat me. He dragged me inside and up the stairs. I hit back at him, my hand went through a glass door, and I had a cut on my wrist streaming blood" (16). She did not tell the doctor that she received the cut in, as she puts it, self-defence [sic]." Her mother, who was living nearby at the time, sided with Hepburn and called the police when Wickham ran away. What happened a few days later was "one of the most horrifying experiences that could happen in life" (16).

At some earlier point, the perceptive reader of Wickham's autobiographical "Fragment" might have realized that it began as both a justification of and an apology to her parents, her husband, and her heirs. It is also her way of telling the stories behind the stories in her poems. But Anna Wickham never discarded her heritage. Her artistic and personal agonies created her poetry, "dashed off in pain, for fun, in anger, with glee, for cash, or in desperation," and it remains "a record of her frustrations and her triumph over them" (R.D. Smith 1). The leap to the upper middle-class provided respectability, but respectability was anathema to most young artists of the early 1900s. They were trying to escape the stodgy conventions of the villa-dwellers, not embrace them. These two opposing desires warred within Wickham all her life. As the Victorian child-angel in the house she must see, understand, and yet forgive, all. Wickham carried this charge into her marriage where she was determined to fulfill the dreams of both her mother and father by marrying up and by becoming a successful singer or poet. She felt sure that the intellectual Patrick Hepburn would understand these disparate impulses of hers and be able to overcome the prejudices of his class. It was several years into their marriage, after they had two children that she realized he could not. Yet all firsthand accounts of Wickham and Hepburn acknowledge their sincere love for each other.

R.D. Smith compares Wickham's sense of responsibility to W.H. Auden's saying, "she took all vows and commitments as binding, even when they were not formalized" (8). This is why she says that when she saw her marriage (of "true" minds) deteriorating, she then saw her motherhood as a way out of the past, as a way to redeem her mother's abuse of her. But it is not. By the middle of "Fragment" she is apologizing to her dead husband and her sons, and stating, "My contract with my father to get into the news began to haunt me" (149). One hundred pages earlier she had said:

> It is with loathing I see that destruction originated with my father. Its root was in his preoccupation with my powers of expression, and in his ambition for my fame and success. Until the time of his death I thought his pride in my poetry was from his love of me, but then I saw that he was bitterly jealous of my work and was interested in me only as a justification of himself, who had failed in self-expression. My writing was his fulfillment and his excuse: this fills me with a sense of utter hopelessness, and a sense of doom. I obeyed my father by expressing something important to him and ruined my husband. [. . .] Our story is of a decadence of which my verses are the index. ("Fragment" 53)

Wickham's marriage to Patrick Hepburn was a marriage of complete opposites, duplicating her parents' marriage. While her father, Geoffrey Harper, longed for a proper wife who would create the environment in which he could expand as philosopher, critic, and writer, Alice was racketing around Australia teaching elocution and reading faces, making the kind of money that made the family's life much more comfortable and middleclass. Geoffrey Harper never could accept nor imitate his wife's accomplishments. He remained a piano salesman forever. Patrick Hepburn wanted a wife who would put his needs as an intellectual above her own, just as Geoffrey Harper had. Hepburn wanted a fellow enthusiast to share his passion for Romanesque churches and astronomy. As R.D. Smith relates, "Their bitterest clash was caused by Anna's need to write and publish her poems, and Patrick's insanely furious reaction to this" (16–17). Their son, James Hepburn, explains, "He was not a conventional man, save only in his concept of what should be the role of a wife" ("Preface" xx).

The Hepburns settled into a marriage that mirrored the Harpers'. Violent disagreement would be followed by tender reconciliation. Patrick Hepburn retreated into his law work and his enthusiasm for astronomy. Meanwhile, Anna Wickham, poet, presided in the home. Their houses in

Hampstead, 49 Downshire Hill, and 68 Parliament Hill, became salons where Wickham provided music, entertainments, and lectures for a variety of groups. Hampstead, although suburban, has been the home of artists and intellectuals since the times of Constable and Keats. Hepburn resented this diversion of attention away from him, and his family resented the odd types from all social classes that they would sometimes meet there. After Patrick's death in 1929, the Parliament Hill house was completely thrown open to writers and artists. Both Malcolm Lowry and Dylan Thomas, among many others, took advantage of Wickham's hospitality.

David Garnett in his memoir, *The Golden Echo*, relished his first meeting with Anna Wickham, which occurred when she came across the street to his parents' home. Most people who quote Garnett's memories of Wickham use his description of her looks, which is indeed striking. He says Anna had a "nectarine coloring," was carelessly dressed in beautiful clothes, and spoke in a warm contralto. Judging from other things he says, this visit must have happened in late 1911 or early 1912, because Anna's first book, *Songs by John Oland*, had been published in 1911 by the Women's Printing Society Ltd, Brick Street, Piccadilly (R.D. Smith 19). Patrick Hepburn had forbidden Wickham to publish these verses, even though she had explained that she was doing so primarily to please her father. At the Garnett's, Anna was in a great state because she had just been performing at a musical concert, and because she had "lost her temper with her husband and had smashed a glass door with her fist" (235–36). Wickham's "I & My Genius" dates the event in 1913; what she told the Garnetts differs substantially from what she writes of the event. When she returns home from their house, a doctor and two "mental" nurses are waiting to escort her to "a large house on the edge of Epping Forest" for which Hepburn paid fifteen guineas a week (17).

In an eerie precursor to T.S. Eliot's treatment of his first wife, Vivienne, Patrick Hepburn had consulted with some doctor friends who certified that Wickham was mentally unstable.[2] She knew they were waiting at her home to take her to a private asylum as soon as she got back from the concert. Wickham's incarceration differs from that of Mew's siblings only in the fact that she escaped by aping male intellectual behavior so that her male doctors would certify her as sane.

R.D. Smith agrees with Garnett's account, having received a similar story in a letter from James Hepburn, Anna's son. However, James writes that Anna *accidentally pushed* (my emphasis) her hand through a glass panel (R.D. Smith 17). Whichever of the three descriptions of the violence is most accurate (and, curiously, none says how badly or slightly Anna was hurt), this display of unwomanly rage sent Anna away for six weeks. Wickham sums up the emotional blackmail to which both her father and Patrick Hepburn subjected her. "Just as it was necessary to my father's *amour propre* that I should express something, it was necessary to my husband's male integrity that I should not" ("Fragment" 53). Still, Wickham makes the most of her incarceration. She felt that the discipline of a hospital stay was an invaluable regime for her. In those six weeks she wrote eighty poems, but her creation of them was a source of shame rather than pride, because Wickham believed that art should stem from a "deep delight." So here, at the beginning of her career as a writer, she already feels alienated from one of her most desperately longed for sources of joy.

Garnett tells a charming story about her return. He says that she told him, "'I put the whole thing out of my head, [. . .] sent for a copy of Todhunter's arithmetic and spent most of the day doing sums. When the visiting doctors came round they let me out'" (*The Golden Echo* 236). That Wickham was able to do sums all day apparently illustrated her rationality. By aping male, rational behavior, she escaped the fate of Sylvia Plath who is characterized by Porter as "becoming trapped in a patriarchal psychiatry that trapped her in her own past" (123). Still, as Wickham says, "the experience ruined me, and the effect of it has ruined us all. I never forgave Patrick for submitting me to its ignomies and its tortures" ("Genius" 19). R.D. Smith states that Wickham's release was for a probationary month, to see if she could behave; yet soon after she got home she went to the Poetry Bookshop, gave Harold and Alida Monro a copy of *Songs* and thereby launched her poetic career (18). There is no evidence that she ever was sent away again. Nine of her poems were subsequently published in Monro's *Poetry and Drama* in the summer 1914 issue.

What kind of marriage had Anna Wickham made in the house of her soul? It mired her in a state of perpetual conflict. As she says, "there was a spirit in me stirring towards self-expression and independence, and a spirit yearning backwards toward the city of compliance." Still, she never forgave her husband "for the disastrous folly of so dehumanizing me" ("Genius" 20). The time she blossoms as an artist is the time, 1914–19, that Patrick is away at war. This period of her life is when she began to open her house to artists, and when her reputation as a poet grew. Both *The Contemplative Quarry* (1915) and *The Man with a Hammer* (1916) were published while Patrick served as a kite balloon observer for the Royal Naval Air Service and an original member of the Royal Air Force (R.D. Smith 19). During (or shortly before) the war, she met the Lawrences, and Louis Untermeyer, and as Smith says, "her husband being away, Anna became more 'Bohemian'" (20). In other words, during the war she did not have to live the lie, and could let her personality blossom without fear that it would offend her husband, or cause her any more nervous prostration.

One of the things that Wickham decided to do was develop her relationships with her artist and writer friends whether her husband approved or not. David Garnett says in *Great Friends* that he introduced Wickham and D.H. Lawrence early in 1915 and that they liked each other (85), but R.D. Smith quotes the artist Nina Hamnett's 1932 autobiography,

Laughing Torso, as saying that, in 1913 when Hamnett was ill with influenza and Wickham had taken her in to nurse her, the Lawrences and Katherine Mansfield came several times a week to visit Anna (388 n.)[3] Hamnett says that when Mrs. Lawrence and Katherine Mansfield were upstairs with her, Lawrence and Wickham were downstairs singing hymns together. The correct date is probably Garnett's because the Lawrences lived on and off at 1 Byron Villas, Vale of Health, Hampstead from August until the end of December 1915 (Sagar 231–32). The friendship between Wickham and Lawrence has never been investigated in detail. They had many life experiences and attitudes toward writing in common. Yet at the heart of their relationship was a gulf that never could be bridged.

These attitudes were developed in lively discussions between them. As Wickham states in "The Spirit of the Lawrence Women":

> Our communion was profound and exceedingly serious, and Lawrence very kindly did not insist on its being in the form of his monologue. He not only let me talk but appeared to be interested in what I said. He relieved me of the burden of my mind, and at the same time tried to reveal what was in his mind to me. Our words plumbed beyond meaning. (*WAW* 355)

Both Wickham and Lawrence had experienced the horrors of Board-school teaching, he as a teacher, and Wickham through her mother's stories. They shared a love of music, but most importantly, they shared an attitude toward poetry. Aldous Huxley begins his introduction to Lawrence's letters with words from a letter that Lawrence wrote during the period he was friends with Wickham.

> I always say, my motto is "Art for my sake." If I want to write, I write— and if I don't want to, I won't. The difficulty is to find exactly the form one's passion—work is produced by passion with me like kisses—is it with you?—wants to take. (*ix*)

This is Wickham's artistic credo as well. What Wickham shared with Lawrence was their past and a jumble of artistic sensibilities. However, unlike Lawrence, Wickham could laugh at the pretensions of the latter. She wrote two poems to (and about) Lawrence which sum up their relationship:

> Multiplication
> (For D.H.L.)
> Had I married you, dear,
> When I was nineteen,
> I had been little since
> But a printing machine;
> For, before my fortieth year had run,
> I well had produced you
> A twenty-first son.

Your ingenious love
Had expressed through me
Automatic, unreasoned, fecundity.
I had scattered the earth
With the seed of your loins,
And stamped you on boys
Like a king's head on coins. (WAW 318)

This poem fantasizes about where both of their creative efforts might have gone if they had been married to each other. Certainly both acknowledged that the urge to write was close kin to the urge to procreate, although Lawrence worked his whole *oeuvre* around this concept while Wickham joked about it in hers. Another poem, "Love Letter," said by R.D. Smith to be an "uncharacteristically bad poem [. . .] [which] catches D.H. Lawrence's hectoring sententiousness," is being misread. I believe that it, too, simultaneously displays her affection for Lawrence while also teasing him about, as Smith puts it, "his monstrously absurd machoism [sic]" (41).

A Love Letter
You have given me some quality of the male,
While I have given you some qualities of myself.
You are the father of my action,
While I have begotten in you new courage.
Maybe we are completed by love,
So that we are beyond sex.
We have found the miraculous unity,
To which existence itself implies increase.

I do not grieve away my days
Because you are gone from me,
My mind is stimulated forever by the idea of you,
I do not ask that your love should be faithful to my body,
It is impossible that your soul should be faithless to my soul.
It is well I cannot eat with you all my days,
I would not take my soup from a consecrated cup.
I have before me a wealth of happy moments when I shall see you.
They are like holy wafers, which I will eat,
For stimulation, for absolution, and for my eternal hope.

I ask nothing of you, not even that you live,

If you die, I remember you

Till the blood in my wrists is cold. (*Selected* 37)

That this poem is a wicked parody of Lawrence's ideas about the relationship between the sexes never seems to have occurred to R.D. Smith. Trenchant criticism of Lawrence's style and ideas pervades Wickham's long essay "The Spirit of the Lawrence Women." In it she makes the distinction that the writer Lawrence is not the friend Lawrence who was honest with her about intellectual matters. This essay mourns the lively mind that she knew and claims that when Lawrence committed his thoughts to paper they hardened into dogma and dialectics. Anna Wickham felt betrayed by Lawrence's attitude toward women while feeling that because they inhabited the same social space she could understand him in ways that many of his aristocratic and upper middle-class friends (including his wife Frieda) could not. While she excoriates J. Middleton Murry's deification of Lawrence's male persona, certainly the phrases she uses to describe his writing about the relationship between women and men come from an emotional response. She calls Lawrence the scourge and betrayer of women who uses words to deliberately obscure meaning. With his rhetoric, Lawrence creates emotional effluvia, which are "allowed to arise like an odour from a decay of phrase," and she sums up his work as a "miasma of menace towards women who detach any considerable portion of their energy from their purely sexual function" (*WAW* 357). At the same time, she has the grace to be ashamed of speaking in such a harsh way about an old (and dead) friend who cannot defend himself.

Anna Wickham was always fair and kind to the friends she adopted even if they did not repay the kindness. Lawrence was one who did, writing on September 23, 1915, to Edward Marsh, the editor of *Georgian Poetry*, "I don't believe you've seen these poems by Anna Wickham [. . .] I think some of these poems *very* good. You may like them for *Georgian Poetry*" (*Letters* 262). Unfortunately for Wickham, Marsh did not take Lawrence's suggestion. Like Mew, Wickham did not fit the Georgian aesthetic, which encompassed "spiritual buoyancy," "new tendencies," and the prevailing scorn for "Victorian lushness" and "*fin de siècle* enervation" (Ross 118–20). Yet, as Amy Lowell says in a review, "Weary Verse,"

> One cannot help wondering on what principle [the four volumes of *Georgian Poetry*] are edited. Scarcely on that of presenting all the best poetry of the moment [. . .] since Richard Aldington, F.S. Flint, the Sitwells, and Anna Wickham have never been included. (258)

Another who thanked Wickham for her kindness to him was the American editor and poet Louis Untermeyer. Like David Garnett, Untermeyer was charmed by Wickham's looks and verve. As he says in his autobiography, *From Another World*, "she had more color and character than many of the poets who were so quickly acclaimed" and he never wavered in his high opinion of her verse, including her in his anthologies of modern British and American poetry (340). He bemoans the fact that Wickham is unrecognized by her compatriots. Untermeyer claims that it was Wickham who introduced him to the seventeen-year-old Stephen Spender's poems, but Spender does not acknowledge this in his autobiography (341).

Obviously Anna was not giving up her artistic friends and her poetry for Patrick, but the crucial artistic relationships developed only when Patrick was away. At the same time she was not neglecting her family; rather, she was increasing it. The Hepburns had a third son, Richard, in 1917, presumably conceived while Patrick was home on leave, and their youngest, George, in 1919, after Patrick returned home for good. By 1920 Wickham was responsible for the physical and emotional well being of her husband, four sons, and any artist friends who needed a place to stay. Anna Wickham was never able to bar the door. Wickham is frank about the untidy nature of her house and the failure of the woman artist:

> I have never believed in my art. I have never been interested in it. I have been interested in men. My desire has not been to make art but to create an artist. I have believed in being a woman, and my notion of my *métier de femme* has been to stay in my family and order my house. ("Fragment" 53)

This both reflects the influence her mother, Alice Whelan Harper, had on her, and rejects it. By writing the above, Wickham is playing to, and playing against, the character of her mother and her husband. She, unlike her mother, did stay in her family, but neither ever ordered her house. The legacy from Wickham's grandmother, Martha Whelan, of hidden illegitimacy and then the forcing of the Board school experience on Helen and Alice, was thought by Wickham to have placed the family in a social no-man's land from which a marriage to Patrick Hepburn was to have redeemed her. For a time after the birth of the second set of sons, Wickham again tried to settle into the wife and mother role. As an upper-middle-class housewife she had a cook, a live-in housemaid, and a student ballet dancer to help with the baby, George. While she was content with her children, Wickham still suffered from a spiritual malaise connected to her deteriorating relationship with her husband and her desire to resolve her parents' conflicts through her personal achievements.

The spiritual legacy from her mother was a mish-mash of Theosophy, and early feminist principles. These were hopelessly confused by the rudiments of Catholicism, which Wickham received from her schooling in Australia, and her father's Darwinian agnosticism and Positivism. No comfort there. At the same time, both Alice Harper and Anna Wickham were trying to make their intellectual houses *in* man's land. This incursion was not acceptable; it was even frightening for their marriage partners. A social and spiritual limnality became for Wickham an artistic marginality as well.

But in the early twenties this was some years away. Even though Wickham says she enjoys motherhood, she also never loses her desire to be a creative personality, which she feels is essentially bisexual. Yet she feels that no one can be a creative androgyne in a traditional marriage such as the one she had with Patrick.

Still, the momentum of her writing continued. In 1921, the Poetry Bookshop published *The Little Old House*, and in America, Harcourt Brace published her two previous volumes as one, with a glowing introduction by Untermeyer. He says, "'But already a small and widely-scattered group of women are taking stock of themselves—appraising their limitations, inventions and energies without a thought of man's contempt or condescension.'" (qtd. in R.D. Smith: 21). Untermeyer groups Wickham with May Sinclair, Virginia Woolf, and Dorothy Richardson and says that the rigorous self-examination recorded by the new group of women poets is typified by its best "seeker and singer," Anna Wickham. Who knows where the career of Anna Wickham might have gone if her son Richard had not died of septic scarlet fever in the winter of 1921 (Hepburn *xxi*)? The grief and guilt that this event caused haunted Wickham for the rest of her life.

After Richard's death, she left London with James, her eldest son, to spend six months in Paris getting herself sorted out. R.D. Smith says that these months in Paris were used not only to grieve for Richard but also to try to resolve the conflict inside her between her artistic obsessions and her duty to her family (21). During this time she met Natalie Barney, and associated with a group that included Ezra Pound, Sylvia Beach, Djuna Barnes, Robert McAlmon, and other expatriates from England and America. In the preface to *The Writings of Anna Wickham*, James Hepburn quotes "Song to Amidon," an imagist poem that Anna wrote after she had spent the morning with Pound at the Cafe du Dome: "Dear fragrance,/Be no more a man/But a small hill of herbs" (*xxi*). This poem illustrates my belief that Wickham could be an excellent poet when she surrounded herself with like minds. However, left on her own, she, like many who are unsure of their poetic voice, overwrites. So, in David Garnett's 1971 edition of her *Selected Poems*, what was once an imagist gem becomes this:

> Song to Amidon
> Dear Fragrance,
> Be no more a man,
> But a small hill of herbs.
> And I will take you in my hands
> And press you to more intimate fine scent;
> Then I will hold you to my heart,
> Till I know grace.
> The hungry winds shall woo me for your sake,

Incontinent, I'll fling you to high air

And you, ascending to poor God's assault,

Shall burden Heaven with your subtle sweet

Till He repents him of old odorous smoke,

And flings out bolts to throw the altars down. (23)

Although the second version of "Song to Amidon" is a more complete poem in the sense that its meaning is clearly wrought, it lacks the mystery of the first three lines standing alone. Wickham's first three lines "made it new," but then she stumbles and remakes it old. A phrase like "He repents him" casts a specious archaism into a poem that does not need it. Wickham's distrust of her reader, and that reader's reception of her poetic persona's sexual vision, causes her to mask her meaning with stale "smoke."

After Paris, James and Anna's return to Hampstead signaled a return to domesticity, but it was an increasingly fragile peace. According to James, in 1926 Patrick filed for a judicial separation, in the terms of which Anna and the three boys were to have four hundred pounds per year as long as she made no attempt to "approach her husband" (*Preface xxii*). R.D. Smith says that during this time Wickham increased her literary contacts, joining P.E.N., giving poetry readings, and keeping up with the crowd at the Fitzroy Tavern.[4] For a time, she and the boys stayed at Alida Monro's in Bloomsbury, but by 1928, the year the judicial separation lapsed, the family reunited in Hampstead (R.D. Smith 23). However, this peace was short-lived.

During the Christmas holidays of 1929, Patrick went alone on a walking tour of the Lake District. On Christmas Day, he fell off a mountain and died of exposure. Although neither James Hepburn nor R.D. Smith mentions it, the authorities investigated his death before it was declared death by misadventure. The December 30th and 31st editions of the *London Times* carry articles about his death. Under the headline "Astronomer's Death: Drowning Accident in the Lake District," the December 30 1929 *Times* [London] quotes witnesses at the inquest into his death who testified that after arriving at the Swan Hotel in Grasmere at seven a.m. Christmas morning, Hepburn decided to hike from Grasmere to Borrowdale, starting around one p.m. James Sandelands of the hotel staff states that Hepburn was advised not to go as the weather was very bad and the hour late. Leaving a parcel to be sent to his home address in London, Hepburn set out anyway. "'His mind seemed to be perturbed, and he was very restless,' Mr. Sandelands added" (7). The next day, a shepherd found his body lying in a stream. The coroner concluded that Patrick Hepburn accidentally drowned, but he added that Mr. Hepburn had done things that were highly unusual and he took a risk that "very few people who knew the Fells would have taken" (7).

Was this death an accident or suicide? The answer to this question will never be known. R.D. Smith apparently accepts the verdict of accidental death, but he does mention that Hepburn had been on other solitary walking holidays in the Lake District, and, in fact, the above-mentioned article from the *Times* also quotes another innkeeper (who identified the body) as saying that Hepburn had first stayed with him in September 1926, and on that occasion Hepburn had been "stumbling about in the dark on Sty Head Pass, injuring his leg" (7). If we can assume that Patrick Hepburn was well aware of the risks he was taking, and that he preferred to be by himself instead of with his family on Christmas and Boxing days, what should we conclude about the Hepburn's tattered marriage? A misogynist might decide that Anna Wickham had caused Patrick Hepburn's death, especially if he had read her 1921 poem, "The Homecoming":

I waited ten years in the husk
That once had been our home,
Watching from dawn to dusk
To see if he would come.

And there he was beside me
Always at board and bed;
I looked—and woe betide me
He I had loved was dead.

He fell at night on the hillside,
They brought him home to his place,
I had not the solace of sorrow
Till I had looked at his face.

Then I clasped the broken body
To see if it breathed or moved,
For there, in the smile of his dying,
Was the gallant man I had loved.

O wives come lend me your weeping,
I have not enough of tears,
For he is dead who was sleeping
These ten accursed years. (*Selected* 47)

Is it conceivable that unconsciously Patrick Hepburn responded to the emotional import of this poem? Perhaps Wickham is acknowledging her part in his death, or her guilt at her imagined part in his death, when she says "[he] made the most heroic attempts to [. . .] batter the love of words out of me. He failed and died of it. [. . .] Our story is of a decadence of which my verses are the index" ("Fragment" 53). The correspondence between art and life here is similar to the connection between Mew's death and May Sinclair's story about a fey artist.

It took two years for Anna and James to wind up Patrick's law practice. R.D. Smith says that they were finished by 1932, that there was little cash, and that Anna Wickham was now free to be herself and promote her career as a poet (23). Yet did the alterations, the renovations, she made for her parents, her husband, her sons, and her literary friends and *protégées* finally nail her into what Lionel Birch, in an April 1946 article for the *Picture Post*, called "A Poetess Landlady?" Was Anna Wickham someone who had rented out her creative space? Surely she agreed with her French friend, Lucie Delarue-Mardrus, who believed that no one was ever cured of his childhood. Because the home and the house became so problematic for Wickham, she had a hard time developing the poetic intimacy of space that Bachelard considers essential for the creative spirit. Early on, when she left home several times to try to make a life for herself by singing, she always returned to her husband and sons because she did not want to be robbed of her children. Returning once, she kissed the door because she loved the house, even though it was a prison of torment for the artist in her. Both Mew and Wickham became prisoners of the structures they inhabited. Middleclass Englishmen and their wives embraced the angel in the house metaphor, but this angel signaled death for the artist, not life.

Wickham did take her urge to write poetry seriously, but she also relied on a mask of humorous disparagement of her own work to disguise its truth. Some critics might characterize the wit of her poems as masculine. It is often bitter and cruel, scathingly attacking society's mores and male/female relationships. Because her message is so blunt, she jokes about it and allows her friends and her family to joke about it and her outward manifestations of it to diffuse the impact of her work. Wickham had to become a universal mother figure on the one hand, and the eccentric bohemian gypsy on the other, in order to give the predominantly male literary establishment identities for her with which they would feel comfortable. Unfortunately, these identities, while allowing for cordial personal relationships, also effectively negated any careful considerations of her work. Some critics, editors, and fellow poets were awed by Wickham's personae and their prophetic pronouncements. Others thought she was a silly, self-indulgent fool. Jones characterizes Wickham's work as "opinionated, argumentative terse statements" that have a "hard-edged, punchy quality" like D. H. Lawrence's poems in *Pansies* (300).

The direct artistic result of Wickham's widowhood was a spate of new publication. A 1936 *Richard's Shilling Selections* featured thirty-six of her poems, thirty of which were new. In 1937 her work appeared in the anthologies *Edwardian Poetry* and *Neo-Georgian Poetry*. All three of these efforts were undertaken under the aegis of the poet John Gawsworth (Dowson 166). In America, Louis Untermeyer continued to include her in his anthologies. R.D. Smith declares that she had an (undeserved) international reputation, which elevated her sections in anthologies above those of Robert Graves, Walter de la Mare, and, in a few instances, W.B. Yeats (23). Inclusion in anthologies was so important to the poets of the day that even as great an artist as Thomas Hardy was concerned that his work appear in the right ones (Jones 98). During this fertile period, Wickham's cultivation of her friendship with Natalie Barney, whom she had met in Paris in 1921–22, was perhaps her most significant artistic and personal relationship. In 1938 she was asked by the Friends of the Library of Chicago to organize a collective tribute to Harriet Monroe, the deceased editor of *Poetry*. She also joined Charlotte Haldane in a group feminist effort for which she wrote a manifesto, *The League for the Protection of the Imagination of Women. Slogan: World's Management by Entertainment*. In 1939, the BBC contracted her to take part in a television program, but the program was cancelled because of the outbreak of World War II (R.D. Smith 23–27).

This period, when her Hampstead home began to be known as *La Tour Bourgeoise*, earned Wickham that dubious sobriquet, "poetess landlady." Housekeeping had always seemed to overwhelm her ability to keep up with it and now she entered what she herself called her slattern period, advertising to her frequent house guests via a hand-made sign in her hall, "Anna Wickham's. Stabling for Poets Painters and other Executives. Saddle your Pegasus here! Creative mood respected. Meals at all hours"(Birch 23). Poets were welcome to scrawl verse on the kitchen walls, and the landlady often answered. Her generosity was a boon to several young struggling writers. In 1937, the newlyweds, Dylan and Caitlin Thomas, stayed with Anna Wickham. In a letter to Lawrence Durrell, written in December 1937, Thomas mentions their first meeting at Anna's, implying that Anna threw them out at midnight. He thanks her for her hospitality in the following:

> But I wonder what Anna will make of [Henry] Miller's books. I know her well. Morals are her cup of tea, and books are just beer: she swallows them down without discrimination of taste or body or brew, and judges them by the effect they have on her bowels. For her a good book produces a bad poem from her, containing an independent moral judgment, but the poem could really have been written without the book. And I think it insulting to books to take them as a purgative in order to void material which, with a little constriction of the muscles, could have been voided anyway. (266)

On January 3rd, 1938, Thomas writes to George Reavey,[5] "We were, as you know, staying with Anna Wickham, but a difference of lack of opinion [sic] made us return to the country" (267). Thomas's low opinion of

Wickham's intellect and poetic skill, and his bad manners, speak for them-
selves. In other letters Thomas is scathing in his attacks on John
Gawsworth, the editor of *Neo-Georgian Poetry* and *Edwardian Poetry*,
and a proponent of Wickham's work. Thomas calls Gawsworth "that left-
over, yellow towelbrain of the nineties soaked in stale periods" in a March
5, 1939, letter to M.J. Tambimuttu, the Ceylonese editor of the magazine,
Poetry (London) (361). R.D. Smith comments on Thomas's ill-mannered
treatment of Anna Wickham, and others who helped him, by saying,
"Then, in a not uncharacteristic way, he later bit the hand that had fed and
watered him" (28).

Another young writer who boarded in *La Tour Bourgeoise*, Malcolm
Lowry, had much nicer memories of Wickham. In 1932 the writer John
Davenport introduced Lowry to Wickham, "who had probably already
heard of him from Nina Hamnett, a regular at the Fitzroy, or from
Charlotte Haldane, now in London and in touch with Wickham through a
feminist group in Hampstead" (Bowker 142). Apparently Lowry tried to
adopt Wickham as a substitute for his own mother, but, even though they
stayed up late discussing poetry and exchanging poems for critical com-
mentary, Anna declined the position as surrogate. In a letter accompanying
several of her poems she says to Lowry, "'[c]oncerning the difficult matter
of parenthood, for the next hours I am your nice little daughter. So you will
permit my performance'" (qtd. in Bowker: 143). Her desire to be designat-
ed as daughter rather than mother should not be read as coy flirtatiousness.
Rather, it shows that Wickham, even late in life, still viewed herself as the
child-angel in the house. While she was still enmeshed in wifely and moth-
erly duties, after her stay in Epping Forest, she hired a "lady's-help" whom
she had met in the institution. While chaperoned by the lady's-help,
Wickham carried on chaste flirtations with a number of men. She sent to
her father all the love poems she wrote detailing these brief encounters
("Genius" 20).

It is obvious that Wickham devoted much of her time in the thirties to
coddling young male talent. Both Dylan Thomas and Malcolm Lowry even
then were known for their prodigious drinking bouts. They needed some-
one to take care of them. They also were chronically short of money, so a
free place to stay had its attractions. That Wickham both enjoyed and
resented their involvement in her life is evident when she writes to Natalie
Barney about Lowry, calling him "'one of the boys'" (Bowker 174). That
she felt she could learn from the boys is evinced in the coy note she sent to
Lowry with a sheaf of her poems. That they could learn craft from her was
not an idea that they seriously considered. Yet she was serious about her
craft and her poems are carefully wrought according to her standards. She
sums up her stance in "Comment":

Tone
Is utterly my own.

Far less exterior than skill,

It comes from the deep centre of the will.

For nobler qualities of Song,

Not singing, but the singer must be strong. (WAW 185)

Because she is, as Birch says, "a poet of a flavour which you won't find anywhere else" (23), Wickham's work has been overlooked by both her more famous modernist contemporaries and the current critics who were trained in the formalist manner. Making sense of Wickham's aesthetic is a necessary part of the revision of modernism; not only do her literary contacts put her beside the writers like Ezra Pound, T.E. Hulme, and D.H. Lawrence who are among the shapers of modernist theory, but her poetic choices illustrate the dilemmas faced by a woman writer who wished to create a tone "utterly my own." She embraces a conservative, genteel style to contain multiple feminist epistemologies. A careful study of her literary mentors and their effects on her work will expand on the groundbreaking work that Celeste M. Schenck has accomplished in "Exiled by Genre."

Wickham's poetry would seem to some formalist critics to be mere doggerel, but what these critics are missing is the fact that she uses doggerel deliberately as a vehicle for her poetic politics. When doggerel does not suit her purpose, she does not use it. Wickham's main theme, the spiritual, emotional, and intellectual life of a modern woman in all her various moods, was not one that male modernists appreciated. Kime Scott states that T.S. Eliot's poetic theories deny validity to the "artist who writes of experience that has not been taken up adequately in literary monuments—women's experience" (Refiguring 128). If a writer such as Wickham takes a "nonvalid" subject as her theme, then her use of a debased poetic structure could only strengthen her poetic exile. We can re-figure Wickham's place in modernism and how her stance will alter our perceptions of the movement only when we acknowledge that her artistic choices are deliberate.

R.D. Smith, Schenck, and Dowson have all made much of Wickham's life in Australia to explain her poetry's alienation from the poetic movements of the early twentieth century. However, none of them explains this idea in detail. Applying post-colonial critical theory to the discrepancies and disjunctions of Wickham's poetry can help to build a critical house for Wickham. She has been unhoused and unsung for too long. A poetic politics of exclusion caused Anna Wickham's neglect. Although no critic has yet addressed this mysterious neglect, I believe it to be compounded by Wickham's conjunction of feminism, form, and freedom. This stance places her on the edge, but it should also make her more interesting to contemporary critics for whom the liminal state is desirable.

Is an angry, but at the same time loving female poetic persona who does not hide her sexuality inherently expatriate? If so, perhaps until we read Wickham's poems as her way of repossessing her (soul) house, we are not reading them as she intended. In the effort to make others feel the honored guests, the privileged readers, can an author write her *self* out of that particular home? Or is the effort to keep the female self in the work so fraught with danger that the woman poet must declare as a prelude to every book:

> Here is no sacramental I.
>
> Here are more I's than yet were in one human.
>
> Here I reveal our common mystery.
>
> I give you 'Woman.' (R.D. Smith 1)

Wickham castigates men for placing women into the sacramental/sacrificial position when she says in "Angry Woman":

> If I must fly in love and follow in life,
>
> Doing both things falsely,
>
> Then am I a *mime*,
>
> I have no free soul. (*WAW* 204)

In the end, Anna Wickham fails to integrate her various selves. What should have been a productive middle age was interrupted by an accident of history. All of Wickham's sons went off to fight in World War II with her blessing. A firebomb that destroyed some of her manuscripts and many letters damaged the house in Parliament Hill, the most devastating loss to scholars being the letters Natalie Barney wrote to Anna over the course of twenty years. When the war ended, James, John, and George were alive, but involved in new careers and people.

In April of 1947 Anna Wickham hanged herself. The manner of her death and her son James's explanation of the reasons behind her suicide constitute the final mystery of Anna Wickham. Gordon Bowker tells this story of Anna's death. "In fact, this strange women [sic] had failed at her first attempt, sat down, wrote a poem about the experience, and then done it a second time successfully" (413). Neither R.D. Smith nor James Hepburn gives this account of the circumstances, but Smith does say that her son George, who found her, "was amazed that she, so clumsy with her hands, had succeeded in tying an efficient knot." Smith continues, "[t]his came to him at the first moment of shock: later he ran into the street howling wordlessly like a dog" (28). James Hepburn says that Anna killed herself because she was tired and "we were well set up and no longer needed her—that we would be better off without her" (*Preface xxiii*). In "Anna Wickham" for the *Women's Review,* Hepburn includes the death poem that begins, "I hung myself/I was unconscious on the floor" (41). Once again, as with Patrick's death, art creates life, or more accurately, the end of life, rather than the other way round. These bizarre details seem, in a way, to be a fitting end to a life that was never easy, and to an art that Wickham herself characterized in the opening stanza of her poem "Self Analysis" as "The tumult of my fretted mind" [which is] "faulty, harsh, not plain—/My

CHAPTER SEVEN

Anna Wickham 1911–1947
"I am a raw uneasy parvenue"[1]

Formalist

As men whose bones are wind-blown dust have sung,

Let me sing now!

I'll sing of gourds, and goads, of honey, and the plough.

I am a raw uneasy parvenu,

I am uncertain of my time.

How can I pour the liquor of new days

In the old pipes of Rhyme? (*WAW* 195)

In spite of her self-designation as a parvenue, Edith Alice Mary Harper, as Anna Wickham, wrote poetry all her adult life, and published in periodicals such as *Poetry and Drama*, *The New Republic*, and *Poetry* between the years 1914 and 1947. She wrote over 1,400 poems, about one fifth of which were published during her lifetime in five books of poetry. She was also widely anthologized from the 1920s to the 1940s, then forgotten until the late 1970s when a brief flurry of interest in her poems arose in connection with feminist gynocriticism. However, these rediscovery articles focus primarily on Wickham's themes as they relate to feminism and freedom for women, and neglect the wide range of subject matter and styles that Wickham employs to sing her song.[2] A more thorough discussion of Anna Wickham's *oeuvre* must begin with the works that she read and acknowledges as germinal. The only clues she leaves to the development of her poetic self are contained in the autobiographical "Fragment." These clues are concealed in her accounts of family history, and at first glance appear contradictory. Oblique and ambiguous, the clues can be read several ways, just as the clues in Charlotte Mew's work leave themselves open to multiple explanations and interpretations. Wickham makes an honest assessment of herself in the poem "Formalist." She believed herself to be a

literary as well as a social *parvenue*. An examination of her upstart men-
tality and style will reveal the motivations behind her inconsistencies.

In the academic and critical endeavor to develop a modernist canon,
poets such as Charlotte Mew and Anna Wickham were disregarded
because their work did not fit neatly into the whole and because their
woman-centered subject matter was not considered to be as important as
the themes of their male colleagues. As I have argued in my discussion of
Mew's poetry, she deserves to be included in our re-vision of modernism.
So does Anna Wickham. Although neither of these poets belonged to a par-
ticular school or group of poets, and although both "poured the liquor of
new days/into the pipes of Rhyme," they did pioneer a voice for women
"degraded and alienated by family structures" (Scott "Introduction,"
Gender 15). Schenck reminds readers that both Mew and Wickham were
simultaneously exiled both from and to poetic form. Today's reader, freed
from the constrictions of the formalist critical mode, might see their flex-
ibility as strength, not flaw. Experimentation with form, even an ironic
flirting with the clichés of previous poetic dogmas or the speech of con-
temporary life, is a modernist given. However, when women poets produce
these kinds of freewheeling or ironic pastiches, they are often misconstrued
as naive or slavish imitations. Until very recently, few critics acknowledged
that either Mew or Wickham were forerunners in the development of a
feminine poetic aesthetic.

A case could be made for Wickham as a pioneer of *post*modernism
because her poetic impulses were often spur-of-the-moment reactions to
contemporary phenomena; they were dashed off in haste and thrown in a
drawer or scrawled on the wall of her kitchen in response to a comment
made by a child or a visitor. Wickham's barrage of poem-making could
happen anywhere. In a July 20, 1922 letter to Edmund Wilson, Edna St.
Vincent Millay says, "She writes ten thousand poems a day, writes them on
the café tables, on the backs of menus, on the waiter's apron [. . .] (154).
Wickham brought home the habit from the Fitzroy Tavern crowd, who
wrote couplets or quatrains as asides to each other, or as ironic commen-
tary on the general conversation, while they were drinking. Garnett com-
ments, "Anna often pulled pieces of paper out of her bag and passed them
over to me . [. . .] Sometimes something I said struck her and instead of
replying she would reach for a pencil, scrawl a few lines and push them
across the table. Her answer to my remark was a poem" ("Introduction"
Selected 9). Wickham was always more interested in *what* her poetry pre-
sented as her immediate *now*, rather than in *how* it said she was a woman.
In "Examination" she states, "If my work is to be good,/I must transcend
skill, I must master mood" (*Selected* 15). Epistemologically, stance is more
important than style. Her stance is that she will, moment by moment, tell
us *"woman."*

In Wickham's aesthetic, poetry must be a daily activity written in response to life. If we realize that this attitude colored all Wickham's work, then her kitchen and pub table scribbles should be recognized as a link in the chain that joins American Indian ritual songs to the poems pasted on the Democracy wall in Beijing during the student-led protests. The idea of the poet as high priest(ess) or philosopher-king(queen) would only have appealed to Wickham if she were using it as a spoof of another writer. Wickham's poetry is down-to-earth and domestic on the one hand, and yet it harks back to the university wits on the other. She could be categorized as a magazine poet, a groundbreaking feminist, a non-Georgian, a writer of doggerel, and an early advocate of free verse. Wherever she is placed in the history of modernism by scholars, they must begin their reassessment remembering that Wickham's aesthetic grew out of her lived life, through her contact and conflicts with family, other writers and artists, her incidental reading, and the society she inhabited. Although this truism could be applied to most writers, it is especially important for an understanding of Wickham's style because, like Mew, she had no academic background to provide a codified philosophy to progress from, or to react against.

In the family tradition of her grandmother and mother, Anna Wickham insisted on her right to constant re-vision. Family stories could be told in multiple versions, from antithetical stances, in warring tones. However, this kind of polyglossia, which Wickham employs in tone and style, in both her prose and poetry, makes her poetry hard to categorize, hard to attach to a school and, therefore, easier to dismiss, using the most current critical clichés of each succeeding era. Hers is defiant poetry from the margins. She also creates a problem for herself by siding with the forces that believe amateurs to be truer writers than professionals. Whether she professed this view out of misguided loyalty to her ineffectual father's ambitions for himself, or out of her embarrassment regarding some of her mother's so-called "professional" artistic ventures is hard to judge. It is also possible that her later friendship with Natalie Barney influenced her thinking on this matter, placing Wickham's stance as a poet on the side of the private, coterie writer as opposed to the public, professional, and even academic type best exemplified by T.S. Eliot.

Eliot's influence on the later twentieth-century assessment of modernist poetics has been thoroughly discussed by many scholars and critics. His attitude toward women writers, reviewers, and editors has been analyzed in many books and essays, including Gilbert and Gubar's three volumes of *No Man's Land: The Place of the Woman Writer in the Twentieth Century.* Eliot's own letters to his parents and Ezra Pound, among others, reveal his negative response to women in the literary arts. On May 13, 1917, in a letter to his mother announcing his new position as a contributing editor of *The Egoist,* Eliot remarks, "At present it is mostly run by old maids"; in September he writes to Pound about a reading series at the Poetry

Bookshop, "I thought too many women—it lowers the tone: [. . .] perhaps there should be a special evening for males only, as well as this. Eeldrop on the feminisation of modern society" (*Letters* 179, 198). To his father he writes that he distrusts the "Feminine" in literature and that he tries to keep *The Egoist*'s writing as much as possible in male hands. On July 11, 1922, he reiterates this position to Pound, commenting that he feels there are only a "half a dozen men of letters (and no women) worth printing" (*Letters* 204, 593).

Perhaps Eliot was trying to distance himself from the anxiety of influence caused by his mother's poetic aspirations. Peter Ackroyd discusses the complex emotional and literary relationship between Eliot and his mother. Much as is the case with Wickham and her parents, Eliot was "the late son of two parents who were thwarted artists," and Charlotte Eliot was very much like Alice Harper in her frustrated ambitions and dedication to the "militant mould of her generation." Ackroyd continues, "a fleeting image of the mother can be glimpsed in much of Eliot's own work" (21–22). Veiling themselves from the parental gaze entailed a physical distancing for both Eliot and Wickham. Both only began their artistic careers in London, after escaping the antipodes, the landscapes of their youth. Both were also shaped by their connection to another escape artist, Ezra Pound.

Critics and scholars have variously described Ezra Pound's contributions to modernism. Hugh Kenner calls the whole enterprise the Pound era while Shari Benstock in *Women of the Left Bank*, and other feminists, remind readers that Pound's agenda for modernism included isolating and then dropping the women who contributed to this movement because he felt they had no talent (21–23). If the development of modernism is viewed in terms of mastery and control, then Pound first and Eliot later could be called the masters of the fate of many other writers' places in the era's history. Recently, the evaluation of modernism has expanded to include both female and male writers who were previously thought to have little, if any, significance in the shaping of the modernist aesthetic. Scholars such as Bonnie Kime Scott have embarked on a project to refigure modernism. Scott states that "Modernism becomes a much more variable text when we consider the versionings of it by women helping to direct one another as writers" (*Refiguring* 230). The place of the Brontës, Alice Meynell, Olive Schreiner, May Sinclair, and other women writers and editors as influences on both male and female writers of the period is opening new vistas. In terms of poetry, what these new views show is that there was much activity in circles that were known to Pound and Eliot, but disparaged by them.

The most important circle for both Mew and Wickham is centered in the Poetry Bookshop. But because both of these women viewed their poetic lives as separate from their domestic lives, even the supportive and benign culture of the Poetry Bookshop circle was problematic. For Wickham, the problems associated with her connections to it arose from her perceptions of how her class and sexual politics might be perceived. Jones mentions James Hepburn's comments that Alida Monro loathed Anna because of Anna's overt sexuality. He also describes one poem, "The Indictment," which is wickedly cruel about Alida's devotion to her dogs (105–06). James Hepburn says of his mother's relationships: "To anyone who offended her code she could be devastatingly rude. [. . .] Any attack, real or imaginary, would be emphatically resisted" (*Preface xx*). While the Monros were the most important early supporters of Wickham's work in England, by the end of their relationship Wickham felt neglected and betrayed, as is evidenced in the following diatribe:

> To Harold Monro
> You bloody Deaconess in rhyme,
> You told me not to waste your time—
> And that from you to me!
>
> Now let Eternity be told
> Your slut has left my books unsold—
> And you have filched my fee. (*WAW* 332)

As always with Wickham, an untangling of her motivations has to begin with a close examination of her family life. The constant war between her father's sisters' Royal Academy belief that true art is the province of the professional, only achieved through the pain of hard work, and the legacy of her mother, Alice Whelan Harper, who believed that art was a product of the artist's charisma and overpowering emotion, created the poetic persona, Anna Wickham. Her artistic self-searching layered every word that she wrote. She never saw herself as a model in the rapidly changing fashions of modern poetry. As she said on one occasion, "'Harold Monro ruined my life by encouraging me to be a poet. I should have been a maker of popular mottoes!'" (R.D. Smith 18). Monro believed that the successful modern poet had a vast instinct for self-aggrandizement, which is the opposite of Wickham's instinct for self-disparagement.

Add to her poor artistic self-image the reality of her parents' lives, in which her father, whose family privileged the professional, became the eternal amateur. His great novel never made it from the mind to the page. Alice Whelan Harper, whose spirit-induced art seemed spontaneous, became the major financial contributor for the family through her professional artistic endeavors. Her parents' conflict, between the professional amateur, Geoffrey Harper, and the amateur professional, Alice Whelan Harper, never resolved itself. Therefore, the only way to understand Anna Wickham's work is to read it both ironically and sincerely, because that kind of schizophrenic pose was bred into her by heredity and circumstance.

One reason Harold Monro backed Wickham's efforts to publish her verse is that he could see its worth. As he said about the poems of another woman, Emilia Stuart Lorimer, they are "'the raw and inevitable product of personality, or nothing. Sometimes [they] may seem almost ingenious through the sheer force of [their] sincerity'" (qtd. in Grant: 50). Harold Monro looked for poets who could sincerely express a unique personality, and, even though Anna Wickham might play down her stylistic facility, she would not dispute that she had a unique personality, which she tried to express sincerely. In fact, the majority of her poems try to do just this.

Wickham's peculiar literary schizophrenia is also evident in her choice of mentors. Along with the artistic attachment she formed for the wealthy ex-patriot American lesbian Natalie Barney, Wickham confessed to Louis Untermeyer that her favorite American poet was Ella Wheeler Wilcox (340). As muses, these two women stand for antithetical aesthetics. Barney's emphasis on coterie production, lesbian aesthetics, and salon performance was completely different from the domestic, magazine verse style favored by Wilcox. Where the two merge is in their love of rhymed verse, aphorisms, and the belief that poetry is not diminished when it is used to commemorate an occasion. As well, both Barney and Wilcox celebrate women's sexual natures and romantic feelings. They did this through the veil of classical and literary allusion, distancing their personal selves from the passionate personae of their poetry. In forming her mature poetic voice, Wickham learned a great deal from both Barney and Wilcox. However, what Wickham learned from Wilcox and Barney came to fruition when she was an adult. Wickham's earliest poetic and philosophical models, the Reverend Richard Harris Barham, author of *The Ingoldsby Legends*, Charles Stuart Calverley, a nineteenth-century translator and minor poet of light verse, and Olive Schreiner, whose *Story of an African Farm* is the only novel mentioned by Wickham in "Fragment," all contribute significantly to aspects of Wickham's style and subject matter.

Various critics trying to describe Wickham's work have called it "New Elizabethan," metaphysical, "poet's poetry," wildly mystic on the order of Blake or Emily Brontë, "pebbles of fine prose," and extreme feminism. In an omnibus review in *The Nation*, Mark Van Doren writes of Wickham, Marianne Moore, and Edna St. Vincent Millay that they would be prized more highly in seventeenth-century England than they are in their own times and countries. He continues, "It [*The Contemplative Quarry and the Man with a Hammer* (1921)] is the work of an inspired metaphysician [. . .] a very contemporary John Donne" (484). A description of Wickham's poetry as metaphysical would place her as a modernist. T. S. Eliot's influential essay, "The Metaphysical Poets" appeared in the *Times Literary Supplement* in 1921. In it he draws a line from the poets of the seventeenth-century to the late nineteenth-century symbolists and on to the moderns, praising these poets' ability to translate idea into sensation (Menand

146–47). Most of her contemporaries who mention her work do classify her as a modern poet, but when the New Critics codified the modernist poetic canon, she was not included, although Marianne Moore was. The neglect of Wickham's contributions to modernism is understandable only when both her lifestyle and her poetic style are considered together.

Wickham's style, subject matter, philosophy, and her overt feminism all contribute to this neglect. Aside from the most obvious observations about her feminist stance, no critic has ever seriously discussed Wickham's ontology. Wickham's association with the important modernist philosopher and poet, T. E. Hulme, has not been explored. Because Wickham never completely eschewed rhyme and because her subject matter is domestic for the most part, her affinities with Hulme's ideas have been overlooked. Her work is undeniably modern when readers realize that one of the driving impulses behind it is Hulme's view that modern poetry expresses momentary mental phases, vague moods, and the maximum individual and personal expression. For Hulme, the modern poet remains tentative and half-shy (Levenson 43–44); or in Wickham's words, a parvenue. On the other hand, the modern poet is constantly struggling against the seductions of metaphysics, a seduction to which Wickham frequently succumbed because she needed a metaphysical brace for her *outre* feminism. Unfortunately for Wickham's reputation, the interest in *fin de siècle* philosophies that she inherited from her parents stuck her in this early phase of Hulme's ideas. If we accept Nietzsche's remark that philosophy is autobiography, we can understand why Wickham could not follow Hulme when he modified his Bergsonian romanticism to embrace classicism and anti-humanist and geometric art (Levenson 80–98). Because Wickham was so intent on merging the desires of her parents into her art, she remains a poetic impressionist "rooted in Victorian values, Edwardian social aspirations and Fabian politics" (R. D. Smith 27).

While her father attended Fabian and Positivist Society lectures, read Aristotle, and preached Walter Pater and the joys of amateur enthusiasms, her mother orchestrated the four-year-old Wickham's performances of "whole passages from *The Ingoldsby Legends*." As Wickham ruefully confesses, "there is no school of facile composition better than these verses" ("Fragment" 86). *The Ingoldsby Legends*[3] contains stanzas such as the following from the poem "The Babes in the Wood":

> Moral
> Ponder well now dear Parents, each word
> That I've wrote, and when Sirius rages
> In the dog-days, don't be so absurd
> As to blow yourself out with Green-gages!
> Of stone fruits in general be shy,
> And reflect it's a fact beyond question

> That Grapes, when they're spelt with an *i*,
>
> Promote anything else but digestion. (338)

Actually, it is amazing that Wickham's own poetry survived this early infusion of doggerel. Perhaps some readers would say it did not.

Yet today's scholars forget that an explosion of doggerel, designed to shatter the mannered, genteel verse of the later nineteenth and early twentieth century, was hailed as a modern breakthrough. The question of the place of doggerel in modernism and its influence on other modern poets has not been thoroughly explored. At the time that Wickham was placing herself among the group of poets considered modern, Harold Monro says that interest had been awakened in a style that Wickham adopts. In *Some Contemporary Poets* Monro writes, "the rapid free doggerel of 'The Everlasting Mercy' [by John Masefield], its modernity, its bald colloquialism, and its narrative interest"(23) revived an interest in contemporary poetry in 1911. As Masefield (and Wickham) use it, doggerel critiques class structure and bourgeois tradition. Celeste Schenck points out that Wickham's use of it in "Nervous Prostration" is both closer to folk balladry than the genteel verse favored by the suburbanites Wickham is excoriating, and is a "formal as well as a political spoof on bourgeois values" ("Anna Wickham" 615). Wickham learned this kind of rollicking irreverence from the Reverend Barham.

The Ingoldsby Legends also directed Wickham's subject matter. The book is full of fairy tales and a spurious medievalism; "As I Laye A-Thynkynge" is the final poem. These poems and tales influenced Wickham to the extent that she writes in "The Mummer":

> Strict I walk my ordered way
> Through the strait and duteous day;
> The hours are nuns that summon me
> To offices of huswifery.
> Cups and cupboards, flagons, food
> Are things of my solicitude.
> No elfin Folly haply strays
> Down my precise and well-swept ways.
>
> When that compassionate lady Night
> Shuts out a prison from my sight,
> With other thrift I turn a key
> Of the old chest of Memory.
> And in my spacious dreams unfold
> A flimsy stuff of green and gold,
> And walk and wander in the dress
> Of old delights, and tenderness. (*WAW* 178)

This poem has a medieval gloss; in fact, this poem might be categorized as the poetic equivalent of Charlotte Mew's Kendall ancestor's Neo-Gothicism. The most interesting aspect of Wickham's use of outmoded poetic device and diction is that she employs it in the service of a very contemporary feminism. Here the formal, and some would say anti-modern, versification is being used to structure a rage of dis-order. It is apparent from the title that the persona of this poem is acting in an ancient performance (marriage), the religious meaning of which has been obliterated by the modern disjunction of the ritual act from its original intent. Mourning the loss of pagan "elfin Folly," the speaker feels imprisoned by the convent(ional) nuns/no-ones into the hollow "offices" and "well-swept" (empty) rounds of housework supposed to satisfy the female half of a marriage. Not only are the hours nuns and no-ones (not one's own), they are also the time of *nones*, the mid-afternoon prayer and contemplation for those dedicated to a religious order. For (superior) mothers, it is the time when the children are down for their naps and the woman can turn her mind to other affairs. A codified religious ritual is compared to a no less codified domestic ritual. Domesticity, in this sense, is ironically equated with prayer, and pagan folly with whatever the speaker is giving up for the nonce (nuns).

The second stanza, just as the first turns on the multiple puns on the word "nun," and the whole line, "The hours are nuns that summon me" is leveraged by line three, "With other thrift I turn a key" and the weight of the word "thrift." Of course, thrift means economy in the household sense, but readers can only understand the import of this line when they remember that thrift comes originally from the Norse word *thrifask* meaning to thrive. In Middle English thrift meant prosperity, a flourishing, profit, or savings. The spurious medievalism then becomes a necessary setting, revealing the persona's hatred of the prison of the daily grind, the religious domestic's delight, and setting this hatred against the continuous joy of dreams and desire, fueled by memory, "the dress of old delights." All domestic economy, presented in this poem as a remnant of the dark ages, turns to ash if it does not rekindle tenderness in the night. Certainly desire, struck against "Cups and cupboards," is "flimsy stuff." It can vanish altogether, except in dreams. In the "The Mummer," published in 1915 in *The Contemplative Quarry*, Wickham has provided us with a hollow woman to set before Eliot's hollow men. But instead of "Lips that would kiss/ form[ing] prayers to broken stone" (Eliot *Collected* 58), the mummer's lips pray at/to *nones* (no ones). The effect is the same. Society's hypocritical expectations for the individual crush the persona's ability to love. Certainly the complicated wit of the central images of "The Mummer" justifies Van Doren's "inspired metaphysician" label.

Besides *The Ingoldsby Legends*, one other poetic influence that Wickham mentions in "Fragment" is the poet, Charles Stuart Calverley.[4] A

Judge Paul, an Australian high court judge whom she met when she traveled alone, aged eleven, to meet her parents during the school holidays, gave a volume of his poems to her. The journey included an overnight boat trip and a long ride on the steps of a "corridor coach." During this trip the judge also gave her a copy of Laing's *Modern Science and Modern Thought,* and she also read a copy of a children's annual. Her reading on this epiphanic journey reflects the liminal state in which one experiences intellectual and emotional *stimulae* that profoundly affect the future. Recalling this betwixt and between time, Wickham states: "The poems by Calverley I have always remembered" ("Fragment" 107–08). A.A. Milne, a devotee of the writer since childhood, believed that Calverley was the best at a form he thought both lovely and difficult—light verse. Milne declared light verse the hardest type to write because it is the most severely technical of forms. Still, he acknowledges that most writers are ashamed of writing it. Yet Milne was still recommending Calverley to aspiring writers as late as 1945 (Thwaite 70, 270, 464). What Wickham remembered were parodies and pastiche such as his poem "The Arab," which tricks the unwary reader into thinking that it is about an Arabian horse when it is really a description of a magazine-selling street urchin. The poem begins "On, on my brown Arab, away, away!/Thou hast trotted o'er many a mile today" and ends "And the bit in thy mouth, I regret to see,/ Is a bit of tobacco-pipe—Flee, child, flee!" (Spear 62). Spear also points out that this poem echoes a line from *The Ingoldsby Legend*'s "The Witches' Frolic" which Wickham would have known (62 n.).

Wickham turns the horse/person metaphor to her own ends in one of her most powerful poems, "Mare Bred from Pegasus," which appeared in *Richard's Shilling Selections.* In it, rather than gently pulling the reader's leg as Calverley does, Wickham rails against a male writer's condescending comment to her. When he says, "Make Beauty for me!" she replies:

> For God's sake, stand off from me;
> There's a brood mare here going to kick like hell
> With a mad up-rising energy;
> And where the wreck will end who'll tell?
> She'll splinter the stable and eat a groom.
> For God's sake, give me room;
> Give my will room.

Later in the poem, she sneers, "My pretty jockey, you've the weight/To be a rider, but not my mate," and ends several stanzas later with "Run, run, and hide you in some woman's heart,/In a retreat I cannot kick apart!" (*WAW* 283). Rather than amuse the reader, as does Calverley with his pun on arab as a name for one of the best breeds of horse and as the slang term for homeless urchins (street arab), Wickham throws her metaphor into an unnamed male poet's face. Her point is that a woman poet, the mare bred from Pegasus, would stand beside male poets to fashion a contemporary poetry only if male poets accept her as an equal. If these male writers choose to view women as sex-objects and mother-figures only, then the stable of their art will be kicked to pieces.

Of the many poems Wickham has written about the plight of the woman poet, this one is the most passionate and direct. It chronicles the "fierce hope and more fierce distrust" of the woman writer who is asked by a fellow artist to "make beauty." The Victorian social assumptions that this demand reflects demean the intellect of the woman writer and limit her to a subject not highly prized by the avant-garde. Instead of being encouraged to use "all my wit, all imagination,/ And every subtle beauty of creation"; the woman poet is mocked by the condescension of the command to the point where "Desire rose up [. . .] to strike you dead,/ With that mad mare my will/ To lash and smash her fill"(283). The "masterless hard state" kicked against by Wickham's mare is the location of the exiled woman poet, "the quintessential stranger in the paradise of male letters" (Marcus 270). In the mare's rage to bring the whole stable down is also the energy to create her own poetics so she will no longer have to laconically "cower [. . .] at your dying fire" nor "blow [. . .] at your chill desire"; Wickham is predicting a time in the future when male writers will retreat to the comfort of non-writing women's hearts to hide from the wrecked male aesthetic stable that the women writers and critics have smashed. She was furious that she would not be alive to see the day. In letters to Natalie Barney Wickham's anger flares at Harold Monro and John Middleton Murry. She castigates them for giving women writers, and herself in particular "little stimulus" and rails against the "subtle and dangerous sexual assault" of male editors' corrections of her phrasing (qtd. in Jones: 71). Contemporary critical theory has wrecked the stable canon of modernism, and a reevaluation of women writing in the modernist era is part of that wrecking.

It is significant that the two poets that Wickham cites as early influences are high Victorian light-verse writers. Both Barham and Calverley's poems were most often published as occasional verses in popular weeklies and monthly magazines, including *Punch*. Yet no contemporary of Wickham's approached her verse as parodic writing, and neither have later critics. An exiled voice often becomes a mocking voice. Discarding the weighty concerns of the eminent Victorian writers, Barham and Calverley make fun of many aspects of British life. A case can be made for a primary parodic impulse in many of Wickham's poems. And as Milne asserts, light verse should be taken as seriously as serious verse because "'in modern light verse the author does all the hard work, and in modern serious verse he leaves it all to the reader [. . .]'" (qtd. in Thwaite: 271). In his later career, even T.S. Eliot might have agreed with this sentiment. *Old Possum's*

Book of Practical Cats qualifies as serious light verse. Wickham's small imagist poem written after a session at the Cafe du Dome with Ezra Pound parodies "the better maker." Perhaps her poem, "Imperatrix," written to commemorate a bit of gossip about Frieda Lawrence and a younger lover (told to Wickham by David Garnett), might also qualify. The point that Spears is careful to make about Calverley—that his poetic style is like a mockingbird—is also a point to explore as a way into the poems of Wickham. If many of her poems are mockeries, parodies in other voices, then the inconsistencies of style and subject matter that critics have stumbled over in their efforts to categorize Wickham's place in the modernist experiment are understandable. These different voices also ally Wickham's work to Mew's, whose dramatic monologues capture a more serious side of the woman poet's attempt to find a voice. The misreadings that critics have fostered about both Mew's and Wickham's work could explain why their verse has not received a more sympathetic hearing.

From these tutors, Anna Wickham's aesthetic was formed. What they taught her has more of the wit of the late seventeenth and early eighteenth centuries than characteristics of the nineteenth century's high Victorian seriousness. Barham and Calverley are certainly minor writers, but both write poems full of *jeux d'esprit* perhaps not as apparent in the major writers' poems. Mark Van Doren calls Wickham "a very contemporary John Donne," and he continues his praise by saying she is "one of England's most honest and inviting minds today" (484). What she may be is a twentieth-century Aphra Behn, Katherine Philips (the Matchless Orinda), Anne Finch, Countess of Winchilsea, or even a Lady Mary Wortley Montagu.[5] Van Doren's impulse is correct, though he may not have known the work of these women poets. Wickham's yoking of the metaphysical, or even sometimes the magazine-Victorian, style to her feminist and bohemian critique of the villa-dwellers, places her as a modernist because it is proof that she willingly takes from a variety of styles and impulses to fashion her own form.

Wickham's brief against the society in which she found herself after her marriage to Patrick Hepburn has also been categorized as the attitude of the colonized to the colonizer. Both Jane Dowson and Celeste Schenck believe that Wickham's years in Australia stamped her with an outsider's skeptical view of the establishment. Even further, Schenck postulates that Wickham's Australian childhood endowed her with a sense of "robust [. . .] sexual entitlement" and "freedoms unavailable to Englishwomen" ("Anna Wickham" 614). These gross generalizations, about both Wickham and the social conditions of late Victorian Australian life, try to slip Wickham's case into a current critical theory. There is no evidence that either of these statements holds true. Rather, Wickham's Australian experience seems to have left a negligible impression on her. She never uses images of Australian flora or fauna or Australian language patterns. R. D.

Smith concurs. He believes that the sojourn in Australia made Wickham more aware and proud of her Englishness, not less. "Her outback life [. . .] imprinted in her some of the old-fashioned Empire patriotism, which her more intellectual friends found surprising in a poet of feminist rebellion, and an opponent of the old class, bureaucratic establishment" (43). Even the latest critical response from Australia concurs. It was only at the peak of her writing career that she felt comfortable enough to publish in *The London Aphrodite*, a short-lived, irreverent journal designed to outrage modernists, reactionaries, academicians and sentimentalists. This journal, edited by two Australians, Jack Lindsay and P.R. Stephensen, poked fun at everything pompous and British; its brief existence allowed Wickham one time to "pronounce her affinities with the Australian larrikin" (Jones 76, Vickery 33–34).

If Wickham exhibits the traits of an exile in her writing, she received her perceptions of colonialism not from her own experience in Australia, but from her reading of the third of her earliest influences, Olive Schreiner. Books, along with "kippered herrings and Cross and Blackwell's pickles" were a way for the Harpers to "keep in touch with the old life" ("Fragment" 92–93). In this context, while the young Wickham felt she "belonged to a civilised family: the bushwacker who lived in the bush in a log hut seemed to be immeasurably distant from us," she read *The Story of an African Farm* ("Fragment" 92–93). While her family adopted the role of lonely exiles from the politics, culture, and art of the continent, stuck unwillingly in a colony of philistines, Wickham read about another girl who considered herself an exile. Lyndall Gordon, the heroine of Schreiner's novel, is both an intellectual and a sexual exile, even while she is still living amid the *kopjes*, *kraals*, and *Kaffirs* at the Boer farmhouse of her Tant' Sannie. In this novel, those who seek and strive for social, intellectual, and sexual freedom, Lyndall and her soulmate, the farm-boy, Waldo, rebel and die. While the reader's first impulse would be to see the clear reasons that Wickham could equate her own young self to both Waldo and Lyndall, in the sense that "The barb in the arrow of childhood's suffering is this: its intense loneliness, its intense ignorance" (Schreiner 43), the more accurate reading of the importance of this text to Wickham's life and work looks at the parallels that it provides to her parents' situation and the stylistic choices it opens. Schreiner's style, which Showalter characterizes as "a genuine accent of womanhood, one of the chorus of secret voices speaking out of our bones, dreadful and irritating but instantly recognizable," taught Wickham how to say her themes (*A Literature* 198).

The connection between Olive Schreiner and Alice Harper is through Eleanor Marx. Schreiner was Marx's best friend; she told their mutual friend, the author of *The Psychology of Sex*, Havelock Ellis, that she had a horror of Edward Aveling. Aveling's reputation as a sexual predator is well documented. He might have been the father of Alice and Geoffrey Harper's

first child. Around the same time that the Harpers married, Aveling began
living with Eleanor Marx; they posed as husband and wife, although he
was legally married to yet a third woman (W.S. Smith 73–83). In
Schreiner's novel, Lyndall Gordon has a child with a man she will not
marry. Another man, Geoffrey Rose, is compelled by his love for her to
dress as a woman and nurse her during her decline into death, after the
death of her child. Intellectual, emotional, and physical freedom mean
more to Lyndall Gordon than life. She wants neither a master nor a slave;
neither a he-man nor a she-male. In *The Story of an African Farm*,
Schreiner delineates the issues that obsessed the New Woman. New Women
like Alice Harper, Olive Schreiner, and Eleanor Marx wanted Lyndall
Gordon's freedoms and more. They wanted the sexual freedom that some
men possessed. They wanted to be considered equals in all ways. Most
importantly, they wanted their work to be considered of equal value.

For Alice Harper at least, freedom seemed most possible in a less civi-
lized locale. She responded romantically to the lure of the antipodes. She
sailed off, without her husband, but with the young Anna, when the child
was only eighteen months old, and returned for a much longer stay, when
Wickham was about six or seven ("Fragment" 79, 90). Post-colonial criti-
cism can help the scholar explain Alice Harper's response and how it affect-
ed her daughter's art. The question posed by Alan Lawson, "'Who am I
when I am transported?' is an inevitable colonial question" (168). A com-
pletely new linguistic, social, cultural, historical, and metaphorical self can
be created. Lawson continues, saying that the discrepancies between a dif-
ferent place and the old language we use to describe that place pose a prob-
lem for a people who feel culturally disadvantaged; therefore, the language
undergoes great strain (168–69). What Lawson does not factor into his cul-
tural equation are the metaphorical implications of his use of the word
"transported." Alice Harper and Olive Schreiner possess this linguistic site,
and it is the birthplace of Anna Wickham's poetry. Literally, Anna
Wickham, free-woman and poet, was born on Wickham Terrace, Brisbane,
Queensland, while she was standing with her father listening to great gusts
of hymns roll out of two opposite churches. Figuratively, Anna Wickham,
free-woman and poet, was born out of her mother's struggles with the
question, "Who am I when I am transported?"

Although she did not know it, Wickham received the answer to her
mother's always unspoken question, "Who am I when I am transported?"
as she was reading *The Story of an African Farm*. Lyndall Gordon is most
comfortable and truthful with herself when she is talking with Waldo about
the life of the mind/spirit, and what it means to be a woman. Lyndall
explains to him the pitfalls of sexual allure and the opposite pull of the
New Woman's needs:

> A little weeping, a little wheedling, a little self-degradation, a little careful
> use of our advantages, and then some man will say—'Come, be my wife!'

with good looks and youth marriage is easy to attain. There are men enough; but a woman who has sold herself, ever for a ring and a new name, need hold her skirt aside for no creature in the street. They both earn their bread in one way. Marriage for love is the beautifullest external symbol of the union of souls; marriage without it is the uncleanliest traffic that defiles the world. [. . .] When we ask to be doctors, lawyers, lawmakers, anything but ill-paid drudges, they say,—No; but you have men's chivalrous attention; now think of that and be satisfied! (190)

This statement serves as both an indictment and a defense of Alice Harper's actions as they are detailed in earlier chapters. What Wickham learned from *The Story of an African Farm* is contempt for her mother's solutions to her problems, but she also learned to justify a woman's need for complete freedom. She learned this without understanding its significance as an explanation of her parents' behavior toward each other. Wickham also never directly articulated how her reading of *The Story of an African Farm* influenced her poetry, but a perusal of any of her poems reveals it. "Gift to a Jade" expresses Lyndall's diatribe more succinctly:

For love he offered me his perfect world.

This world was so constricted and so small

It had no sort of loveliness at all,

And I flung back the little silly ball.

At that cold moralist I hotly hurled

His perfect, pure, symmetrical, small world. (*Selected* 21)

And again in "The Resource" Wickham rephrases Lyndall's complaint:

When I gave you honest speech

You were annoyed,

When I gave you honest love

Your taste was cloyed.

And now I give you silence,

And a smile you take for chaste.

In these things I am less worthy than a harlot.

And your pride has worked this waste. (*Selected* 27)

To completely answer Alice Harper's question, "Who am I when I am transported?" and to understand its implications for her daughter's work, the critic must first examine the negative meaning that "transport" has for the Australian.

Convicts were the first Europeans who were transported to a land so barren that it was considered useless for any purpose other than a gigantic jail. These outlaws included paupers, prostitutes, and political dissidents.[6] In the mid-to-late nineteenth century, when more people from England began immigrating, they felt a cut above the "natives" whose ancestors were law-breakers. However, if we view Alice Harper's escape to Australia in the light of New Womanhood, we can begin to see just why she transported herself. In Lyndall Gordon's eyes, Alice Harper would have been no better than a prostitute. Seduced by Edward Aveling, she in turn seduced Geoffrey Harper, knowing she was pregnant. She became a "woman who had sold herself, ever for a ring and a new name" (Schreiner 190). She could easily have become a fallen Magdalen.

For the sale of her freedom, she wanted an equal share in the marriage. When she saw that she would not get it from Geoffrey, she convicted herself for her weakness in failing to live up to her convictions. Alice Harper acted as judge, jury, and accused, sentencing herself to penal servitude both in and out of her marriage. In the life and times of Alice Harper the perceptive reader can see in microcosm not only the dilemmas posed to society by the tenets of New Womanhood, but also the problems of a paternal imperialism which was at its height at the turn of the century. Why not go to Australia? And why not work her passage as the ship captain's mistress? If she was already outside of the law (pregnant with an illegitimate child) before her marriage, did not that marriage merely further her "transportation" as a moral exile? If the New Woman's search for freedom often led to the same old imprisonment in conventional society, then could that woman perhaps find her freedom in prison, or, as her daughter found it, in "the regime of the private asylum" which she characterizes as "an invaluable discipline for the woman artist" ("Genius" 19)?

The second transportation practiced by Alice Harper can provide an answer. If the New Woman still could not have ascendancy in sex or work, she ironically could fall back on the position where Victorian women had already been given moral superiority—spirituality. In this instance, Alice Harper's, and to some extent Anna Wickham's, attitudes about the spirit of women mirror Charlotte Mew's. Patmore's ideas about the redirection of sexual energy toward religious ecstasy, and T.H. Green's beliefs about renunciation and sublimation elevating human life, worked to free Alice Harper from her wifely duties. However, from her exiled, colonized stance, the fathers' religion that had made a convict (without convictions) of her would not do. The second sojourn in Australia was marked by Alice Harper's success in transportation of another kind. As Madame Reprah, she practiced Physiognomy, and hypnotism, functioning as an early psychoanalyst and as a medium and contact healer ("Fragment" 103–04). From this position, Alice Harper could retain her distance from the bushwhackers, using her charisma to make money and become a celebrity. Calling her mother a pioneer, Wickham acknowledges the strain Alice's activities put on her parents' marriage. Geoffrey Harper "had a strong sense of *comme il faut* towards the objects of his serious intention and eliminated all subjects not included in[. . .] the *Synthetic Series* of Herbert

Spenser, which neglected hypnotism" ("Fragment" 104). Geoffrey's rational, imperialist position was threatened by (yet in their daughter it blended with) his wife's successful primitivism. Alice's position allowed her to become more aboriginal, to convict and convince the gullible ex-convicts. The Harpers' marriage exemplifies the imperial/colonial paradigm. Poor Alice Harper had to finally remove herself to America, the colony that successfully revolted, before she could enter a community that suited her code of New Womanhood. Because Alice Harper started early to arouse Anna Wickham's emotional response and because of both parents' need to "make [her] all over again and develop [her] into a child worthy of their aspiration," her poetry bears the marks of their parental imperialism. Just as the brightest students from the colonies were sent to England for finishing, so was Wickham. She was sent for the same reason—to serve as living proof that the imperialist agenda could benignly produce heirs worthy of the system.

The kinds of subtle subversions, layering colonized/colonizing/colonizer, practiced by Alice Harper, shape the texts of her daughter. Wickham's feminist themes are imprisoned in the forms of the past just as Olive Schreiner's narrative of feminist inspiration and prophesy is couched in the language and doctrines of Romanticism, because there is no colony where the mind can express itself outside the language of the patriarchy (Colby 69). The endless philosophical musings of Waldo and Lyndall served as an Ur-text for Wickham because reading them was like reading the minds of her parents. That is why echoes of Schreiner's diction and *dicta* can be heard in Wickham's poems.

As well as sharing an interest in spiritualism and Theosophy, Schreiner shared with Alice Harper a delight in celebrity. This pairing also figured in the success of Wickham's American influence, the poet Ella Wheeler Wilcox. Wilcox's sensational and scandalous *Poems of Passion* (1883) gave its author instant celebrity. One offending poem is "The Farewell of Clariomond," which contains the following stanza:

> I knew all arts of love: he who possessed me
>
> Possessed all women, and could never tire;
>
> A new life dawned for him who once caressed me:
>
> Satiety itself I set on fire.

In her autobiography, Wheeler Wilcox confesses that this poem was written after reading Theophile Gautier's story, "Clariomonde" but adds, "certain critics insisted on referring to my poem as a recital of my own immoral experiences!" Her poems were derided as the ravings of "half-tipsy wantons" by Charles Henry Dana in the *New York Sun*, which assured a place for the book on the best seller lists in both America and England (*The World and I* 81–82).

Wilcox's popularity as a magazine poet and celebrity lasted until her death in 1919. She is characterized by Anne R. Groben as "a leader in what was called the 'Erotic School', a group of writers who rebelled against the stricter rules of conventionality. By 1900, a whole feminine school of rather daring verse on the subject of the emotions followed W.'s [sic] lead" (416). Wilcox is also author of those immortal lines beginning, "Laugh and the world laughs with you,/Weep and you weep alone" (*The World and I* 88). Although her poetry was considered shocking, Wilcox herself was deeply conventional and happy in her marriage to Robert Wilcox. She wanted her poetry to please the majority, so she wrote for the level of the general taste. Walker comments, "Her career as a successful *woman*, in her terms, was more important to her than her art" (122).

In her cry that she should have been a motto maker, in her desire not to make art, but to create an artist, in her unselfconscious lines about sex ("My pretty jockey, you've the weight/To be a rider"), we see Anna Wickham's debt to Ella Wheeler Wilcox. Of course, it should be remembered that Wickham's parents wanted her to become a popular poet, not necessarily a good one. For her father, the peak of Wickham's fame would have come when her well-known poem, "The Cherry Blossom Wand," was parodied in *Punch* by William Kean Seymour (R.D. Smith 27/20 n.). EVOE's earlier parody of Charlotte Mew in *Punch* joins these two women poets in an important manner. They would not have been parodied if their style had been like many other poets of the times. They were parodied because their styles were new.

Outside of her family members, the person with whom Anna Wickham maintained the longest important artistic and emotional relationship is the American expatriate writer, Natalie Barney. Yet the relationship was not as reciprocal as Wickham wished it to be. For example, when Wickham read at Natalie Barney's salon in Paris, the Temple *a l'Amitie*, as part of a cultural exchange between French and Anglo-American writers, she was introduced (amid much laughter and applause) as "'only a *demi-revoltée*'" with four sons and no daughters, functioning as both "'pelican and nightingale'" in a household of men (qtd. in R.D. Smith: 25). Barney's comments here, although perhaps meant lightly and delivered on the spur-of-the-moment, could be read as lesbian snobbery, excluding Wickham. That Barney's comments were meant somewhat disparagingly is evidenced by the fact that after her death, Barney's executor discovered, in the back of a disused cupboard, a shoebox full of poems and cards labeled "Anna Wickham" (Wickes 260). These hundreds of Post-card Poems (*Des Cartes à l'Amazone*) could perhaps have been published, but there is no evidence that Barney encouraged her to compile them into a book. In 1929 Wickham was working to help Barney secure a British agent and publisher, and her letters of this time are full of literary advice (Jones 232–36).

Jennifer Jones's access to the unpublished papers and poems reveals that Wickham and Barney had a more complicated relationship than Smith acknowledges. Beginning in 1926 Wickham exchanges poems for money from Barney. This arrangement gave Wickham some financial freedom, but also committed her to a kind of literary prostitution, which she deeply resented. In "Resentments of Orpheus" Wickham excoriates Barney's lesbian circle, naming Gertrude Stein, Mina Loy and Djuana Barnes, among others, before concluding "Euridice, fare-three-well/Since thou has leased thy love to hell,/Let smokes of mediocrity/And such slow fires envelop thee" (qtd. in Jones: 210). In a late letter to Barney Wickham confesses, "'[. . .] I thought that your imagination—was to my imagination as was I to the large blonde whore—& I was sorry for you'" (qtd. in Jones: 240).

Students of women's writing of this period might decide that Barney preferred to encourage writers who worked out of the impetus that Barney categorized as the "aesthetics of indiscretion." In this aesthetic, the woman artist draws the response of others to her life and work, rather than uses her work to forge herself a place in history. "For Natalie Barney, as for Sappho, woman's art was the product of shared experience among women, a social and collective effort by a small group of extraordinary women who separated themselves from society in order to love and write literature" (Benstock 293–94). Certainly, Barney and Wickham differed in their desire to be known through their writing. As Benstock notes, Barney's play, *Equivoque*, about Sappho, explores the idea that Sappho might have chosen to value life over art, and, therefore, she was of the opinion that it was self-indulgent to try to assure one's immortality through one's works. Here, Barney endows Sappho with her own beliefs. Barney privileges the artist's right to control her works and to make informal presentation for a coterie the central focus of the artist's task. Barney's artistic emphasis was to encourage feminist exchanges and dialogues among the women (and men) that she invited to her salon. The poem or play as performance for a select "contemporary Sapphic circle," with herself as Sappho, leading her disciples into a modern Hellenism, was Barney's artistic *desideratum* (290–92). Even after World War I, when her women friends no longer physically resembled Barney's ideal pre-Raphaelite androgynous female whose forms decorated her Temple *a L'Amitie* so gracefully, Barney held to her vision of a modern Sapphic circle where "safe from the intrusion of the outside world, the divided female spirit healed itself, rejoicing in short-lived freedom from patriarchal restraint" (Benstock 306).

Anna Wickham's invitation into this world came in 1922, at a time in her life when she had just lost a son, and when her husband was becoming more and more distant, so she embraced wholeheartedly the chance to rest in a separate walled garden of women where she could, for a time, forget reality. R.D. Smith says that "the attraction was emotional, sexual, and artistic, three areas in which Anna had been parched for years by her fidelity to her husband and devotion to domesticity." He concludes that "Anna was fascinated by Natalie, though never subdued by her" (24–25). Questioning Smith's choice of the word "subdued," I believe the rapport between Barney and Wickham was more artistic than personal or physical, although Smith claims that the previously mentioned shoebox was full of passionate love-letters from Anna; however, immediately afterwards, in parentheses, he says, "which was also a passionate discussion of the problems of being a woman and an artist" (24). Of course it was. Women can have vehement friendships that exclude sex and focus on their mutual passion for an art form. They can also express love and affection for each other without being in love. It is clear from both Smith's and Jones's descriptions that Anna Wickham was never let into the inner circle of Barney's temple. As Wickham wrote, "I might have been your whore—/God was I less or more!—/I was your artist" (qtd. in Jones: 222). The "might" in this poem indicates that she was not, and the next line reinforces this reading. In a 1928 letter, Wickham complains that she was denied entrance by Barney's housekeeper, understanding that the woman would only have been acting on Barney's orders (Jones 225). Because of her family background, any kind of prostitution was anathema to Wickham.

Barney's stylistic choices influenced Wickham's at a critical time. Benstock's description of Natalie Barney's writing could also stand as a description of Anna Wickham's. Benstock says that Barney's forms were Romantic poetry and the epigram, and that "[u]nfortunately for Barney, the twentieth century quickly set itself against the various movements that shaped her intellectual development" (293). Certainly the same could be said about Wickham. Barney might have encouraged Wickham to work on further books; R.D. Smith says that there is evidence that Wickham projected a further volume of poetry, *The Disorderly Shepherdess*, a long dramatic poem, "The Boy and the Daffodil," and that she tried to write a novel for Horace Shipp, agent for Sampson Low, Marston & Co. (24). Barney might have suggested further projects. Both she and the American Griffin Barry, a friend of Edna St. Vincent Millay's, served as disciplinarians for Anna, even though Wickham hated having to prostitute herself in order to get poems written (Jones 217–18). There are still boxes of material in the Parliament Hill house, but Barney's letters to Wickham, along with some of Wickham's manuscripts, were destroyed when a fire-bomb hit during World War II (R.D. Smith 28). Still, Barney called her the "English Verlaine" and, as R.D. Smith states:

> Natalie, even after Anna's death, continued her admiration for her poems, but their correspondence reveals that Anna's mainly long-distance passion for Natalie was not reciprocated. More satisfactory was their artistic rapport. Anna was looking for a collaborator in various literary ventures, and, insofar as the activities at the Temple made her personally and artistically known, she found one. But the lover-soulmate-fellow worker in the

arts she hoped for was not there, despite Natalie's true affection, admira-
tion for the poems, and, in times of crisis, financial help. (25)

It is difficult to judge the intricacies of the relationship between Barney
and Wickham from a distance of more than half a century. However, it is
safe to say that Barney's involvement with Wickham, and the time she
would have given to helping Wickham's career, is negligible compared to
her championship of others such as Renee Vivien, Romaine Brooks,
Elizabeth de Gramont, and Lucie Delarue-Mardrus.[7] It was not Barney
who translated Wickham's poems into French, but Mardrus who included
them in her 1935 *Edition Des Poemes Choises de Lucie Delarue Mardrus*
(R.D. Smith 25). Barney's attitudes toward performance and publication
may have influenced Wickham's desire to fuse her musical skill and per-
sonal charisma into a vehicle to showcase her poetry to a wider audience
than those attending Poetry Bookshop readings. R.D. Smith states that she
had contracted with the BBC to take part in a television program, but the
date was September 3, 1939, so the show was cancelled. R. D. Smith is of
the opinion that Wickham would have been a "tremendous performer in
this infant medium" (27). Certainly Barney's satisfaction with coterie writ-
ings and performances, coinciding with Wickham's parents' ideas (and
quarrels) on the subject of professionalism in the arts, must have created a
tension in Wickham which contributed to her meager publishing record
during the final ten years of her life. Like Charlotte Mew, whose family
problems overwhelmed her final ten years, Wickham published little in her
last years.

A close look at the shoebox full of Wickham's *Des Cartes a l'Amazone*
might reveal that they are her attempt to create an artistic, and, perhaps, a
sexual home. Jones reports that the shoebox also contained a picture of
Anna, reclining nude, draped in sheer fabric (231). It is ironic that
Wickham's hope for a home in which to settle her exile art would be
crushed because her work was not "indiscreet" enough! Barney's belief that
the violence implied in heterosexuality and childbirth made woman a vic-
tim of her sex instead of a celebrator of the female body was in direct oppo-
sition to Wickham's glorification of childbirth and motherhood. Wickham
expressed this disjunction in the following letter that she wrote to Barney
in January, 1928:

> For the love of God don't tell me to write poetry. It maddens me—if you
> want me to write poetry let your will sleep in the storm of my energy.
> Don't ride all over the battle-field, stand on your hill and confer. If I am
> to write poetry I want you to help me in certain definite ways—*I want you
> to love my child*. Get ahead now and love my child (R.D. Smith 389 n.24).

So Anna Wickham's dream of collaboration on a series of poetic post-
cards written by two Amazons was destroyed by sexual politics. Barney
could not love the child that she believed to be the product of violence and
the curtailer of women's freedom, and Wickham could not work with a

person who would not love her child. Whether that child is one of the Hepburn sons, or Wickham's poem doesn't matter. Wickham could find neither her house nor her home in Barney's salon. As a result, her production ends up being much like the "red, dead thing" (perhaps a still-born child, perhaps a heart, perhaps a poem) in Mew's "Saturday Market"— laughed at and buried, because nobody cares.

In her one piece of criticism, "The Spirit of the Lawrence Women," Wickham wrote that she believed that the "creative consciousness of a pure artist is bisexual. There is a marriage in the house of the soul. [. . .] and the result is a work of pure imagination" (*WAW* 368). In an early poem written in the male voice of John Oland, Wickham describes the dilemma of the artist:

> In The House of the Soul
> (Harlequin and a Woman under One Skin)
> Well, they are gone!
> And we are here alone.
> I, the mime, and master of surprises,
> Who have fooled that mob with fifty new disguises—
> You, who sit in the soul
> A quiet wife;
> You, who are Control
> Weaving the long continuous web of life.
> I should have little courage to continue with this jest
> Could I not meet you here, and be at rest.
> Sometimes I think that there is nothing of my winning,
> That all we have of service from our union is your spinning;
> But when of shame my heart is full—
> Then you remind me, dame;
> I bring you wool
> It is our business here to make a song—
> Whoever is sore, whatever is wrong. (*WAW* 270–71)

Here, the persona speaks from two sexes, two voices at once. For once Wickham has reconciled the opposite forces that drive her; however, it is curious that it is the silent, waiting wife, in a direct allusion to Penelope, who stands for both huswifery and creativity (weaving), while the buffoon Harlequin stands for sexuality (procreativity). Perhaps Wickham is directly addressing her bisexuality; perhaps any exclusion repels Wickham's desire. In order to remain the child-angel in her parent's house, Wickham could never leave the polymorphous perverse sexuality of the pre-adolescent. Years after he spoke the words, Wickham remembers her father saying, "I hate women, *old girl,* (my italics) thank God you're not a woman darling"

(*WAW* 102). For Wickham, like Mew, each poem disguises as much as it reveals. Because of Victorian morality, neither could express her real self directly, so each distanced her self by irony, wit, and making in many different voices a very modern babble.

To sum up the impact of Charlotte Mew and Anna Wickham on modern poetics, the critic has to jump generations, leaving out the formalists of the fifties, and proceed to poets of the confessional school such as Sylvia Plath and Anne Sexton. Plath and Sexton are considered by some critics to be the mothers of feminist poetry, but their foremother was Anna Wickham, whether they knew it or not. Her brash voice declaims in "The Fresh Start:"

> O give me back my rigorous English Sunday
> And my well-ordered house, with stockings
>   washed on Monday.
> Let the House-Lord, that kindly decorous fellow,
> Leave happy for his Law at ten, with a well-
>   furled umbrella.
> Let my young ones observe my strict house rules,
> Imbibing Tory principles, at Tory schools.
>
> Two years now I have sat beneath a curse
> And in a fury poured out frenzied verse,
> Such verse as held no beauty and no good
> And was at best new curious vermin-food.
>
> My dog is rabid, and my cat is lean,
> And not a pot in all this place is clean.
> The locks have fallen from my hingeless doors,
> And holes are in my credit and my floors.
>
> There is no solace for me, but in sooth
> To have said baldly certain ugly truth.
> Such scavenger's work was never yet a woman's,
> My wardrobe's more a scarecrow's than a
>   Human's.
>
> I'm off to the House-goddess for her gift.
> 'O give me Circumspection, Temperance, Thrift;
> Take thou this lust of words, this fevered itching,
> And give me faith in darning, joy of stitching!'

When this hot blood is cooled by kindly Time

Controlled and schooled, I'll come again to

  Rhyme.

Sure of my methods, morals and my gloves,

I'll write chaste sonnets of imagined Loves. (*WAW* 240–41)

In this poem, Wickham answers the question about why there is no great, as she puts it, She-Poet. Both Wickham and Mew put into housework much of the energy they needed for writing because their families depended on them to keep the household afloat. In "Dedication to a Cook" Wickham says that the person who asks the above question about women poets should come live with her and he will understand the answer. Fighting against the bonds of domesticity, for artistic freedom, and for a more inclusive understanding of women's sexuality, Mew and Wickham create a poetry as fresh today as it was the day it was written.

And as much as Mew and Wickham depreciate their work, their poems remain monuments to the fact that they could and did write poetry that stands on its own merits. If both women can reach a wider audience now that feminist critics have begun reclamation projects designed to rescue them and others from previous critical neglect, Mew and Wickham will be recognized for their contributions to a literary era. We must recognize, as Bachelard so aptly puts it, "a childhood which dares not speak its name" (*Reverie* 103) in our understanding of Charlotte Mew and Anna Wickham as unredeemed captives of the angel in the house metaphor. It is through the mytho-poetical structures of *bricolage* that we can come to a system that explains their production.

The Angel in the House
"Poetry is a commitment of the soul"[1]

The blending together of several metaphors to describe a new approach to Charlotte Mew and Anna Wickham demonstrates how their careers, themes, prosody, and reputations were at the same time an acknowledgement of and a reaction against certain social, cultural, historical, and literary phenomena. Interdisciplinary investigations are based on a respect for the facts of the times. The importance of the Victorian family structure on modern women poets has not been examined as thoroughly as it should be. Nor has attention been paid to the fact that, while publication of Mew and Wickham's poetry created interest among other poets, both male and female, critical interest in, and a concurrent dissemination of the poems was sadly lacking. Jane Dowson blames a persistent negative cultural representation summed up by the appellation *poetess*. Further, the continuing tendency to produce omnibus reviews of several different women poets, lumped together merely because they are women, displaces the emphasis from product to gender. Along with the development of a critical aesthetic of their own, so that their work will not be judged as mere imitation of male poets, women poets also need to be showcased as important contributors to the cultural and aesthetic mix of their time. A salient point to remember is that while there may not be much critical attention being paid to Mew and Wickham's aesthetic, readers are still being moved by the poems themselves. A quick glance at the many anthologies that contain a poem or two, or a perusal of the Internet confirms that their work continues to speak to readers. Unfortunately, a few women poets, for a number of reasons, some of which I have detailed, were also relegated to the margins or ignored during the early feminist recovery of poetry by women. I have shown in my study of Mew and Wickham's lives and work the dangers of such neglect and the avenues that further investigation can create.

The Oedipal break from the father, which establishes a lone man battling against society's threatening chaos is, of course, an ineffective model for an understanding of female aesthetic development. Therefore, to tell the stories of women modernists, critics need a new matrix. The empty matrix, the empty womb/room, has often been cited as the cause of hysteria in women and female hysteria has been viewed as a negative trait. However, my conjunction of the angel in the house with the child in the house side-steps this problem, because the child's womb is a place of possibility, and imagination with infinite choice, not merely the site of reproductive function. Even when Mew and Wickham struggled with the idea of themselves as children in the house, the trope remained important to their artistic production. Thanks to the pioneering work of feminist Juliet Mitchell, hysteria, when it is understood as a simultaneous acceptance and rejection of the culture's notions of femininity, can be a term that describes a woman's use of masculine language, which enables her to be both feminine and to refuse femininity within her negotiations with the word (Bronfen 405).

This strategy begins to describe the multivocality of poets like Mew and Wickham and positions the woman critic in a location where she can begin to map the effect of these poets' techniques. Sadly, at the time they were producing, the need to write was often interpreted as hysteria, and, as Wickham herself asserts, "I knew that Patrick [. . .] thought it one of the gravest of my symptoms that I imagined myself a poet" ("Genius" 18). Now, many female critics have begun to evaluate women's fiction from the position of critic as hysteric, but because of the overwhelmingly negative stigma attached to the term, not many male critics feel comfortable using this strategy. More work from this critical standpoint needs to be undertaken for both modern and contemporary women poets. As Mew and Wickham matured as women and writers, they shifted voice from child to hysteric. Both of these voices remain marginal, but as I have shown, that can be read as more strength than weakness, because it allows them poetic license to develop unique styles. Unfortunately, at the time they were producing, there was no critical vocabulary with which to explicate their stance. Not one of their contemporaries understood that they were creating a new matrix for modernism. Using the womb metaphor, rather than the previous phallic one, allows critics to read women writers through a womanly metaphor much more suitable for discussing their style.

The substance of a matrix should include those dimensions of Victorian and modern culture which have been either ignored or trivialized by literary historians. So that our sense of what counts as meaningful history can be expanded, we must examine aspects of culture such as housing, spiritualist movements, popular magazines, fashion, the changing concepts of motherhood, and household maintenance. These more domestic concerns, where nature and culture mesh, are coupled in women writers' work with a yearning toward a spiritual domain beyond the constraints of mundane materialism. How some women writers blend the trivial with the transcendent to create an appeal to a wide audience separates them from the modern avant-garde for whom middle-class philistines, suburban hypocrites, traditional religionists, and popular female novelists are anti-aesthetic antagonists. The conjunction of genre, gender, and geography, both literally and figuratively, is where exciting work remains to be done in the ongoing critical expansion of modernism's boundaries.

Charlotte Mew and Anna Wickham have been ignored until now because of past critical polarizations. The space where Mew and Wickham function as producers of memorable literature is hard to map, and when it has been mapped, as it is in this study, it is then hard to separate the product from its production. Thematically and rhetorically diffuse, Mew and Wickham send the critic to a bewildering variety of source material in order to create a critical history that can account for their variety. Because they chose to keep characteristics of earlier forms while at the same time addressing radical subject matter, those critics who prefer to discuss writers who combine radical subject with radical form dismiss them. As well, Mew and Wickham sometimes combine stylistic experimentation with what some critics feel is conservative or clichéd subject matter. Another aspect of Mew and Wickham's poetry that is problematic for feminist critics is their facility with the male narrative voice. The persona in their poems is just as likely to be a man as it is to be a woman. Since they thought that the artist was either asexual, bisexual, or both, gendered readings of their work have to assume a similar fluidity. These poets were skeptical about the importance of their poems and themselves as poets. When artists are so deliberately destabilizing, critics become wary.

However, it is just these characteristics that make them modernists. Mew and Wickham use their poetic voices to disrupt their own production, much as the view of the child as angel in the house disrupts the Victorian stereotype of woman. In their poems when one voice speaks, another is being repressed, when one rhythm predominates, another is echoed or parodied, when mythology intrudes as trope, it is mocked. Erudite international allusions have no place in this polyglossic babble. The purpose of these words is to fashion a new self. As a child experiments with language and disregards adult boundaries in the process of discovering a self, so Mew and Wickham worked toward something new in poetry. In *The Poetics of Reverie,* Bachelard stresses the importance of the image in childhood. He believes that it is more important than anything else because childhood is the origin of a writer's verbal landscape, created before the self separates from the concrete beauties of the world. He quotes Lucie Delarue-Mardrus, a friend of Anna Wickham's from the Natalie Barney *salon,* who says, "'And who then was ever cured of his childhood'" (139). My work shows how Mew and Wickham's poems diagram the intimate space—the body, room, house, home and landscape—that constitutes a poet's most valuable trope. Both women's poetry emerges from their life-long attempts to move beyond the metaphor that I have chosen to use to describe their lives and works. Functioning as angels in the house, they constantly struggled to discard that identity in their work. But that is the purpose of a matrix, a womb. When gestation is complete, something new emerges.

However, not every birth produces a healthy infant, despite the best efforts of the mother. Mew was clearly reacting to a general negative critical reception experienced by women modernists in her chilling poem, "Saturday Market." Critics have variously interpreted "the red, dead thing" in this poem as an aborted fetus, or the persona's heart, but it could also be the artistic product because sometimes what comes forth is perhaps more of a cause for shame than pride. For the woman poet, the poem is something to be concealed because, in the Saturday market, it just causes laughter; no one in the marketplace really cares. This poem's situation in an unidentified rural location, its unspecified time, and its use of dialect successfully mask a scathing condemnation of the same society that she also excoriates in "Fame." One of Mew's strengths as a poet is that she is clear-eyed in her understanding of the game she is playing. Although the work of scholars and critics such as Val Warner, John Newton, Jane Dowson and Jennifer Jones have remembered Mew and Wickham's fine poems, still, so far, very few in the marketplace of English poetry have seemed to care about keeping the work of Charlotte Mew and Anna Wickham alive. Mew's conclusion is that it is best to just "make an end of it." And that is exactly what both Mew and Wickham did by committing suicide.

Although Virginia Woolf misread the identity of the angel in the house, she did not misread the effects of the metaphor on generations of women writers. The existence of this ideal figure, accepted by men and women well into the twentieth century, has, as Woolf asserts, everything to do with imperialism, colonialism, the rise of the middle class, and attitudes toward suburbia and its inhabitants. Of course, mortals really never win in their struggles with conceptual angels. Woolf says she did her best to kill the ideal figure that haunted her, because this figure controlled her thought. The angel in the house functions as the tutelary spirit of the home, the site of all matters of the most vital importance to writers. If Bachelard is correct that the truth of the imagination begins with the child in the house, and if that angel is a girl-child, not the grown woman of Woolf's imaging, then by killing the angel, as Woolf brags that she does, she is killing herself as a writer. In an interior struggle between her imagination and reason, Woolf informs her readers that reason wins. She pulls back because men are not ready for the truth, as it might be told by women. Masking the truth ensures Woolf's acceptance as a great modernist writer, but it kills her just as it killed Mew and Wickham.

Although Mew and Wickham also resort to masks, more often they scorn them in their poems. While they write using different personae, their tone is always authentic, even when it makes their work diverge from the dominant aesthetic. Differing from Woolf, they retain something of the child in the house (its imagination and undifferentiated sexuality) in their poems and this position allows them to write more sincerely than Woolf. They also write from the hysteric position, something the restrained Woolf would never do. That is why they must be acknowledged as important modernists, and it explains why they were not viewed as such in their own time. While they were creating this new matrix, writing with their bodies and from them, they were also writing themselves closer to death. They could not see their effect; they tried many times to extinguish their writer selves. For a variety of reasons, they could only visualize themselves as amateurs. They were even proud to see themselves as such, but, in a world that increasingly relied on the professional, their contributions were disparaged. Wickham's final poem speaks of her "long pride and error" and Mew's poem "An Ending" talks about missing the way. Conceptualizing their work in the way that I have in this study is a way to write over (or overwrite) their deaths to acknowledge their achievement, even though they themselves could not recognize it. Their words continue to speak to us because, as Bachelard says, "Poetry is a commitment of the soul" (*Space xvii*).

At the end, it is most important to remember the poems like Wickham's "In the House of the Soul (Harlequin and a Woman under one Skin)" which enjoins "It is our business here to make a song —/Whoever is sore, whatever is wrong" (*WAW* 271). One of her poems about poetry and the poet, "Soul Colour," which begins "The only real thing in my garden is the scent of flowers" continues:

> There is no reality in my flesh,
> Nor in work, nor in words, nor in possessions;
> All these things are symbols of myself,
> The sum of emotion, thought and desire
> Which I call soul-color. . .
>
> In life I am like a juggler,
> I throw about my symbols, I rearrange them.
> I fling my spheres and rings into the air [. . .] (*Selected* 16)

A close attention to the poetry and the lives of Charlotte Mew and Anna Wickham provides a new way to look at literary modernity. This view builds a matrix, combining a deconstructive approach to the question of identity with a careful attention to the specifics of their lives and literary productions. Both poets simultaneously denied and accepted, resisted and complied with the trope of the angel in the house. A tug of war between what Wickham calls the *sacrificial/sacramental I* endures in their work. In their interactions with society, they pretend to kill the angel by dressing as its imagined antitheses: the ambiguous dandy and the free-roaming bohemian, advertising a sexual stance that neither followed, except in her imagination. Their looks proclaimed their desired politics and poetics, even while the angel trope demanded an altogether different persona. The mysteries surrounding the lives and deaths of these two poets can be summed up by the conundrum from Charlotte Mew's "The Quiet House":

> The things that kill us seem
>   Blind to the death they give:
> It is only in our dream
>   The things that kill us live. (*CPP* 18)

Notes

CHAPTER ONE: THE BOHEMIAN AND THE DANDY

1   Bachelard *The Poetics of Reverie* 118

2   Jennifer Jones reveals that Wickham sent a substantially different version of this poem to Louis Untermeyer, which reads in part, "Here is no *sacramental* I [. . .]" As Jones notes, the difference between "sacrificial" and "sacramental" is great (164).

CHAPTER TWO: CHARLOTTE MARY MEW 1869–1894

1   "Fame" *CPP* 3

2   Thomas Leverton was one of the surveyors of the Government Board of Works with whom H.E. Kendall would have learned his craft. It is probably through Leverton that he received his position in the Barrack Department of the War Office, which he held until 1823. John Nash (1752–1818) is the architect responsible for London's Regent Street and the recasting of Buckingham House into Buckingham Palace for the King, among other projects in the Queen Anne and Vernacular Revival and Georgian Gothic style (Gloag 11–12, 20, Dixon 138).

3   John Gloag succinctly explains the social and moral impact of the Gothic revival style and its practitioners. "Victorian taste was oppressed and distorted by that revival, which gave a religious tone to architecture, as, a century later, progressive beliefs about the structure of society gave a political tone to the modern movement in design. [. . .] the architecture produced by the Gothic revivalists was intrinsically reactionary; those who created it looked back, never forward, so in an age of fantastic material progress, architecture was out of step with science, engineering, commercial enterprise and industrial expansion" (*xv*).

4   Amy Greener's *A Lover of Books* (1916) details her friendship with Lucy Harrison and contains Harrison's literary criticism. Harrison wrote on Jane Austen, Wordsworth, Shakespeare's women, Ann Radcliffe, and Tagore, among other subjects and authors. In fact, she is an astute feminist critic whose pieces deserve a wider recognition than they have. For instance, she opens her essay

"Three of Shakespeare's Women" with the following: "'Where women are honoured the Divinities are complacent; where they are despised, it is useless to pray to God.' If there is any truth in these words of the ancient Eastern Sage, it may not be unprofitable to give a little time to the study of the varying estimates of women put before us in song and story by those who are supposed to be the leaders of thought in their time and generation." Later in the same essay she continues, "Throughout our literature, even up to a late date, women have proved a most convenient butt for the satirist; hundreds of stories find their point in woman's folly, her ignorance, her bad temper, in a word, her smallness of mind. That some women should be silly is hardly to be wondered at. For generations she was carefully and systematically shut out from participation in rational education, nay, any education at all; her mind was left without wholesome food in any shape or kind. Then the very persons who had thus legislated for her, amused themselves by laughing at the product of their own arrangements" (Greener 143–45). No date is given for this essay, but it is interesting to note that Harrison is saying much of what Virginia Woolf repeats in the Shakespeare's sister section of *A Room of One's Own*.

5   "The Governess in Fiction" was published in *The Academy* August 1899; "The Poems of Emily Brönte" in *Temple Bar* August 1904; "Mary Stuart in Fiction" in *The Englishwoman* April 1912.

6   As Gail Cunningham explains, the New Women were only genuinely new if their conflicts with convention were matters of principle; they had high ideals; and they went their own ways according to principles that they had formed through reading, thinking, and discussing them with like-minded souls. Evidence of New Womanhood could be as trivial as short hair, comfortable clothes, cigarette-smoking, and swearing (in the company of close friends only!), but if these activities were accompanied by pronouncements on their liberating effects, then the speaker was a New Woman. She was essentially middle-class, prepared to limit her breeding capacity, and rebelling against personal circumstances, as opposed to the Suffragists who were rebelling against political circumstances (10–16). Charlotte Mew certainly fits this definition.

CHAPTER THREE: CHARLOTTE MARY MEW 1904–1913

1   "Fame" *CPP* 2

2   The Keynotes series was John Lane's idea, which evolved after the publication of George Egerton's *Keynotes* (1893). Cunningham characterizes this piece as "The first work of the neurotic school" (64). A New Woman novel, *Keynotes* is told from the point of view of an emancipated intellectual woman, a Sue Bridehead type. Beardsley designed a special cover for the series, but it had to be subdued for the sensibilities of the circulating library crowd. Cunningham describes the brief flourishing of this movement and states that it was about over by the turn of the century (65, 74–75). Davidow in "Charlotte Mew and the Shadow of Thomas Hardy" makes much of the connection between Mew's farmer's *bride* and his Sue *Bridehead*, [her italics] although I feel the connections Davidow makes are tenuous, at best.

3   The disputed piece is one that Warner's *CPP* includes in an appendix. "A Reminiscence of Princess Mathilde Bonaparte," it was published in *Temple Bar*

78 (1904). Along with two sonnets, jointly published under the title "V.R.I." (*Temple Bar* 72 (1901), it was printed under the initials CM. While Warner and Fitzgerald have accepted the sonnets as Mew's, Fitzgerald's who claims that Mew never signed her initials C.M., but always C.M.M. questions the essay's provenance for Charlotte Mary Mew. As well, Fitzgerald claims that the aunt would have to have been Mary Lenora, the sister of Anna Maria, who was ill and living in Brighton at the time mentioned in the disputed piece (note 255–56). The initial source for the bibliographic information is Davidow.

CHAPTER FOUR: CHARLOTTE MARY MEW 1913–1928

1   "From A Window" *CPP* 37

CHAPTER FIVE: ANNA WICKHAM 1883–1904

1   "The Call for Faith" *WAW* 163

2   George Cruikshank, 1792–1878, a famous illustrator and caricaturist whose cartoons of statesmen, churchmen, and the daily life of London capture the spirit of Victorian England. His over 200 works include the illustrations for Charles Dickens' *Oliver Twist* (1839). He contributed sketches, along with Leech and Tenniel, to Richard Harris Barham's *Ingoldsby Legends*, a copy of which he gave to Martha Whelan. Robert Patton makes a strong case for his philandering. He documents Cruikshank's second family with Adelaide Attree, the former housemaid of his second wife. With Attree, at 31 Augustus Street, Cruikshank sired eleven children. Their descendents believe that Cruikshank is their ancestor ("Fragment" 69, Patton 286).

3   Frank Huddlestone Potter, 1845–87, garnered a critical reception in France more easily than in his native England. Wickham relates that he was engaged to her aunt, Helen Whelan, to whom he "bequeathed his pictures and what money he had," although he "was really in love with my grandmother" ("Fragment" 69).

4   Edward Bibbins Aveling, 1851–98, is infamous for at least two reasons. George Bernard Shaw admitted that Aveling was the model for Louis Dubedat in *The Doctor's Dilemma*, and Aveling carried on a much-publicized "free marriage" with Eleanor Marx, Karl Marx's beloved youngest daughter, even though he was already married. When his first wife died in 1897, and he was able to marry Eleanor Marx, with whom he had had some sort of relationship since 1882, he instead (under the assumed name of Alec Nelson) married a twenty-two-year-old actress, Eva Frye, who was acting in a melodrama in which Aveling had some interest. As an entrepreneur, Aveling had once managed a traveling troupe. Marx committed suicide on March 31st, 1898. This story is told in the chapter "The Secularists" of Warren S. Smith's book, *The London Heretics: 1870–1914*. Aveling is described as a man whose history is notorious because of his philandering. Smith states that he probably also had an affair with the "most brilliant and personable woman in the reform movement, Mrs. Annie Wood Besant" (74). Here we have a man whose place in the Victorian reformist scene is defined in sexual terms, yet he was a scientist whose interests extended to passions for

the theater, poetry, and public education (he was elected to the London School Board on the secular and free education platform); his idols were Shelley, Marx, and Darwin. Aveling, the scientific socialist, was also an emotional and sentimental public reader of verse who could burst into tears and sobs after a recital of the last act of *Prometheus Unbound* (75). Aveling was also unscrupulous about money. He borrowed freely from his friends and mismanaged the expense account of the Socialist Labour Party when he and Eleanor Marx traveled to America on its behalf (80). This man is the person who intersected with Anna Wickham's mother, Alice Whelan, at a critical point in her life.

5   The Secularists were a group of individuals dedicated to reforming England's laws on a number of issues including separation of church and state, birth control, and freedom of speech and the press. The leaders included Charles Bradlaugh, and Annie Besant. In 1877, they led the battle over the obscenity trial connected to the printing of Dr. Charles Knowlton's *The Fruits of Philosophy*, which explained and advocated birth control (W.S. Smith 27–83).

6   Lewis Feuer, "The Marxian Tragedians." *Encounter* 5 (1962): 23–32, and Havelock Ellis, "Eleanor Marx." *The Adelphi* 6 (1935): 342 ff. and 1 (1935): 33 ff.

7   For a full discussion of the amazing lives of Annie Besant, see Warren S. Smith and the two-volume biography of Annie Besant by Arthur H. Nethercot. Nethercot's biography, while accurate and complete, advertises a common male reaction to Besant's significant contribution to British intellectual life. Calling his biography *The First Five Lives of Annie Besant* and *The Last Four Lives of Annie Besant* trivializes the work she did for Socialism, Fabianism, the London School Board, the union movement, and birth control. It seems obvious that the young Alice Whelan, just realizing her own stage presence and charisma, would look to the woman who had won *Woman* magazine's poll and prize contest on "Who is the most eloquent, convincing, rational, and powerful speaker among women of today"(Nethercot 343).

8   W.T. Stead, the editor of the *Pall Mall Gazette*, and *The Review of Reviews*, was a crusader who supported the views of Annie Besant. He later wrote many articles about his heroine, Besant, and served as the editor of the popular *Real Ghost Stories*. In 1893 he started the magazine *Borderlands* devoted to the occult, psychic phenomena, and spiritualism. From the 1880s until he died in the sinking of the Titanic, Stead's "special brand of social reform and religious uplift" carried a worldwide influence (W.S. Smith 256–70, Nethercot 389).

CHAPTER SIX: ANNA WICKHAM 1904–1947

1 "Nervous Prostration" *Selected* 20

2   For a detailed description of the relationship between T.S. and Vivienne Eliot, see Peter Ackroyd's *T.S. Eliot: A Life*; especially pertinent is a section on page 233 which details the drawing up of a "reception order" in the summer of 1938 for the committal of Mrs. Eliot to a private mental hospital where she spent the rest of her life.

3   David Garnett's parents, Edward and Constance, were well-known figures in literary London whose influence helped many young unknown writers, including D.H. Lawrence. Lawrence was writing to Edward Garnett by late summer 1911

(Huxley 11). The Garnetts were neighbors of the Hepburns in Downshire Hill, Hampstead, as were the poets, Ernest and Dollie Radford (*The Golden Echo* 124–25). Dollie Radford was also one of Anna Wickham's friends. R.D. Smith characterizes Radford as "a friend (and patron) of D.H. Lawrence as well as Eleanor Marx and Anna Wickham" and states that a Radford daughter lived as an *au pair* at the Hepburn's during the 1914–18 war (393 n.).

4   The Fitzroy Tavern, a haven for the artists Augustus John, Jacob Epstein (and his first model, Betty May, the Tiger Woman), Henri Gaudier-Brzeska, and Nina Hamnett, as well as Professor J.B.S. Haldane, and his wife, the author Charlotte Haldane, was a home away from home for Anna Wickham. It is likely that she introduced both Dylan Thomas and Malcolm Lowry to the delights of the Fitzroy. See Sally Fiber's *The Fitzroy: The Autobiography of a London Tavern* (1995) for a more detailed description of the pub James Norbury characterizes as "much more than a London public house. It is part of the history of London, in fact it has become part of the fabric of our inheritance, [. . .] a landmark of the literary, artistic and social history of our times" (back cover).

5   George Reavey was a critic, editor and translator connected to the Europa Press. He spent much of his time in Paris and died in 1976 (Ferris 230).

CHAPER SEVEN: ANNA WICKHAM 1911–1947

1   "Formalist" *WAW* 195

2   These essays are Matt Holland's "Anna Wickham: Fettered Woman, Free Spirit," published in *Poetry Review* Summer 1988; Margaret Newlin's "Anna Wickham: 'The sexless Part which is my mind,'" in *Southern Poetry Review* April 1978; and Myra Stark's "Feminist Themes in Anna Wickham's *The Contemplative Quarry and The Man with a Hammer*" in *Four Decades of Poetry: 1890–1930*, Vol. 2, 1978.

3   The author of *The Ingoldsby Legends*, the Reverend Richard Harris Barham, lived from 1788 to 1845. He was a writer and a wit, whose books and light articles in magazines such as *Blackwood's* and *John Bull* made him one of the most popular authors of the nineteenth century. *The Ingoldsby Legends* are folk tales and ghost stories interspersed with long humorous or sentimental "tragical" poems. As mentioned earlier, George Cruikshank illustrated *The Ingoldsby Legends* and gave an expensive copy of the book to the Whelan family. It became one of their prize possessions.

4   Charles Stuart Calverley (1831–84) was a poet who excelled in light verse, parody and pastiche, according to Hilda Spear's account in *The English Poems of Charles Stuart Calverley*. She further states that he was a critic of the pedantic and the "puffed-up," and it is only in his translations from the classics that he is completely serious. Spears ranks Calverley with the great Cambridge parodists A.C. Hilton and J.K. Stephens, commenting that though his literary achievement is slight, it's pleasing, and she continues, "At the same time he evokes an atmosphere of Victorianism. [. . .] He shows us aspects of the life of a limited sector of the community"(11).

5   Aphra Behn (1640–89) has been characterized as the first Englishwoman to make her living by writing. She is most famous for her novel, *Oroonoko*. Like

Anna Wickham, Behn has been characterized as a Bohemian and feminist. Katherine Philips (1631–64) established a literary salon, the "Society of Friendship," which included the poets Abraham Cowley, Jeremy Taylor, and Henry Vaughan; her verses on Vaughan's poems bought her considerable fame, as did her translation of Corneille's *Pompee*. Anne Finch (1661–1720) poetically sparred with Alexander Pope, wrote verse in imitation of Sappho, and was "discovered" by Wordsworth, who praised her verse as a forerunner of Romanticism. Lady Mary Wortley Montagu (1690–1762) also jousted with Pope, and is known for her wit and satire (Bernikow 58–59, 68, 81, 92.)

6 For a fascinating and complete rendering of the early days of Australian settlement, see Robert Hughes's *The Fatal Shore: The Epic of Australia's Founding* (1988).

7 Renee Vivian's (1877–1909) real name was Natalie Tarn. She had an American mother and British father. She wrote poetry in French. Her books were published in Paris by Alphonse Lemerre between 1902 and 1910. In 1934 Lemerre published her complete poems in two volumes. Three of her books, *A Woman Appeared to Me, At the Sweet Hour of Hand in Hand,* and *The Muse of Violets* were translated into English and published by Naiad Press in the late 1970s. She was Natalie Barney's lover for several years before her death. Romaine Brooks, a photographer, became Barney's lover when both were over forty. Shari Benstock characterizes her photographic portraits of Barney's circle as "Amazons in drag" (305). Elizabeth de Gramont, the Duchesse de Clermont-Tonnerre, was a rival of Brooks. Lucie Delarue-Mardrus, also a member of Barney's circle, was Barney's entree into an aristocratic group of French lesbians (Benstock 79).

CHAPTER EIGHT: THE ANGEL IN THE HOUSE

1 Bachelard *Space xvii*

Bibliography

Ackroyd, Peter. *T. S. Eliot: A Life*. New York: Simon and Schuster, 1984.

Alcoff, Linda. "Cultural Feminism Versus Post-Structuralism: The Identity Crisis in Feminist Theory." *Signs* 13.1 (1988): 405–36.

Aldington, Richard, ed. *The Viking Book of Poetry of the English-Speaking World*. Rev. Mid-Century Ed. New York: Viking, 1962.

Altick, Richard D. *Victorian People and Ideas*. New York: Norton, 1973.

Anson, John. "'The Wind Is Blind': Power and Constraint in the Poetry of Alice Meynell." *Studia Mystica* 9.1 (1986): 37–50.

Ardis, Ann. *New Women, New Novels: Feminism and Early Modernism*. New Brunswick: Rutgers UP, 1990.

"Astronomer's Death." *Times* [London] 30 Dec. 1929: 7.

Bachelard, Gaston. *The Poetics of Reverie*. Trans. Daniel Russell. NY: Orion, 1969. 99–141.

———. *The Poetics of Space*. Trans. Maria Jolas. Foreword Etienne Gilson. NY: Orion, 1964.

Barash, Carol. "Dora Marsden's Feminism, the *Freewoman*, and the Gender Politics of Early Modernism." *Princeton University Library Chronicle* 49.1 (1987): 31–56.

Barham, Richard Harris. *The Ingoldsby Legends or Mirth and Marvels*. Illus. by Cruikshank, Leech, etc. London: Frederick Warne. 1889.

Bell, Kathleen. "Charlotte Mew, T.S. Eliot and Modernism." *Kicking Daffodils: Twentieth-Century Women Poets*. Ed. Vicki Bertram. Edinburgh, Scotland: Edinburgh UP, 1997. 13–24.

Benstock, Shari. "Expatriate Modernism: Writing on the Cultural Rim." *Women's Writing in Exile*. Ed. Marilynn Broe and Angela Ingram. Chapel Hill: U of North Carolina P, 1989. 20–40.

———. *Women of the Left Bank: Paris 1900–1940*. Austin: U of Texas P, 1986.

Bernikow, Louise, ed. *The World Split Open: Four Centuries of Women Poets in England and America, 1552–1950*. New York: Vintage, 1974.

Birch, Lionel. "Anna Wickham: A Poetess Landlady." *Picture Post*. 27 April, 1946: 23–25.

Blake, Kathleen. *Love and the Woman Question in Victorian Literature: The Art of Self-Postponement*. Totowa, NJ: Barnes & Noble, 1983.

Blamires, Harry. *Twentieth-Century English Literature*. History of Literature Series. New York: Schocken Books, 1982.

Blain, Virginia. Introduction. *Victorian Women Poets: A New Annotated Anthology*. Ed. Virginia Blain. Harlow, England: Longman-Pearson Education, 2001.1–16.

Boll, T.E.M. "The Mystery of Charlotte Mew and May Sinclair: An Inquiry." *New York Public Library Bulletin* 74 (1970): 445–53.

Bowker, Gordon. *Pursued By Furies: A Life of Malcolm Lowry*. New York: St. Martin's, 1995.

Bronfen, Elisabeth. *Over Her Dead Body: Death, Femininity and the Aesthetic*. New York: Routledge, 1992.

Brontë, Charlotte. *Shirley*. Ed. Herbert Rosengarten and Margaret Smith. Oxford: The Clarendon Press, 1979.

———. *Villette*. Ed. Herbert Rosengarten and Margaret Smith. Oxford: The Clarendon Press, 1984.

Brown, Penny. *The Poison at the Source: The Female Novel of Self-Development in the Early Twentieth Century*. New York: St. Martin's, 1992.

Brownstein, Marilyn L. "Marianne Moore." *The Gender of Modernism*. Ed. Bonnie Kime Scott. Bloomington: Indiana UP, 1990. 323–52.

Burwell, Rose Marie. "A Checklist of Lawrence's Reading." *A D. H. Lawrence Handbook*. Ed. Keith Sagar. New York: Barnes and Noble, 1982. 84, 96.

Cameron, Deborah, ed. *The Feminist Critique of Language: A Reader*. London: Routledge, 1990.

Carey, John. *The Intellectuals and the Masses: Pride and Prejudice among the Literary Intelligentsia, 1880–1939*. New York: St. Martin's, 1993.

Clarke, Bruce. "Dora Marsden and Ezra Pound: *The New Freewoman* and 'The Serious Artist.'" *Contemporary Literature* 33.1 (1992): 91–112.

Clark, Suzanne. *Sentimental Modernism: Women Writers and the Revolution of the Word*. Bloomington: Indiana UP, 1991.

Coffman, Stanley K. *Imagism: A Chapter for the History of Modern Poetry*. New York: Octagon, 1972.

Colby, Vineta. *The Singular Anomaly: Women Novelists of the Nineteenth Century*. New York: New York UP, 1970. 1–14.

Collins, Vere H. *Talks With Thomas Hardy at Max Gate 1920–1922*. 1928. London: Duckworth, 1978.

Crisp, Shelley J. "Meynell's 'The Return to Nature: Histories of Modern Poetry.'" *Explicator* 50 (1991): 28–30.

Cunningham, Gail. *The New Woman and the Victorian Novel.* New York: Barnes and Noble, 1978.

Dante [Alighieri]. *Purgatory.* Trans. Mark Musa. Bloomington: Indiana UP, 1981.

Davidow, Mary C. "Charlotte Mew: Biography and Criticism." Diss. Brown U, 1960.

———. "Charlotte Mew and the Shadow of Thomas Hardy." *Bulletin of Research in the Humanities* 81 (1978): 437–47.

———. "The Charlotte Mew - May Sinclair Relationship: A Reply." *New York Public Library Bulletin* 75 (1971): 295–300.

Day, Gary, and Gina Wisker. "Recuperating and Revaluing: Edith Sitwell and Charlotte Mew." *British Poetry 1900–1950: Aspects of Tradition.* Ed. Gary Day and Brian Docherty. New York: St. Martin's, 1995. 65–80.

De Lauretis, Teresa. "Eccentric Subjects: Feminist Theory and Historical Consciousness." *Feminist Studies* 16.1 (1990): 115–50.

Denisoff, Dennis. "Grave Passions: Enclosure and Exposure in Charlotte Mew's Graveyard Poetry." *Victorian Poetry* 38:1 (2000): 125–140.

Dijkstra, Bram. *Idols of Perversity: Fantasies of Feminine Evil in Fin-de-Siècle Culture.* New York: Oxford UP, 1986.

Dixon, Roger, and Stefan Muthesius. *Victorian Architecture.* New York: Oxford UP, 1978.

Dowson, Jane, ed. "Anna Wickham." *Women's Poetry of the 1930s: A Critical Anthology.* London: Routledge, 1996. 165–74.

———. "'Humming an entirely different tune'? A case study of anthologies: *Women's Poetry of the 1930s*" *Sheffield Hallam Working Papers on the Web: Literature and Value.* <http://www.shu.ac.uk/wpw/dowson.htm>.

———. Introduction. *Women's Poetry of the 1930s: A Critical Anthology.* London: Routledge, 1996. 1–28.

"Education of the Poet, The: A Colloquy with Richard Howard and Marilyn Hacker." *Antioch Review* 58.3 (2000): 261+ Full-Text. *InfoTrac One File.* On-line. Gale Group. Kimbel Library, Conway, SC. 11 May 2002 < http://web6.infotrac.galegroup.com>.

Eliot, T.S. *The Complete Poems and Plays: 1909–1950.* New York: Harcourt, 1971.

———. *The Letters of T. S. Eliot.* Ed. Valerie Eliot. Vol. I: 1898–1922. New York: Harcourt, 1988.

EVOE. "In Search of a Bard." *Punch* 24 August 1921:146.

Felski, Rita. *Beyond Feminist Aesthetics.* Cambridge: Harvard UP, 1989.

———. *The Gender of Modernity.* Cambridge: Harvard UP, 1995.

———. "Modernism and Modernity: Engendering Literary History." *Rereading Modernism: New Directions in Feminist Criticism.* Ed. and intro. Lisa Rado. New York: Garland, 1994. 191–208.

Ferral, Charles. "Suffragists, Egoists, and the Politics of Early Modernism." *English Studies in Canada* 18 (1992): 433–46.

Fiber, Sally. *The Fitzroy: The Autobiography of a London Tavern*. Sussex: Temple House, 1995.

Fitzgerald, Penelope. *Charlotte Mew and Her Friends*. London: Collins, 1984.

Fletcher, John Gould. "Feminism in Poetry." *The Freeman* (1921–22): 164–65.

Freeman, John. "Charlotte Mew." *The Bookman* 76 (1929): 145–46.

Galton, Francis. *Natural Inheritance*. London: Macmillan, 1889.

Gamerman, Amy. "Bringing the Poets to Life: Verse and Verity." *The Wall Street Journal* 13 Feb.1996, natl. ed.: A13.

Garnett, David. *The Golden Echo*. Vol. 1. New York: Harcourt, 1954.

———. *Great Friends: Portraits of Seventeen Writers*. London: Macmillan, 1979.

Gilbert, Sandra M., and Susan Gubar. *No Man's Land: The Place of the Woman Writer in the Twentieth Century*. 3 vols. to date. New Haven: Yale UP, 1988–.

Gillespie, Diane F. "May Sinclair and the Stream Of Consciousness: Metaphors and Metaphysics." *English Literature in Transition* 21 (1978): 134–42.

Gittings, Robert. *Thomas Hardy's Later Years*. Boston: Little, Brown, 1978. 194–203.

Gloag, John. *Victorian Taste: Some Social Aspects of Architecture and Industrial Design*. London: Adam and Charles Black, 1962.

Gorman, Herbert S. "Four Phases of Modern Poetry." Rev. of *The Contemplative Quarry* by Anna Wickham. *The New York Times Book Review* 4 September 1921: 14.

Grant, Joy. *Harold Monro and the Poetry Bookshop*. Berkeley: U of California P, 1967.

Greener, Amy. *A Lover of Books: The Life and Literary Papers of Lucy Harrison*. London: Dent, 1916.

Greer, Germaine. *Slip-Shod Sibyls: Recognition, Rejection and the Woman Poet*. New York: Viking, 1995.

Groben, Anne R. "Ella Wheeler Wilcox." *American Women Writers*. Vol. 4. Ed. Lina Mainiero. New York: Frederick Ungar, 1982. 415–17.

Hamilton, Ian. Introduction. *Charlotte Mew: Selected Poems*. Ed. Ian Hamilton. London: Bloomsbury Poetry Classics-Bloomsbury, 1999. 10–16.

"Hand of the Poet, The. Part I: John Donne to T.S. Eliot" New York Public Library Exhibit, Nov. 3, 1995 – July 31, 1996.

Haughton, Hugh. "Witness to the real thing." Rev. of *Charlotte Mew and Her Friends*. By Fitzgerald. *TLS* 19 Oct. 1984: 1190.

"Henry Edward Kendall, Architect." *The Builder* 9 Jan. 1875: 33.

Hepburn, James. "Anna Wickham." *The Women's Review* 7 (1986): 41.

———. Preface. *The Writings of Anna Wickham: Free Woman and Poet*. London: Virago, 1984. xix–xxiii.

Hickok, Kathleen. *Representations of Women: Nineteenth Century British Women's Poetry*. Westport, Conn.: Greenwood Press, 1984.

Holland, Matt. "Anna Wickham: Fettered Woman, Free Spirit." *Poetry Review* 78.2 (1988): 44–45.

Holroyd, Michael. "'Said to be a Writer.'" *Unreceived Opinions.* New York: Holt, 1967. 153–60.

Houghton, Walter E. *The Victorian Frame of Mind: 1830–1870.* New Haven: Yale UP, 1957.

Howarth, Hebert. *Notes on Some Figures Behind T. S. Eliot.* Boston: Houghton, 1964.

Hynes, Samuel. *The Edwardian Turn of Mind.* Princeton: Princeton UP, 1968.

———. *Edwardian Occasions: Essays on English Writing in the Early Twentieth Century.* New York: Oxford UP, 1972.

Ingram, Angela. "Introduction: On the Contrary, Outside of It." *Women's Writing in Exile.* Ed. Mary Lynn Broe and Angela Ingram. Chapel Hill: U of North Carolina P, 1989. 1–15.

"Inquest on Astronomer." *Times* [London] 31 Dec. 1929: 14F.

Jameson, Fredric. *The Political Unconscious: Narrative as a Socially Symbolic Act.* Ithaca: Cornell UP, 1981.

Jeffries, Richard. *Wood Magic.* 1881. Ware, Hertfordshire: Wordsworth Editions, 1995.

Jones, Jennifer Vaughan. "The Poetry and Place of Anna Wickham: 1910–1930" Diss. U of Wisconsin, 1994.

"Late Mr. Henry Edward Kendall, Architect, The." *The Builder* 20 June 1885: 883–84.

Lawrence, D.H. *The Letters of D.H. Lawrence.* Ed. and intro. Aldous Huxley. NY: Viking, 1932.

———. *Phoenix: The Posthumous Papers of D.H. Lawrence.* Ed. and intro. Edward D. McDonald. New York: Viking, 1964. 517–20.

Lawson, Alan. "The Discovery of Nationality in Australian and Canadian Literatures." *The Post-Colonial Studies Reader.* Ed. Bill Ashcroft, Gareth Griffiths, and Helen Tiffin. London: Routledge, 1995. 167–69.

Leighton, Angela. *Victorian Women Poets: Writing Against the Heart.* Charlottesville: University P of Virginia, 1992.

Leithauser, Brad. Foreword. *Charlotte Mew and Her Friends.* By Fitzgerald. London: Collins, 1984. 1–7.

Levenson, Michael H. *A Genealogy of Modernism: A Study of English Literary Doctrine 1908–1922.* Cambridge: Cambridge UP, 1984.

Lévi-Strauss, Claude. *The Savage Mind.* Trans. George Weidenfeld and Nicolson Ltd. Chicago: U Chicago P, 1966.

———. *Totemism.* Trans. Rodney Needham. Boston: Beacon Press, 1963.

Lidderdale, Jane and Mary Nicholson. *Dear Miss Weaver: Harriet Shaw Weaver 1876–1961.* New York: Viking, 1970.

Light, Alison. *Forever England: Femininity, Literature and Conservatism Between the Wars.* London: Routledge, 1991.

"The Little Old House." Rev. of *The Little Old House* by Anna Wickham. *The New Republic.* 4 May 1921: 304.

Logenbach, James. "The Women and Men of 1914." *Arms and the Woman: War, Gender, and Literary Representation.* Ed. Helen M. Cooper, Adrienne Auslander Munich, and Susan Merrill Squier. Chapel Hill: U of North Carolina P, 1989. 97–123.

Lowell, Amy. "Weary Verse." *The Dial* (1920): 424–31 Rpt. in *Georgian Poetry 1911–1922: The Critical Heritage.* Ed. Timothy Rogers. London: Routledge, 1977. 253–61.

Marcus, Jane. "Alibis and Legends: The Ethics of Elsewhereness, Gender and Estrangement." *Women's Writing in Exile.* Ed. Mary Lynn Broe and Angela Ingram. Chapel Hill: U of North Carolina P, 1989. 270–92.

Maynard, John. "Known and Unknown Desire: Coventry Patmore's Search for Eros." *Victorian Discourse on Sexuality and Religion.* New York: Cambridge UP, 1993. 141–270.

Menand, Louis. *Discovering Modernism: T. S. Eliot and His Context.* New York: Oxford UP, 1987.

Merrin, Jerredith. "The Ballad of Charlotte Mew." *Modern Philology* 95.2 (1997): 200–18.

Messer-Davidow, Ellen. "The Philosophical Bases of Feminist Literary Criticisms." *New Literary History: A Journal of Theory and Interpretation* 19.1 (1987): 65–103.

Metcalfe, Priscilla. *Victorian London.* New York: Praeger, 1972.

Mew, Charlotte. *Collected Poems and Prose.* Ed. and intro. Val Warner. Manchester, Carcanet, 1981; London: Virago, 1982.

Meynell, Alice. *Alice Meynell: Prose and Poetry.* Intro. Victoria Sackville-West. London: Jonathan Cape, 1947.

———. *Preludes.* London: Henry S. King, 1875.

Millay, Edna St. Vincent. *Letters of Edna St. Vincent Millay.* 1952. Ed. Allan Ross Macdougall. Westport, Conn.: Greenwood P, 1972. 157.

Millgate, Michael. *Thomas Hardy: A Biography.* New York: Random House, 1982.

Mintz, Steven. *A Prison of Expectations: The Family in Victorian Culture.* New York: New York UP, 1983.

Mizejewski, Linda. "Charlotte Mew and the Unrepentant Magdalene: A Myth in Transition." *Texas Studies in Literature and Language* 26 (1984): 282–302.

Monro, Alida. "Charlotte Mew-A Memoir." *Collected Poems of Charlotte Mew.* Ed. Alida Monro. New York: Macmillan, 1954. vii–xx.

Monro, Harold. *Some Contemporary Poets.* London: Leonard Parsons, 1920.

Monsman, Gerald. *Walter Pater.* T.E.A.S. 207. Boston: Twayne, 1977.

Moore, Virginia. *Distinguished Women Writers.* 1934. Port Washington, NY: Kennikat Press, 1968.

"Mr. P. Hepburn." *Times* [London] 30 Dec. 1929: 12.

Nethercot, Arthur H. *The First Five Lives of Annie Besant.* Chicago: U of Chicago P, 1960.

———. *The Last Four Lives of Annie Besant.* Chicago: U of Chicago P, 1960.

Newlin, Margaret. "Anna Wickham: 'The sexless part which is my mind.'" *Southern Poetry Review* 14 (1978): 281–301

Newton, John. "Another Handful of Dust." *TLS* 28 April 1995: 18.

———. "Charlotte Mew's Place in the Future of English Poetry." *New England Review* 18.2 (1997): 32–46.

———. Preface. *Charlotte Mew: Complete Poems.* London: Penguin Classics, 2000. xi–xxi.

Norris, Margot. *Joyce's Web: The Social Unraveling of Modernism.* Austin: U. of Texas P, 1992.

Palmer, Herbert. *Post-Victorian Poetry.* 1938. New York: Folcroft Library, 1973.

Patten, Robert L. *George Cruikshank's Life, Times, and Art.* Vol. 2. New Brunswick, NJ: Rutgers UP, 1996.

Pater, Walter. "The Child in the House." *Miscellaneous Studies: A Series of Essays.* New York: Macmillan, 1900. 147–69.

Patmore, Coventry. *The Angel in the House.* 2 vols. London: John W. Parker and Son, 1854, 1856.

Paul, Janis M. *The Victorian Heritage of Virginia Woolf.* Norman, OK: Pilgrim Books, 1987.

Persoon, James. *Modern British Poetry 1900–39.* Twayne's Critical History of Poetry Studies. Ed. Alan Shucard. NY: Twayne, 1999.

Porter, Roy. *A Social History of Madness: The World Through the Eyes of the Insane.* New York: Weidenfeld & Nicolson, 1988.

Rado, Lisa. "Introduction: Lost and Found: Remembering Modernism, Rethinking Feminism." *Rereading Modernism: New Directions in Feminist Criticism.* Ed. Lisa Rado. New York: Garland, 1994. 3–19.

Raitt, Suzanne. "Charlotte Mew and May Sinclair: A love song." *Critical Quarterly* 37.3 (1995): 3–17.

———. "Charlotte Mew's Queer Death." *Yearbook of Comparative and General Literature* 47 (1999): 71–79.

Reynolds, David S. "Biography Can Give the Humanities a Firm Scholarly Backbone." *Chronicle of Higher Education* 25 April 1997: B4+

Ricks, Christopher. ed. *The New Oxford Book of Victorian Verse.* New York: Oxford UP, 1987.

Ross, Robert H. *The Georgian Revolt: 1910–1922.* Carbondale, IL: Southern Illinois UP, 1965.

Sassoon, Siegfried. Autograph letter to Edith Sitwell, March 28, 1928. Berg Collection, New York Public Library.

Schenck, Celeste M. "Anna Wickham." *The Gender of Modernism.* Ed. Bonnie Kime Scott. Bloomington: Indiana UP, 1990. 613–21.

———. "Charlotte Mew." *The Gender of Modernism.* Scott 316–22.

———. "Exiled by Genre: Modernism, Canonicity and the Politics of Exclusion."
    Broe and Ingram 225–50.

Scott, Bonnie Kime, ed. *The Gender of Modernism: A Critical Anthology.*
    Bloomington: Indiana UP, 1990.

———. *Joyce and Feminism.* Bloomington: Indiana UP, 1984.

———. *Refiguring Modernism: The Women of 1928.* Vol. 1. Bloomington: Indiana
    UP, 1995.

Seymour-Smith, Martin. *Hardy: A Biography.* New York: St. Martin's, 1994.

Shepherd, Valerie. "The Language of Women and Men: 'Nervous Prostration' by
    Anna Wickham With particular reference to Jonathan Swift's 'The
    Furniture of a Woman's Mind.'" Literature and Language. London:
    Routledge, 1994. 117–32.

Showalter, Elaine. Introduction. *Daughters of Decadence: Women Writers of the
    Fin de Siècle.* Ed. Elaine Showalter. New Brunswick, NJ: Rutgers UP,
    1993. vii–xix.

———. *A Literature of Their Own: British Women Novelists from Brontë to
    Lessing.* Princeton: Princeton UP, 1977.

———. *Sexual Anarchy: Gender and Culture at the Fin de Siècle.* New York:
    Viking, 1990.

Shrimpton, Nicholas. "Rogue and maiden." Rev. of *His Arms Are Full of Broken
    Things*, by P.B. Parris. *TLS* 28 Feb 1997: 21.

Sinclair, May. "The Pin-prick." *Harper's* February 1915: 392–97.

Sitwell, Osbert. *Collected Satires and Poems.* London: Duckworth, 1931. 171–180.

Skinner, Shelly. "The House in Order: Lesbian Identity and *The Well of
    Loneliness.*" Women's Studies 32.1 (1994): 19–34.

Smith, R.D., ed. *The Writings of Anna Wickham: Free Woman And Poet.* London:
    Virago, 1984.

Smith, Warren S. *The London Heretics 1870–1914.* New York: Dodd, Mead, 1968.

Spear, Hilda, ed. *The English Poems of Charles Stuart Calverley.* Leicester:
    Leicester UP, 1974.

Stark, Myra. "Feminist Themes in Anna Wickham's *The Contemplative Quarry*
    and *The Man With A Hammer.*" Four Decades of Poetry 1890–1930. Vol.
    2. 1978. 101–06.

Stubbs, Patricia. *Women and Fiction: Feminism and the Novel 1880–1920.* Sussex:
    The Harvester Press, 1979.

Swinnerton, Frank. *The Georgian Literary Scene 1910–1935.* Rev. ed. London:
    Hutchinson, 1969.

Thacker, Andrew. "Dora Marsden and *The Egoist*: 'Our War Is With Words.'"
    English Literature in Transition 36 (1993): 178–96.

Thomas, Dylan. *The Collected Letters.* Ed. Paul Ferris. New York: Macmillan,
    1985.

Thwaite, Ann. *A.A. Milne: The Man Behind Winnie-The-Pooh.* NY: Random
    House, 1990.

Tuell, Anne Kimball. *Mrs Meynell and Her Literary Generation*. New York: Dutton, 1924.

Turner, Victor. "Betwixt and Between: The Liminal Period in Rites of Passage." *Betwixt and Between: Patterns in Masculine and Feminine Initiation*. Ed. Louise C. Mahdi, Steven Foster, and Meredith Little. LaSalle, IL: Open Court, 1987. 3–19.

Untermeyer, Louis. *From Another World: The Autobiography of Louis Untermeyer*. NY: Harcourt, 1939. 319–42.

Van Doren, Mark. "Women of Wit." Rev. of *The Contemplative Quarry* and *The Man with a Hammer*. *The Nation* 113 (1922): 483–84.

Vicinus, Martha. Independent *Women: Work and Community for Single Women 1850–1920*. Chicago: U of Chicago P, 1985.

Vickery, Ann. "Between a Modernist Passport and House Arrest: Anna Wickham and the Question of Cultural Identity." *Soundings: Poetry and Poetics*. Ed. Lynn Jacobs and Jeri Kroll. Kent Town, South Australia: Wakefield P, 1998. 26–36.

Walker, Cheryl. *The Nightingale's Burden: Women Poets and American Culture before 1900*. Bloomington: Indiana UP, 1982.

Warner, Val. Introduction. *Collected Poems and Selected Prose*. By Charlotte Mew. Manchester: Fyfield-Carcanet, 1997. ix–xxv.

———. "Mary Magdalene and the Bride: The Work of Charlotte Mew." *Poetry Nation* 4 (1975): 92–106.

———. "New Light on Charlotte Mew." *PN Review* 24.1 (1997): 43–47.

Wickes, George. *The Amazon of Letters: The Life and Loves of Natalie Barney*. New York: Popular Library, 1978.

Wickham, Anna. "I & My Genius." *The Women's Review* 5 (1986): 16–20.

———. *Selected Poems*. Intro. David Garnett. London: Chatto & Windus, 1971.

———. *The Writings of Anna Wickham: Free Woman and Poet*. Ed. and intro. R.D. Smith. London: Virago, 1984.

Wilcox, Ella Wheeler. *The World and I*. 1918. New York: Arno Press, 1980.

Wilkinson, Marguerite. "Here Are Ladies!" Rev. of *The Contemplative Quarry* by Anna Wickham. *Bookman* (1921): 383–85.

Wolf, Janet. *Feminine Sentence: Essays on Women and Culture*. Berkeley: U of California P, 1990.

Woolf, Virginia. *The Letters of Virginia Woolf*. Vols. 2 & 3. Ed. Nigel Nicolson and Joanne Trautmann. NY: A Harvest/HBJ Book—Harcourt, 1976, 1977. 419,140.

———. *The Pargiters*. Ed. with intro. Mitchell A. Leaska. New York: Harcourt, 1977.

Zegger, Hrisey D. *May Sinclair*. T.E.A.S. Ed. Sylvia E. Bowman. Boston: Twayne, 1976.

Index